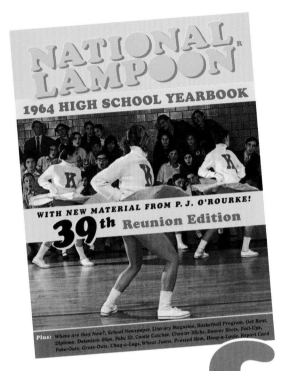

BEFORE
ANIMAL HOUSE,
THERE WAS
HIGH SCHOOL!

THE CLASSIC
PARODY

NOW ALLOWED
IN MOST
BOOKSTORES!

&

COMING IN
JUNE 2004

BEFORE
JAY LENO'S *HEADLINES*,
THERE WERE
NATIONAL LAMPOON'S
TRUE FACTS!

A Hilarious,
Indispensable
Compendium of
Stupidity

NATIONAL LAMPOON · 10850 WILSHIRE BOULEVARD · LOS ANGELES · CA 90024 · USA

RuggedLand

RUGGED LAND · 276 CANAL STREET · FIFTH FLOOR · NEW YORK CITY · NY 10013 · USA

RuggedLand

Published by Rugged Land, LLC

276 CANAL STREET • FIFTH FLOOR • NEW YORK CITY • NY 10013 • USA
RUGGED LAND and colophon are trademarks of Rugged Land, LLC.
NATIONAL LAMPOON and colophon are trademarks of National Lampoon.

PUBLISHER'S CATALOGING-IN-PUBLICATION DATA
(Provided by Quality Books, Inc.)

National lampoon's big book of love / edited by Scott
Rubin, Sean Crespo, and Mason Brown.
p. cm.
ISBN 1590710185

1. Love--Humor. 2. United States--Social life and customs--1971---Humor.
3. American wit and humor. I. Rubin, Scott. II. Crespo,
Sean. III. Brown, Mason.
IV. Title: Big book of love. V. Title: National lampoon.

PN6231.L6N38 2004   818'.602
                           QBI03-700687

RUGGED LAND WEBSITE ADDRESS:WWW.RUGGEDLAND.COM

FEBRUARY 2004
1   3   5   7   9   10   8   6   4   2

BIG BOOK OF LOVE

Editor in Chief:	**Scott Rubin**
Classic Material Selected by:	**Sean Crespo, Mason Brown, Steve Brykman, Joe Osterle, Scott Rubin**
Remastering by:	**Jay Naughton**
Page Layout by:	**Rugged Land**
New Material Edited by:	**Scott Rubin, Sean Crespo, Mason Brown**
Art Direction:	**MoDMaN**
Page Layout and Design:	**Cory Evens, D2 Studios, Kathy Wu, Joe Osterle**
Production Direction:	**Jay Naughton, Cory Evens**

Additional contributions by:

Photography:
　　"Are you a Skank / Manwhore?" - Montemagni Photography,
　　"Tool Magazine" cover - Don Ward, interior - Raegan McCain

Illustration and inking:
　　"Condoms Thru The Ages" – MoDMan, Cory Evens
　　"Look of Love" concept drawings - Margaret Maat

Prop construction:
　　"Look of Love" - Nick Flynt Design

Models:　"Look of Love": Angela Hogg, Alex Berger, Lauren Stanfield
　　"Are You a Skank / Manwhore?": Elina Aghili, Michael J. Anthony
　　"Tool Magazine": Ren Oden, Steve Brykman

Additional written material:
　　"Are You a Skank / Manwhore?" - MoDMaN, Allison Kasic,
　　Leah Wasserstrum, Kari Grove
　　"Orifice Shortage" - Jon Eckman

Design:　"Tool Magazine" - Raegan McCain

Assistance in compiling of original material: Phil Haney

BIG BOOK OF LOVE

TABLE OF CONTENTS

PAGE

Page	Title	Author
6	Classic Cover	Mara McAfee
9	From The Editor-In-Chief	Scott Rubin
10	Letters From The Editors	Rubin, Crespo, Brown
11	Letters From The Editors	Rubin, Crespo, Brown
12	News On The March	Rubin, Crespo, Brown
13	News On The March	Rubin, Crespo, Brown
14	Classic Cover	Neil Selkirk
15	**TOOLS OF LOVE**	Illustration, Daniel Peacock
16-22	My Penis	John Hughes
23	Rape Mysteries	P.J. O'Rourke
24-31	My Vagina	John Hughes
32	Condoms Through The Ages	Steve Brykman
33-36	Sexual Aptitude Test	Leslie Fuller
37-39	What Every Young Woman Should Know	Jeff Greenfield
40-43	First Blow Job	Doug Kenney
44	Two-Way Comics	Ed Subitzky
45-47	How to Tell What Girls Are Like Under Their Clothes	John Hughes, Illustrated by Trina Robbins
48	Foto Funnies	
49-52	Clampax Instructions	Emily Prager
53	Playbore's Dirty Jokes	Doug Kenney
54-57	How to Drive Fast on Drugs While Getting Your Wing-Wang Squeezed and Not Spill Your Drink	P.J. O'Rourke, Illustrated by George Perez
58	Underwear for the Deaf	Michael O'Donoghue, Photos by David Kaestle
59-62	Worst Case Scenario Handbook	Pete Cummin, Art by Cory Evens
63	Gray's Anatomy of Love	Sean Crespo, Illustration David Griffith, Cory Evens
64	What Kind of Man Reads Playboy?	Doug Kenney
65-69	How to Write Love Letters	P.J. O'Rourke
70	Classic Cover	Mara McAfee
71	**QUEST OF LOVE**	Montemagni Photography
72	19 New Ways to be Offensive at a Wedding	Ed Bluestone
73-79	Nancy Reagan's Guide to Dating Dos and Don'ts	Doug Kenney
80-82	How to Talk Dirty in Esparanto	Henry Beard, Richard Bonker, Illustrated by Bruce Cochran
83-88	First Homosexual Experience Comics	Doug Kenney, Ted Mann, Illustrated by Joe Orlando
89	David Eisenhower's Rubber Riot	Doug Kenney
90-93	The Engagement Guide	John Hughes, Illustrated by Trina Robbins
94-95	Valentine's Day Massacre	Stan Watts
96	Foto Funnies	

BIG BOOK OF LOVE

TABLE OF CONTENTS

PAGE

97-102	Time Bastard	Sean Crespo, Mason Brown, Joe Osterle, Jeremy Engel, Illustrated by MoDMan
103-110	Third Base Magazine	John Boni, Henry Beard
111-112	How to Be Loathsomely Repellant to Women	Sean Crespo, James Pinkerton
113-118	Old Love Stories	Ed Subitzky, Illustrated by Joe Orlando
119-121	Pornography for the Dumb	Norman Rubington
122	Foto Funnies	
123-126	Mothers Little Helper	Anne Beatts, Ed Subitzky
127-129	Love: The Gathering	Mason Brown, Sean Crespo, Art by Keith Newton, Richard Carbajal
130-131	AOL Joe's Guide to Understanding Online Profiles	Joe Osterle, Mason Brown
132	Classic Cover	
133	LOOK OF LOVE	Scott Olsen
134	Foto Funnies	
135-142	This Magic Moment	Tod Carroll, John Weidman, Photos by Pedar Ness
143-146	Spicy Tales	Commander Barkfeather
147-151	Art or Porno	Geoffrey de Mandeville
152	Foto Funnies	
153-156	Try a Little Tenderloin	Tony Hendra, Ron Barrett
157-159	Fredrick's of Toyland	Michael O'Donoghue, Mary Mitchell, Illustrated by Neke Carson
160	Foto Funnies	
161-163	Tool Magazine	Steve Brykman
164	Foto Funnies	
165-169	Love Is	Mason Brown, Art by Joe Osterle
170	Foto Funnies	
171-179	Special Danish Section	Michael O'Donoghue, Sean Kelly, Robert Heit Cartoon: Joe Orlando
180	Classic Cover	David Kaestle
181	LITERATURE OF LOVE	Illustration, Emek
182-185	I, a Splurch	John Weidman, Illustrated by Peter Bramley
186-188	My Parents Met in a Chat Room	Pete Cummin
189	Strange Sex We Have Known	William S. Burroughs, Terry Southern
190	True Facts	
191-192	Parents of the Girls of the East-West Conference	Michael Reiss Photos by James Salzano
193-195	Father Aiken's Day Planner	Mason Brown
196-197	How to Write Dirty	Michael Reiss, Al Jean
198-202	Obligatory Sex Scenes	P.J. O'Rourke
203-207	History of Sex	Shary Flenniken
208	Foto Funnies	

FROM THE EDITOR IN CHIEF

Oh precious Love, that elusive spiritual treasure we all must discover to find completion. But what is Love? Is it the defining moment between the union of man and woman? Is it just a word? Is it a foolish, ambiguous emotion? Oh Love: it has plagued human existence since Man emerged from apes and realized that he was, in fact, very erect.

"How silver-sweet sound lovers' tongues by night,
Like softest music to attending ears!"
—William Shakespeare

For Man, Love can only be described as caring about someone deeply and then wanting to penetrate them even deeper. The two seem at odds with each other. How can you care about someone and then want to shove a hard object inside at least one of their body cavities? You would think that humans would have been designed differently. After all, we have dominion over the Animal Kingdom; where's our innate civility?

Why isn't rubbing feet enough? A massage? Even a good game of Lawn Darts?

Unfortunately, Man is doomed.

If Love is such a beautiful, intoxicating emotion, then why do we need the act of copulation to clinch it?

I love football, but I don't want to fornicate it. I love a really good movie, but I don't run up to the screen and hump it. I love cars, but I don't hang out at Jaguar Dealers so I can insert my rod into the glistening tailpipe of a new XK8.

I love women, but somehow this Love is different from all the other Loves. It's simply not enough to admire a beautiful woman: I want to enter her; ride her; poke her; pork her; bonk her; boff her; rub my member between her mounds; and, of course, flip her over and repeat… and this is normal. Normal, I tell you! Oh I'm not done… I want to handcuff her; spank her; zip her head into a rubber mask; take pictures of her; and then put it all on the Internet. What is wrong with me? With us? (I hope I'm not alone here.) Man shouldn't be allowed to continue on this earth until he can control his lust for the opposite sex.

"If love is rough with you, be rough with love. If love pricks you, prick it back, and you'll beat love down."
—William Shakespeare

Johnny Cochran once said, "It's all about race." But is it? Isn't it really all about sex? Look at his name, for God's sakes. Even white racist, redneck slave owners had sex with their black slaves. It's all about the sex act! Love is simply the prelude, the curtain before the peep show begins. It's reaching in your pocket to find that twenty that you know is in there to get that final lap dance. Love is that obsession a guy feels after sitting behind a tattooed, thong enhanced, partially exposed derriere while attending a two-hour seminar on the plight of salamanders.

Don't misunderstand me. I love Love. I really do. I cry at movies. I feel pain and empathy for my fellow man. But show me a pair of naked Thai twins performing fellatio on each other while straddling a spiked, Laotian coital trapeze and, well, I'm feeling stuff, but it ain't love.

How empty of me to be so full of him   —Janet Jackson

So what happened? We created an entire world to justify man's need to enter the female species. Skyscrapers built. Companies created. Yes, I'm even writing this article to ultimately impress some elusive, supermodel fantasy woman. But I'm surely not writing it out of Love. I don't love writing. I love watching football, and damn it, I'm missing the game! Here's the thought process: The book becomes a bestseller, I'll claim I wrote every word; get some press, appear on the "Today Show" with Katie Couric; some hot babe from high school--whom I never had a chance with--will see me (please be Pam Zurack – I'll never get over that rack), she'll find me on Classmates.com, send me naked pix of her, and rendezvous with me in a Motel 6 in Fontana for a night of euphoric, flesh pounding bliss.

Love is simply a momentary, self-induced distraction
to buy a guy a little peace between screws.   —Me

I was told as a child that when two people are in Love, they would blissfully hold hands, skip through endless green meadows, hop on two white horses and ride off to that golden rainbow in the sky. Maybe. But I still only see donkeys and uh, well… But don't give up. Thankfully, at National Lampoon, we're a collection of points of view. Our legendary writers are all here and some of our new resident comic geniuses as well. So, don't despair, maybe you'll find true Love after all.

With Love,

Scott Rubin
Editor in Chief
National Lampoon

LETTERS

Sirs:

They say love conquers all. But what about the U.S. military? If we went to war with love, who would win? I've heard stories of battles being won by women soldiers seducing the other side with sexual favors then killing them while they were doing it. I think I would enlist for that war. Up until the part where I would die.
Gen. George S. Patton Jr. (no relation)
Fort Knox (Not that one)

Sirs:

You want one?… Eeeeeeeech …Don't push back on my head so far … aaaaaaaaaaaaach…Here, have another…Ow…aaaaaaaach, one at a time, one at a time, ow…eeeeeeeeeech…Cherry, that's right…aaaaaaach…don't push so hard, you wanna give me whiplash?
A Pez Dispenser

Sirs:

What would I do for a Klondike Bar? Well, if you are referring to a bar of gold from the famous "rush" instigated by the 1898 Yukon Act, then I would say that I would do anything within my means to acquire this wealth. I would lie, cheat, steal, rape, kill, misreport my taxes—any manner of insubordination necessary.

However, if you are referring instead to the ice cream sandwich with a hard chocolate shell, I would probably not be so active in its acquisition. Perhaps I would not kill, but only go so far as to rape for a Klondike Bar. Come to think of it, I'd rape for anything, loose change, gum under a desk, or even tickets to the Denver Nuggets, and just about anything else of little to no value, if it must be known. I just like rape. What guy doesn't?
Skip Rutherford
Juno, Alaska
P.S. Incidentally, the ratio of men to women in Alaska is 10 to 1, hence the several references to forced intercourse. We're not monsters. We're just single. And horribly violent.

Sirs:

The author continuously employed the concept of the horrific and brutal act of sexual violence known as rape as some sort of punchline. The only thing worse would be a joke about cancer, something like this maybe, on board a flight, the pilot announced there was engine trouble and everyone was about to crash into the ocean.

In the stunned silence that followed, an angry voice spoke out, "Dammit! That stupid doctor of mine! He said I was going to die of cancer."
Dr. Harold Aswar,
Chief Oncologist,
Juno Presbyterian

Sirs:

Damn this infernal poverty! How can a fellow possibly get any saucy maidens to pose for him without a decent cash advance from the King. Whoever said babes love painters? Rich painters, maybe, but not a poor bastard the likes of myself. All I can get are these desperate, fat palookas just grateful to have someone stare at their tits for an hour and a half.

The deeper in debt I get, the bigger the dolls get. It's been weeks since I sold anything. I ask you: who's gonna pay for a picture of a big fat naked chick? Listen, I don't care how you do it, but please, whatever you do, GET ME SOME NICE SKINNY YOUNG MODELS WITH BIG JUGS AND A TIGHT CAN or pretty soon I'll have to declare chapter eleven!!
Peter Paul Rubens
Wherever the Flems come from

Sirs:

Do you guys make up your letters or are they for real?
Bob Guccione
Penthouse magazine
New York, New York

Sores:

Sure, eet's a bommer being blind, but you don't need to see a hand chob.
Jorge Luis "Gorgeous Jorge" Borges
Buenos Aires, Argentina

Sirs:

Take my wives… Please!
Brigham Youngman
Colorado City, Arizona

Sirs:

Every time I write "Sirs," this pathetic paper clip pops up on my screen, and asks me if I "want help?" Fuck him. I can write a goddamned letter by myself.

But there are times he could help. Why just last night, I was searching for an Asian Teens site. It would have been nice for that paper clip to pop up and say, "It looks like you're trying to masturbate to Asian Teens, do you want help?" "Yes, of course I want help, Mr. Paper Clip! My wife and kids will be coming home any minute and I don't want to be caught, so get me some yellow muffin pronto!"

But was the paper clip there for me when I needed it most? No.

Thanks Microsoft. I thank you, my wife thanks you, and my two scarred children thank you. Fortunately, my attorney will also be sure to find Mr. Paper Clip helpful when he writes out my lawsuit.
Frank Sporacio
In his den,
With the door locked this time

Sirs:

I have a question about sexual etiquette for the swingin' seventies, and I wonder if you could make like Harry Reems and, you know, fill me in. What I want to know is: when a girl gives a fella a hand job, who should provide the hanky? My most recent sexual partner says the government should, but he's a Commie and also unemployed.
Edna Fingers
Los Angeles, California

Sirs:

I fucked a Mellon.
Mr. Mellon
The Mellon Ranch

Sirs:

I'm not really a homosexual. I'm just trying to stay out of the Army.
Chevy Chase
NBC Stock Pen
Saturday Night, New Jersey

Sirs:

Howdy! I want to get something off my mind that's been pesterin' me for years. What I actually meant to say was "I never met a man I didn't lick." Ya see, I was never much for spellin', and this was in the days before spell check. But boy did I love lickin' men. I plum loved to run my hot wet tongue from the tips of a man's toes, up his calves, between his thighs… the works!

Don't get me wrong. I'm not gay. I'm just a people-person. A male-people-person.

Just wanted to clear that misunderstanding up.
Will Rogers
A rest area near you

Sirs:

Recently I read an article in Gallery about the practice of autofellatio, you know, blowing yourself. Well, I tried it, and wow! It's great! There's just one problem. How do I keep my hat from falling off?

Bob Hawkins
Columbus, Ohio

Sirs:

The cover of this new book of yours really made me nostalgic. It's as if you transported me back in time to a Leno monologue from a few years ago. Could your next cover please feature an O.J. joke? I think that would be funny. Thank you for catering to me.

Middle America
Middle America

Sirs:

This is a "drag letter." I'm pretending I'm a woman while I'm writing it. I happen to be a married man with two kids, but I find it stimulating to occasionally write letters like this. I don't think it hurts anyone. It's not like I "dress up" or anything. I don't even use scented stationery or funny-colored ink, although I do sometimes dot my i's with little tiny circles. I wonder if any of your other readers share this interest?

Eleen (Bob) Arkins
Richmond, Indiana

Sirs:

Knock knock.
Who's there?
Menandwomen.
Menandwomen who?
Menandwomen sure are different.
Watch my Premium Blend spot and check out my subversive point of view on this and other benign issues. (I also cover how L.A. and New York are nothing alike.)

Generic Comic
Ha-Ha Factory
Cerritos, California

Sirs:

I'm a 45-year-old dentist who used to think your magazine was a real hoot, all those funny articles about women and how dumb they are and everything. I'm very happy to hear of the release of your Big Book of Love. As someone who casually, regularly takes advantage of anesthetized women, it's good to know there's still a place for us guys on the bookshelves. Remember the drunk-girl scene from *Animal House*? I do.

Ed Hadley, DDS
Framingham, Massachusetts

Sirs:

I love you, but more as a brother. Please let's not spoil what we already have. I'd be devastated if I lost your friendship.

Every hot girl you ever wanted
The part of the past you cannot escape

Sirs:

Speaking of love.... you know what I would love? I would love it if James Gandolfini would stop farting on me. Jesus, that guy's farts are enough to make you want to puke.

James Gandolfini's chair
North Haledon, New Jersey

Sirs:

All you need is love. Oh yeah, and a bulletproof vest.

John Lennon
Rock-n-Roll Heaven

Sirs:

That whole "two hearts beat as one" thing is way overrated. Take it from us.

The Conjoined Iranian twins
Separate coffins, Iran

Sirs:

Why is there so much hate in the world? (sigh) My guess is television.

Gerry Adams
Sinn Féin President
Belfast, Ireland
Secret Meetinghouse at 45 Finnegan Lane
(Please ring bell, then knock twice.)

Sirs,

I'm 58 and finally going through puberty. I wasn't into girls when you were still publishing the magazine. It's a pretty lucky thing this book came out just now cause I have to get some stroke time in before I die! Never mind. I died. But thanks anyway.

Treat Gravus
Lotion, Pennsylvania

Sirs,

What's hard, smooth, and wet all over?
This book, if it were dunked in water or any other fluid.

Ed Myna
The Land of the Obvious

Sirs,

Sting is a liar. I had a team of doctors build a fortress around my heart. It blocked almost every artery, vein, and capillary in my upper body. Damn thing almost killed me.
Well, what kind of logic can you expect from a man fatigued from 8 straight hours of doing it.

Nick Yasouf
Surrey, England

Sirs:

Love, Love me Doo?
You know I love me doo! That's why I'm called Seamus, the Scat-loving Leprechaun.

Seamus, the scat-loving Leprechaun
Ireland
The Brown-Jewel of the United Kingdom

Sirs:

Just yesterday I took the old towel I wash my car with and threw it on the kitchen floor. Then I asked my wife to stand on it. When I pointed out to her that she was quite literally "on the rag," she did not laugh. Women have no sense of humor.

William Safire
The New York Times

Sirs:

I'll tell you, if women had seven-inch long clits that shot hot mucous, your oral sex picture would sure be different.

Women
Everywhere

Sirs:

What's the worst thing you can put in your mouth? I've heard varying opinions on this. I need to know because I'm Catholic.

Connie "The Bomb" Scuzapelli
Chicago, Illinois

Sirs:

My next film is called *De Lighthousen unt de Menen*. It is about a lonely man who moves to a lighthouse on the Swedish coast, in wintertime. He goes to this barren outpost so that he will have time to brood about past failures, to berate himself for past foolhardiness, and to agonize over long-dead love affairs.

People often ask me, why are all my films so stifling and dark? Why so unremittingly depressing and hopeless? I will tell you why. It is because I lived with Liv Ullmann for many years, and in all that time she never once gave me a blow job. Not once. Not even a little one. Can you conceive of how depressing that was?

I forgot to tell you the last part of the film. It seems that the lighthouse that the lonely man moved to had been built only the same morning, at low tide. After the desolate man moves his few miserable belongings into the lighthouse, the tide comes in, the lighthouse is engulfed by the sea, and the man is drowned. The lighthouse, you see, was too short. Now leave me alone; I have a film to make and then I am going to kill myself.

Ingmar Bergman
Negatyevv Fjord, Sweden

Sirs:

Not only does everything taste better *on* a Ritz, some things even taste better with a Ritz jammed way up them.
If you catch my drift.

Andy Griffith
Mayberry, R.F.D.

Love Among the Lesions
Universal Herpes Act to assure future security of U.S.

IT BEGINS WITH A PARADOX: A burning, itching sensation in what should be the body's focus of purest pleasure. Next comes a devastating fever. And, throughout it all, there are the telltale sores: small red lesions informing their victims that they are participating in the greatest sexual epidemic in American history. They have herpes.

Now, in an effort to control the effects of the disease, Congress has authorized the Centers for Disease Control in Atlanta to herpeate the drinking water of the entire United States.

"It's really a very simple process," according to CDC spokesman Dr. Abner Clayton. "It's just like fluoridation, only a lot easier, because these little germs grow like mad. We nurture them in huge Petri dishes, and then just dump 'em in the reservoirs. It won't be long before every man, woman, and child in the United States has the disease, and then we can all just go ahead and forget it!'

Helping publicize the new universal herpes program, cast members of television's "Love Boat" show off newly formed eruptions and, not coincidentally, newly uninhibited attitudes toward having sex.

The action was made necessary, according to Clayton, "because people who have the disease—and there are untold millions of them—just aren't copulating anymore. Either they're in too much pain, or they're in remission but afraid of giving it to somebody else. And the people who haven't caught it aren't copulating either, because they're so afraid of getting it. In this liberated age, even husbands and wives are terrified of each other. The result is that virtually everyone in the country is walking around frustrated and edgy. Our industrial output is dropping. And, of course, no one is having any babies. A few more years of this and we'll be easy prey for the Russians."

The only sensible solution, Clayton says, was "to let the other shoe drop and give it to everybody. Now we can all stop worrying about when we're going to get it and who we're going to get it from and get back to the business of living. It's a practical, cost-effective way to keep America copulating and populating."

Clayton beamed. "Why, my wife got her first lesion yesterday, and I woke up this morning feeling a little tender down you-know-where. Once the initial pain and fever subside in a few weeks, we're planning on a second honeymoon."

MEDIA

Porn Industry Predicts Orifice Shortage

SAN FERNANDO VALLEY, CA–Members of the adult film industry met yesterday at the Holiday Inn in Torrance to discuss possible steps regarding what they see as a growing orifice shortage in their films. Or, as one insider joked, "To get this hole fucking thing figured out."

For years the twin cornerstones of the adult film industry–the vagina and the mouth–never failed to arouse millions of fans. The last few years, however, has seen more of a focus on hot anal action. Now porn industry exporters are finally acknowledging a fear that's been in the back of their minds since the industry started. "We're running out of areas of the body to put a nice hard cock," said producer Saul Rubens.

In the nineties, to combat growing apathy toward the vagina, directors had begun to explore other areas. This led to a proliferation of scenes depicting both sodomy and perhaps even the more graphic, facial ejaculation shot. But now the question is, where do you go from here?

The answer, unfortunately, is not so easily found. The bar has been set so high that many industry insiders are hoping for something close to a miracle and are willing to look anywhere to find it. Vicious Video CEO Harvey Glick explains, "There's going to be a time–a year from now, maybe less–when guys out there will get just plain bored of seeing a woman take it up the ass or swallow a man's load. And we sure as hell better be prepared for that day or we'll all be screwed." Amen to that.

If current alternative orifice acceptance is any indication, directors and producers seem ready to take it to the next level. Evidence of this can be seen in one recent porn film with a cock very close to a woman's ear. The ear is one of the orifices up for consideration, as are eyes, flared nostrils, and the armpit. "The armpit might seem unappealing to some, but that's probably the same reaction men had the first time they saw *Ass Bandits*," said Stu Weiner, director of *Ass Bandits 6, Return to Darkness*.

There has also been scientific discussion regarding the possibility of creating an artificial orifice. "Several colleagues of mine have explored the potentiality of a side orifice–the soft area below the ribcage but above the pelvic bone – that sounds like one place a man might find pleasurable… I guess," commented Dr. Sydney Katz.

Another place industry giants are taking a look is at the emerging adult independent film market as well as foreign films ("Hey, you don't have to worry about dubbing a French woman moaning"). It's in the adult "indies" that one can see true risk-taking–actors and actresses less interested in being typecast and more interested in giving it up to the camera.

The conference ended on a positive note with many deciding to view challenge as opportunity. "It's a very exciting time to be in the business. We need to get back to the basics–focus on what's exciting the American male now?" concluded Harvey Glick. "Once thing is for sure, the porn industry has faced crises like this before and come out on top." They better or there's going to be a lot of horny men walking the streets.

Housewife Furious After Exchange of "Fantasy Fling" List

EL SEGUNDO–After spotting Burt Reynolds in a local Circle K convenience mart two days ago, Gail Collins jokingly warned her husband Don that "if I weren't married, I would have definitely gone out with him." To which, Don amicably replied: "If you can get Burt Reynolds to sleep with you, go right ahead."

A good-natured Gail then suggested that the couple imitate an old "Friends" episode and each create a list of five names of "lifetime fantasy flings." According to the show's premise, Don and Gail would then be officially able to have an affair with any names from the list without guilt or fear of repercussion.

Don readily agreed to the scheme and both set to work on creating their lists, unveiling them over a romantic dinner at a nearby Appleby's the next evening.

After the waiter brought the couple their order of potato skins, Gail revealed her list first.

Don was unfazed by his wife's first four selections of Brad Pitt, Mel Gibson, Johnny Depp, and Colby from *Survivor*. Don seemed bemused by Gail's fifth choice, Tom Cruise. "Good luck on that one," he smirked knowingly. "Might as well add Nathan Lane to your list. Go ahead. It's a freebee."

Don then gave Gail his list and, according to restaurant patrons, it was here that the fighting began.

"Your list has three co-workers, somebody named Linda1983@aol.com and my sister, Shawna!" screamed Gail. "What the hell is that about?"

"Well, it's pretty obvious that Shawna is way hot," explained Don. "And I'm fairly certain she likes me. That last cookout we had at your parents' house, she kept brushing up against me and asking whether or not I needed more suntan lotion. That was a real turn-on. And the fact that she's your sister. That is definitely a huge fantasy for me.

"As for Martha Winchester from accounting," Don continued, "she always wears really frumpy white blouses and glasses, but one time I noticed that she was wearing thigh-highs underneath that flannel business skirt. Man, I bet she's wild once you get her going."

"And Carla Donnelly has fucked about half my sales department," went on Don. "Everyone says she likes it nasty. My friend Rick said she even likes it in the ass. That's something I never get to do, especially not with a true butt slut who begs for more. Talk about hot!"

"What about Sarah Burnes?" fumed Gail. "For Christ sakes, she's nothing special!"

"Sarah, Sarah, Sarah," mused Don "I don't know. She reminds me of you about ten years ago." "She's nice. She laughs at my jokes. She wants kids, just like you did before we had the twins. We went out for drinks after a convention meeting in Vegas and we really hit it off. You two should get together. You'd like each other."

It was at this point that Gail Collins threw her drink at her husband, called him an "asshole" and stormed out of the restaurant.

When Don returned to his house, he found his belongings in a suitcase on the front porch. He decided to take refuge at Sarah Burnes' condo.

"It's just a silly little 'fantasy fling' list," stated Ms. Burnes. "I don't know why Gail's making such a big deal out of it. I'm sure that this will blow over. She seems like a really nice woman, but sometimes I wonder whether she knows what a prize she has in Don."

Linda1983@aol.com apparently agrees.

"We have the most meaningful conversations," wrote Linda1983 when contacted for this article. "He IM's me, and it's like I'm talking to the most sensitive man in the world. He really understands what a girl like me is going through. He reads my poetry and everything. I can't wait to meet him offline."

"We're scheduled to meet for Linda's prom," said Don. "I had said I couldn't go with her. That it would be wrong. But now, I figure I can. I mean, what the hell, she's on the list."

U.S. Fish and Wildlife Service Releases Sexual Predators Into the Wild

WASHINGTON, D.C.–Thrilled by the successful reintroduction of grey wolves into the wild, U.S. game wardens have released 34 convicted child molesters back into their natural habitats—basement apartments near elementary schools.

"We're very excited to get these men out of captivity and back to the suburbs where they belong," stated Ken Besson, spokesman for U.S. Fish and Wildlife Service.

Early results have been mixed. Seven of the sexual predators have been shot by residents who claimed to have mistaken the felons for rabid coyotes. And one pederast died due to a lethal combination of easy access to Internet kiddie porn and an insatiable desire for autoerotic asphyxiation.

Still others, however, have thrived.

"We have found torn and tattered cotton panties by the bedsides of most of the remaining predators," beamed Besson. "And approximately 15 preschoolers have disappeared from nearby neighborhoods. Children are their natural prey, so that's a great sign."

But many locals are not as pleased.

"We hope they come to their senses and that the American public will say enough is enough," said Carla Winchester. "Children are dying here! It seems like the only people benefiting from this whole fiasco is the Milk Carton industry."

Besson refuses to be swayed by such "inflammatory rhetoric." According to him, "sexual predators are an invaluable part of natural selection, culling overly trusting children from the human herd before they can grow up to be scammed by boiler-room telemarketers. "

"To some people," continued Besson, "seeing the corpses of sexually assaulted children dripping blood and semen from every orifice is ugly, but to me it's all a beautiful part of God's grand design."

If the sexual predator program does succeed, the Fish and Wildlife Service will proceed with its plans to reintroduce roaming packs of Puerto Rican youths to New York City's Central Park.

"Take Your Kids to Work Day" Shatters NBA Playoff Attendance Record

LOS ANGELES – Last Thursday's Game 2 match-up between the Los Angeles Lakers and the Portland Trailblazers shattered all prior NBA attendance records, as players from both teams wholeheartedly embraced "Take Your Kids to Work Day."

The stands at the 20,000 seat Staples Center started filling up early as the first of Sean Kemp's offspring began arriving. Within minutes, security knew they had a potential problem on their hands.

"We're a good-sized arena," stated Director of Operations Kyle Hadley, "but we've got limits! We've only got a few hundred will-call tickets available. We can't be expected to seat all of the Trailblazers' kids! Especially not after they traded for Strickland!"

Hadley quickly set aside the entire loge for children of the visitors. But his problems were exacerbated by the fact that both Stacey Augmon and Greg Anthony went to UNLV during the Tarkanian years, meaning that anyone born in Nevada in the past 10 years is presumed related. Moreover, Portland Center Rasheed Wallace, the league leader in technical fouls, has been as loose a cannon off the court as on it.

Tensions rose even further when one legitimate child showed up, escorted by his mother. Legions of strippers, escorts, groupies, and junkies started hurling spent syringes at the pair, and accusing them of "not keeping it real."

Fortunately for Hadley, trouble was averted when Sean Kemp's children realized that their father was not at work, but rather at drug rehab for cocaine abuse. By game time, most of his 7,500+ boys and girls drifted out of the Staples Center, leaving plenty of room for rabid LA ticketholders to arrive at their traditional time, midway through the second quarter.

Commissioner David Stern noted that "this unfortunate incident has made us much more aware of some of the problems that our league faces. For instance, if Sean Kemp were ever to face Larry Johnson on a future Take Your Kids to Work Day, the game would have to be held in the Rose Bowl. It seats over 100,000." ☐

TOOLS OF LOVE

MY PENIS

by
Karen
Wheatley
as told to
John
Hughes

One day last fall, I woke up with a…with this…with a…well, it was, it was all covered with hair and um, it was, oh, it was big and, ah, it was a…you know, it was a…what it was was a…it was like a, well…it was a penis. A real one. It scared me to death!

I had all the right kind of privates when I went to bed, I think, but when I got up I had a you-know-what and some other things from a boy's "down there" and it was terrible. Can you imagine being a sixteen-year-old girl who is very popular and who has a really neat life but suddenly grows a ... penis? Oh, God! I thought it was the end of the world or something because I wanted to be a wife or a girl friend, at least, and a mother, and wives and mothers and even girl friends don't have you-know-whats. And if I wasn't a girl anymore, I would have to take boys' gym and shop class and I would have to quit cheerleaders and the girls' gymnastics team. I'd have to get all new clothes and bedroom furniture and I could never be pretty again. Plus I'm sure it would really make my relatives upset.

I don't know how this happened to me. It just did. But I think it had something to do with my hormones, because at my age hormones are really screwy and it doesn't take too much to make them even more screwy. Just before this happened, I had a serious pimple attack, so my hormones must have been wrong already for that to happen. I also was drinking a lot of Cokes and eating a lot of French fries and I went through this period when I kind of craved Kit-Kat candy bars and I think that maybe all that stuff affected my hormones that were not too good in the first place. Also, about a week or so before I woke up with the ... with that "thing" "down there," I noticed my little thingie that's in my "down there" and is hard to find because it's so small and all wrapped up in stuff, I noticed that it was kind of sore. I thought it was just a virus or a "girl problem," but then it got, like sort of, you know, it was like swollen? And then a couple of days later it looked a little bigger. And then, that morning ... I mean, I don't spend a lot of time staring down at my personal area, if you know what I mean, so I tend to miss things that go on "down there."

But I sure couldn't miss this. It was as big as a carrot!

"It," the "thing," that is, the "thing" I woke with, was, to describe it, well, it was the stiff kind and as long as my hand and thicker than a bottle of Ban roll-on. It was the color of a Mexican person's skin and it had a whole bunch of gross veins all over it. And the tip part there was like a knob with a hole in it which is for both kinds of stuff to go out of, you know. Then down below were the whatchamacallits and they were really ugly!

I was somewhat terrified by all of this and I really, really missed my girl privates and I wondered where they went and would they ever come back. I didn't want to tell anybody because I didn't want to end up in one of those newspapers at the grocery store that have weird people and stories in them. I felt like the "thing" belonged to somebody else and I just couldn't get used to it poking out of my pajamas. Plus, I had to go the bathroom super-bad and I had no idea at all of how to use one of those things. Also, how do you walk with one so that your family doesn't know about it?

I tried walking a couple of different ways. They all looked ridiculous. Finally I had to bend way over like my grandmother, who has curvature of the spine, and walk with my legs stiff. I looked out my door. There wasn't anybody around so I went down the hall real quick and into the bathroom. I locked the door and pulled up my nightie, and then I saw myself in the mirror with my, up on the top with my — how do I say it? — with my chest with my bosoms on it and then down "below" with a "thing" It looked pretty weird but, you know, sort of cool, but sort of scary but also not so bad, but actually, probably, gross.

And then I found out pretty fast that girl going-to-the-bathroom is a lot easier than boy going-to-the-bathroom. First of all, you know, the "thing" was going up and the toilet was down. So, if you think about it, the number one would go up and then

come down, but how far up would it go and how hard and where would it come down? I'm no genius in math so I couldn't exactly figure it out, but oh God! I had to go so bad! And I couldn't do it like I usually did because that would mean it would go up and come down in my lap, which would not be too cool. So instead, I stood over the toilet like I was going to sit down only more like straddling it and I didn't sit down either; I leaned way, way back and put my head against the wall (I'm on the girls gymnastics team), and I figured the number one would go up and come down in the toilet, but that's not what happened at all. I relaxed my going-to-the-bathroom muscles (they are the same in boys and girls, for your information), and yucky number one blasted out of the "thing" and it went all over! It was out of control, spraying like crazy all over the towels and the toilet paper and the floor, and when I turned around to try and point it into the toilet (they don't bend), it squirted all over the sink and the toothbrushes (yuck!) and my makeup (brand new!!) and the hair dryer. Boys and dads talk about how they have it made because they can go out in the woods. Well, they don't have it made at all because it's just a mess! Also, those things are practically impossible to, you know, to wipe. Because you wipe off the end and it still drips and drips. No matter how much you wipe it, it still leaks.

After going to the bathroom, the penis became an unstiff one. I was so relieved because I thought that it was going away, but a couple of minutes later, when I tried to put on my underpants, it went and got bigger again. What a pain! Plus, when it's small it's even uglier. It's shrively and wrinkly and it looks liked dried-up fruit.

Speaking of underpants, if all girls grew "things," there sure would be a lot of girls' underpants given to the Goodwill because "things" and whatchamacallits don't fit into girls' underpants at all. Even when it was small it wouldn't fit into my underpants, not even my great big period panties, so I had to steal a pair of my brother's underpants, and if you think it's not sickening to wear somebody else's boys' underpants, you're crazy! Also, boys' underpants are extremely ugly. They have this funny opening in the front and they're white and made out of dumb material and they have real wide waistbands and they're not pretty at all. Plus, the penis kept falling out of the opening, which I don't know why is there if the penis falls out, do you? I had to put it back, but it got twisted around and bent under. And whenever I touched it to move it, it got bigger and that made it harder to move and so I had to touch it more and pretty soon it was all tangled up and it took about ten minutes to fix it and by then my mom was screaming for me to come down and eat breakfast.

It is so embarrassing to eat and talk with your mom and dad and brother with a "thing" in your pants. Plus, it was hard to walk when it was stiff. But it was okay because by the time I sat down, it was small, but then when it was small, it stuck to the skin on my leg and that felt just icky. The good thing about girls' "privates" is that even though you get a "visitor" every month, the stuff stays the same size all the time and it doesn't make it hard for you to walk. You know, lots of boys walk funny sometimes, and I'll bet this is why.

Anyway, after breakfast I said goodbye to my parents, who were going to play tennis because it was Saturday, and I said good-bye to my brother, who was going camping with his friends, and when everybody was gone I went back upstairs and looked at myself some more.

This may sound really queer, and please understand that I *don't* do this often and I never did it before, but I laid on my back naked (it sounds icky but it wasn't at the time, really), but I laid there and, um, I looked down, and sort of, sort of, well, I didn't have my clothes on and

I looked between my "busts," I looked between them and down at the penis thing and to see both of them at the same time was "interesting."

I kind of experimented with it, like, I found out that by squeezing my rear end muscles I could make the "thing" jump, and then when I let go it dropped down, which was neat, sort of, and was something I could never do in a million years with girls' parts. Like I said, it was real ugly, but after looking at it for a while, I sort of decided that it was cool-ugly (the guy who sings for Queen is super-ugly but still cool).

The whatchamacallits, however, are just plain regular ugly. They are in this bag thing that is made of skin that is as saggy as anything! Sometimes it was loose and felt sort of like a hairy glove and then like if a breeze blew in the window or I touched the mirror to it and the mirror was cold, it shrunk up and looked like the sides of an accordion.

Way, way back behind the whatchamacallits was the rear end, and I think it was the one I always had, except it had hair around it.

As I was "down there" I kind of wondered, and I don't mean that I thought about this right away, it sort of just flashed in my mind and I'm not into this at all and I was not a big fan of this sort of stuff when I was completely girl and had all the girl stuff, but I wondered about what would happen if I did to it what sometimes happens with boys. Do you know what I mean? Let me start over. I should probably *never*, ever, ever tell anyone about this and I'm sure that right now my common sense is having a s—fit, but I've, like, made love with my hand about ten times to my boyfriend Chuck (this is embarrassing), which is called a "hand job," which, if you don't know, is sex with your hands. And, to make a long story short, I wondered a little bit if I could do the same thing to myself that I did to Chuck.

I didn't know if it was different when you do it to a boy than when you do it

to yourself because I never had a "thing" before and so how could I know? So I decided, and this may sound real sick, but it's what happened and I guess it was kind of gross, but it wasn't, if you knew what I felt like then. I guess you had to be there. But anyhow, I did it like I did it to Chuck, that was, I put my fingers around it and I counted one-two-three like I always do but this time I counted out loud (I don't count out loud with Chuck). I counted one-two-three and then I started going up and down like I was shaking up a can of whipped cream, and boy did it ever hurt! Ouch! Ouch! OUCH! I pulled off some skin. Poor Chuck!

I sure had a lot to learn but it was fun, sort of, learning. I should probably tell you that when a girl gets touched in a "certain way" in a "certain place," if you get what I'm saying, it sort of tickles, then it feels good, then it tickles again, then it feels good again, then it tickles again, and so on until you have to go home or you get scared. But with a boy's "thing" it feels better and better and better until bang! You shoot sperms all over yourself. That part feels great! You don't even care if you got sperms in your face and your hair and on the curtains that your mom just made for you.

Let me be the first to say that sperm is the absolute grossest! Even when it's your own. Uck! It smells like Comet cleanser and it looks like runny nose. Plus, it is sticky gooey and it splatters out of the penis in warm, gucky glumps and glops and it keeps coming out even after you get dressed. After you finish, you don't remember how cool it felt, you just feel stupid and guilty and sick with yourself for doing it and getting sperms all over everything, and sperms are living, you know — they're like bugs, and they get all over. On top of that, the penis gets small and ugly. The only thing that is better about boy "sex" by yourself than girl "sex" by yourself is that with boy "sex," you know when it's over.

That afternoon I had gymnastics practice. I rode my ten speed over to the school and, let me tell you, all that riding with a "thing" and the other stuff is a lot different. Mainly because the "stuff" squishes around and you probably already know that when that "stuff" squishes around, the "thing" gets stiff, which it did, and when it's stiff you can't pedal, believe me.

One more thing about a penis. It doesn't look very good in a leotard. Because it shows and it's no secret that you have a penis when you wear one, so I had to bring a pair of culottes and blouse that matches to practice. I'd rather have everybody think I'm retarded than to have them know that I had a penis, because with that I couldn't be in a girls' gymnastics meet, Could I? I will say, though, that wearing culottes and a blouse in gymnastics is about as queer a thing as you can do in high school.

I was fifth up on the balance beam, which is my specialty. I was second runner-up at the All-State Girls' Invitational Round Robin Suburban Central Division Finalist Prep Meet and I've practiced a lot since then. My main stunt on the beam was a handstand and then a swing down into a straddle position.

Everything was going just perfect and I felt like I was in the Olympics until I went into my handstand and then swung down into the straddle position and landed on everything "down there"... and it felt like somebody shot a bullet up my rump and clashed cymbals on my head. Then I rolled off the beam and onto the floor and laid there all curled up and screaming.

Naturally, anytime a girl falls down in gym, everybody thinks she's broken her female organs and will never be able to have babies. But I just said I was okay and that some wind got knocked out of me and if it was okay, I'd just go home. My best friend, Roberta, helped me into the locker room. So far, this penis was a real stupid thing.

Roberta has always been my best friend since about three years ago and I like her a lot, but I didn't want her to see "it" because if I didn't like "it" too much and if she was grossed out by "it," I'd feel even worse than I already felt. But Roberta sticks like Super-Glue and I knew she wouldn't leave, and besides, deep down inside, way, way down in the most secret caves of my personal self, was a little voice that said, "Show her," because secretly I wanted to show someone but then again I didn't.

I said, "Roberta, are you my best friend?" And she said, "For sure!" And I said, "Can I trust you completely?" And she said, "For sure!" And so I said, "Even if it was sort of gross?" And she said, "What?" And I pulled down my culottes and she said, "Yeast?" And I said, "No! Look!" And she saw the underpants and she gasped and said, "Boys' underpants!" I said, "Worse," and I pulled down the underpants (girls pull down their underpants a lot when other girls are around and it doesn't bother them). Roberta bent over just a little bit to get a better look and she was watching really intense and then all of a sudden the penis flipped out and Roberta's mouth dropped open and her retainer fell out on the floor, I swear to God! Then she screamed, "A thing! A thing! *You have a thing*!" She was shrieking. "Oh, my God! God! God! A thing! A thing!"

I yanked up the underpants as fast as I could and I shouted, "You jerk!" in my most mad voice. But she just kept shrieking, "A thing! You have a thing!" She's really immature sometimes.

Obviously she had never seen a penis before. She probably never even saw her dad's and she doesn't have any brothers and she's not very popular with boys because she's fat and not altogether beautiful and so I guess I can't blame her for being as shocked as she was. It was just kind of depressing to have someone act like you're a freak because you have something that you never asked for and have to have anyway.

Roberta acted hysterical for a little while longer and then she sort of calmed down (I think she got tired) and then we sat and stared at each other and I told her how I woke up with "it" and everything like that and she said she was really shocked at first but now it didn't seem so bad. Then she asked if she could look at it again.

Roberta really studied it close and made a lot of remarks about it and asked a whole bunch of questions about stuff that I didn't know about, so I just told her that it was a real, actual man's penis and that was all I knew. And then she asked if she could touch it.

I didn't know about that. She was a girl and I was a girl. But I wasn't a girl "down there" because girls don't have "those." So I guessed that it couldn't be queer because it's only queer when girls' parts and girls' parts touch. So I said, "Go ahead and touch it because it's not queer to touch it." And she picked it up like it was a little white mouse in biology lab or something and then she looked under it and pulled it and squeezed it.

Can you guess what happened when she did all that? Right! And it got stiff all of a sudden in one big spurt and it flew out of Roberta's hand. It slapped her chin and scared the life out of her and she screamed and jumped and put her hands up to her mouth like in the movies. I started to laugh, it was just so funny, and Roberta started to laugh, too, and we got real hysterical!

But it wasn't too safe to be out in the locker room with a "thing," so we went into the towel room and locked the door so I could show Roberta how cool it looked to have a "thing" plus boobies. You'd probably do the same if you were in my situation, she was my friend and all. Then Roberta got real excited and she was laughing and she grabbed it and I got that weird feeling in my butt and my hips started moving all by themselves and I crouched down and closed my eyes and then, you know, well, it just, it ... I squirted sperms all over Roberta's sleeve.

It completely grossed Roberta out to have sperms on her sleeve. She grabbed a towel and started rubbing like crazy and I thought she was going to throw up, but then she asked me if that was a "hand job" she'd just done and I said I guessed so and then she seemed to look sort of happy, real happy all of a sudden, and she said, "I did a hand job? That was a hand job?" and she forgot all about the sperms that were swimming on her blouse because she was so relieved to find out that "hand jobs" don't hurt or make you bleed and you don't have to put anything gross in your mouth. But I was still really surprised when she said, "Let's go over to your parents' house and have 'sex relations' with it." Which was what she said next.

You see, although Roberta and I are virgins, I am less of a virgin than she is, and anyway, we both know that a man puts his ... you know, there's a woman's too and together they put this, um, oh, let's see, they, he, she, he puts the ... penis in her, you know what it is, it's a vagina and he puts "it" in there. In other words, he sticks his in hers.

So, the first thing to do at my house was to get naked, which we did, and although I've seen Roberta naked about a million times (we have gym together), I thought it was kind of gross, but now it didn't look too bad. She bent over to take off her underpants and I sneaked a look up at her bottom. Now that sounds very sick, but at the time it was okay.

Then we had to decide which way to do "it," so I just said for Roberta to bend over and we could do "it" like "that" and she said no because then she couldn't see. It was her idea for us to lay on top of each other, but I said that our boobies would be touching and, if that happened, it would definitely be "lezzie" plus how could she see that way and she said she could point toward the mirror, but that was icky. We tried sitting in a chair, but Roberta was too fat and the "thing" bent and it hurt.

We thought about it for a while and then finally we cleared all the junk off

the top of my desk and Roberta climbed up on it and laid down (this gets a little weird and embarrassing) and her legs hung over the edge so that I could stand and point "it" at "hers" The part that was the worst was opening up her legs because when I did, I saw all of the most private, private parts on the inside and that should be a complete secret from everybody and I felt kind of sick and didn't want to do it but I thought that I'd better in case this "thing" went away tomorrow. Anyway, I pointed "it" at her "place" and it looked pretty big and her ... vagina looked pretty small. Roberta said, "It won't fit. It'll hurt."

I personally didn't think it would fit either, but I didn't tell Roberta because, well ... actually I really wanted to do this now. I mean, I don't know why, I just did. (Are you sick yet?) And so I put "it" on her skin and stuff and pushed. Roberta said, "Oww! Let's not do this, okay?"

I pushed harder and harder and harder. Roberta gritted her teeth and moaned and then all of a sudden, whooooooosh! It slid in all the way and bumped into something and squirted sperms inside of Roberta just about under her belly button. Roberta grunted really loud, like a pig, and her hips started going back and forth so fast that I could hardly see them, they were all blurry. It was disgusting to see, but the "thing" felt the *best*. "Intercourse," for all the bad things you hear about it, was pretty cool.

Roberta stopped moving and grunting a couple of seconds later and she laid there and then she started to cry. I pulled out the "thing" and it was coated with gunk from Roberta and some sperms were still coming out of it and that was the grossest part, so far, of all, about having a "thing."

Incidentally, when you have "sex" girl-style you feel warm and cuddly and you want to hug and kiss and get married and have a house and children, but with boy "sex" you just want to get up and go outside and never think about

girls again. So I didn't want to hang around and listen to Roberta cry. She was moaning and saying that her vagina hurt and that it was probably all stretched out and wrecked and she couldn't tell her husband that she was a virgin and she was only fifteen and all that stuff, and I didn't want to hear it. Then she was putting on her bra and I was putting on my blouse and we both stopped and looked at each other and said, "The sperms!" There were sperms inside Roberta and we had forgotten all about what they can do to girls our age.

But by dinner time I was real comfortable with the penis. I wasn't upset about Roberta anymore because she called and said that the sperms came out in her underpants on her way home and just as a precaution she jumped up and down 100 times and put two Midols in her vagina. And also I didn't really care all that much at the time because I figured that would be her problem and, besides, who would make two girls get married?

I noticed one thing and that was that I felt like I was stronger. A lot stronger. For example, I did twenty push-ups (boy push-ups, not on-my-knees kind) and I chinned myself ten times and before I couldn't even do one. That was neat. I guess it went with the penis.

I had a date with Chuck that night and he came over sort of early and had to stay downstairs and talk to my parents while I got ready, which took me a long time because for some reason or other, it was real boring to do my hair, which I usually like to do and I also hated putting on my makeup and I had to do it over about five times. But finally I got ready and I put on jeans and a long sweater and when I walked downstairs, I put my hand in front of my lump.

Chuck took me to a party and it was strange because I knew he was going to take me to a party and try to get me drunk or stoned, which is what he did, and I knew he was going to drive out to the pumping station and park, which is also what he did, and I knew he was going to do all this because that was what I wanted to do, too. Which was really strange.

Anyway, I let Chuck rub all over my boobies. I usually don't let him do that right away and I still don't, because I think a girl shouldn't make herself available to that sort of stuff just like it was there for the taking without any meaningful relationships or anything, but that night it was okay, I guess. (But I don't do it anymore.) But, anyway, it felt super and it made my "thing" get stiff.

He took my blouse off, which I hardly ever let happen because it's kind of embarrassing to be almost naked in a car, but it felt great when he rubbed on my bare boobies. By this time, my "thing" was huge! It was twisted and bent under and I had to move my legs and shake my hips to get it into a more comfortable position. Chuck was having the same problem. When we got our penises fixed, he put his mouth to my boobie and his tongue licked on it. Next he took my hand and put it on his "thing" outside his pants and he said in a real panting voice, "Take it out." So I pulled down his zipper and his "thing" flopped out. Meanwhile he pulled my zipper down and my "thing" flopped out. We were kissing at the time and Chuck's tongue was feeling my teeth and suddenly it stopped feeling and just stayed still. He went up and down on my "thing" with his fingers and then he broke away from the kiss and looked down. I think he thought he was holding his own "thing," but what he saw were two "things." My big one and his sort of smaller one.

I said to him, "I grew a thing!"

Chuck let go of it like it was a dead rat and he looked at his hand and I thought he was going to cry, and he wiped it on the seat and started breathing fast and making choking sounds. He was so emotional about it that I got kind of worried.

I don't think Chuck felt too good and he looked real white and he started to shout, "What's going on?" What is this? Is it a joke? Are you a guy? What is this?" And I said, "It's okay, Chuck. It's still me."

Then he got really mad and screamed, "I touched a prick, I touched a cock, a pecker, a cock, a prick. I touched a priiiiiiick!" He was berserk!

He grabbed me and shook me and said, "Who are you? What are you?" Which I thought was a little overdramatic. He was ten thousand times worse than Roberta, and boys were supposed to be more insensitive than girls. I couldn't stand all his shouting anymore, so I had no choice. I punched him in the face.

Then I explained to him that it was okay. I said, "I'm me and there's nothing wrong except that I have a 'thing.' You have a 'thing' and I never acted like this when I touched yours." And he got all emotional again and said, "Don't you understand? This is gay! This is fag stuff. You can't be a guy and touch another person's cock!" And I had to explain to him that a gay is a guy who loves guys and I'm not a guy so how could I be a gay? That didn't seem to make much difference, so I leaned over and grabbed him by the shoulder and gave him a big kiss and he struggled like mad, but I kept kissing until he gave in and enjoyed it and we kissed and kissed.

I asked him if it was okay if, you know, if I held onto him "down there" and he said, "I don't know." But I did anyway and he didn't seem to mind. I used all the stuff I learned that morning and I must have learned pretty good because Chuck was breathing real hard. Then in the middle of a great big kiss, I moved his hand down to my "thing" and I was expecting him to get angry but instead he just grabbed it and started going real fast up and down and he did it very well, which means he probably practices at home a lot. I started going faster on him and Chuck was in a

sort of frenzy and he was making funny noises in the back of his throat and I'm pretty sure he was crying.

Then he started to lick my boobies again and it was then that I whispered something in his car that he whispers in my ear a lot. I whispered, "Use your mouth."

He got very mad and sat up and let go of my "thing" and said, "This is sick, I'm not going to do it anymore!" He tried to pull away from me but I grabbed his shirt and held him. He said, "You're disgusting. We're going home!"

I took my hand and grabbed Chuck by the hair on the back of his head. I pulled it just enough so that it hurt and Chuck was really scared because at that point I think I was stronger than he was and he couldn't move. "No," he said, "don't!" I slowly forced his face down into my lap. Then I used my thumb and fingers to squeeze just below Chuck's cheeks and force his jaws open. I pushed his open mouth down on my you-know-what.

It was over in about three minutes and it was super! Chuck almost choked and he almost barfed and all the way home he spit out the window and gagged. But all in all, he did a real good job.

I don't see Chuck anymore because he's not around. After that night, he got kind of strange and he beat up a lot of people including his aunt and he's at military school now. As for my "thing," it got smaller the next day and then smaller the next day and so on until about a week later it was all gone and I got all of my girl stuff back and I'm happy about it. Roberta never got pregnant from me but she likes "intercourse" quite a bit and she ended up getting pregnant from some Italian guy who works for her Dad and she's a lot different now. I never told anybody about the ... penis, and I don't think anybody found out. I hardly ever think of it anymore, but I am very careful about what I eat and I never, ever, squeeze pimples on my face. □

MY VAGINA

by
Larry
Taft
as told to
John
Hughes

One morning last winter, um, I woke up and, well, I was asleep and then I woke up, and what I found was, um, well, I woke up and there it was, and my...what should have been there wasn't and what was there was...it was...a vagina. I mean, *I was a sixteen-year-old guy with a box!* I had a damn ugly, hairy woman's privates and it was gross and sickening, and I was so pissed off I wanted to punch it right in the face!

When I went to bed I had a regular guy's cock and nuts and pubic hair. But when I woke up and looked inside my pajamas, all that stuff was gone and instead I had this ... vagina and hardly any hair down there and a butt that was pink and bald. It was so disgusting I'm surprised I didn't just march downstairs and go out in the garage and not pull up the door and start my mom's station wagon and die. How could I be a guy when I had a twat? I mean, what was I? Where was my "dick"? Where were my balls? Why did all of this happen?

I thought about it a lot and I think what *maybe* happened was I tried to get high off the gas that's supposed to be inside a can of whipped cream and I was also smoking a lot of Kools, and I eat real shitty and I always sit too close to the TV and I never read with good light and I ... well, like a lot of guys my age I ... do a lot of ... "self-jacking off." It was either that or God did it.

But anyway, there I was with a vagina. Oh, by the way, it isn't polite to say this and I'm not being conceited, but the dick I used to have was a pretty good one. It wasn't so big that it was gross and it wasn't so tiny that it was a joke, and it didn't have moles or spots on it like that of a guy who was in my gym class two years ago (Jim S.), and it didn't bend over to one side when it was in a "hard-on." My balls were O.K., too, and my hair was decent and my rear end was normal, and I was overall happy with that stuff and I was supersorry to see it gone, really.

So, like, there I was, you know, on the edge of the bed looking down into my lap, and instead of seeing this thing I just saw this shitty little wad of hair. I wouldn't exactly say I cried, but I will admit that I felt so bad that my eyes got really runny, and I felt sad because,

you know, I was All-Conference in three sports and I wanted to eventually get a football scholarship to Michigan State or USC, and I had just bought a motorcycle (Kawasaki) and a new stereo (with Bose speakers, MAC amp, and Nakamichi deck), and I had started to shave, and all my friends were friends because I was a guy, and who the fuck but a girl would ever want to be a girl except a homo and I am *not* a homo! That's a fact. Even though I had a pussy I was not a queer! I hate that and I hated it then and I will hate it all of my life, and I looked up "homosexuality" in the dictionary and in a bunch of other books, and having a vagina doesn't make you a homosexual. Liking guys makes you a homosexual, but you have to like them so much that they are like girls to you (and that is a requirement), and I didn't so I wasn't a homo, I swear to God.

Well, anyway, there I was. I had this pussy and I was feeling real pissed off because I thought my life was over. Then it occurred to me: like, there was a girl's thing only about a foot and a half from my eyes and only about two inches from my hand, you know. So I figured that it's not every day that a guy my age gets to look at an actual living girl's thing, and as long as I wanted to in the daylight and do to it whatever stuff I wanted to do to it, it was O.K., you know? So I sort of "forgot" about how I was freaking out and I opened the thing up and took a peek.

I never saw one in the light. I only felt them in the dark, and, of course, I saw a few hundred in magazines, you know, but never one in the light that was a 3-D one. It was quite a shock to see how big it was. I measured it with a sheet of notebook paper, which is eight-and-one-half inches wide, and it was almost as long as the whole

sheet of paper was wide from the top of the hair down to the edge of the butt. A vagina is not like a dick, you know. A dick is just a thing, which is just a stick with a knob on the end and two balls, and that's it and it's real simple. But a vagina is a whole bunch of stuff all crammed in there and buried in a whole bunch of skin and called a vagina although, according to my dictionary, the vagina is only the actual hole part.

Starting at the top, which was the closest part to me and which was just a lot of hair: it was a nice V shape and it didn't spread out all over and become leg hair, like on a guy. It was pretty soft hair, sort of like camel's hair sport coat material only longer and curlier, and sort of darkish-brownish blond. You know how guys' hairs are really weirded out, you know, all twisted up and strange? Girls' hairs are perfect and cool.

O.K., so then I moved down to the middle part and I poked around in there and I found the beginning of the inside skin part. Do you know that the Mississippi River is so small up in Minnesota, where it starts, that you can step over it? That's sort of like the same with a vagina. It's very small at the top and then it gets big and complicated. Where I had my thumb was like the "source" and it was just the beginning, and there weren't any holes or flaps or anything. Just a small curve.

Then all the skin started. Boy, is there ever a lot of skin! There is probably enough extra skin down there to make a whole face. It's all tucked in and wrinkled up, and at first, it doesn't make any sense. It just looks like somebody got it drunk and just mushed everything in there. That skin is sort of two-tone. It's fleshish/pinkish outside and then when you get inside it's redder, like inside-the-mouth skin, and it is very soft and sticky. And it gets stickier the closer you get to the hole, and then it's just "wet." It also can be, like, "molded," and I made a bird shape out of the real long flaps that sort of hang out.

Anyhow, it's all defined into things called, I think, lips, and I think there are about four, sets of them, although I'm not sure because they are all attached to each other. Inside all those lips is the actual hole. I'm not-sure what all that skin is for except maybe for "show" because, who knows, when we were cavemen maybe guys thought all that stuff looked cool. But anyway, the hole itself isn't even just a hole. Like, it has lots of ridges and bumps and stuff in it, and it's not really a hole like a hole in the ground is a hole—it's more like an opening because it's sort of closed up, and it moves around and opens up and closes; like if you cough, it shuts and if you yawn, it opens up.

It was as deep as a Little League trophy and it stretched, too. So, like, it fit a Magic Marker, and it also stretched big enough to hold a Polaris submarine model. There is a lump up at the end of the hole, and I don't know what it is exactly because it's awful dark in there, even if you take the mirror off your desk and lay it on the floor and squat over it and shine a great big hunter's flashlight up there. But I guess it's just all that reproduction stuff that girls have.

Also, another kind of gross thing about a vagina is that it smells kind of bad. Pardon me for being kind of sickening, but it's true. I smelled one before on my old girl friend and then it smelled O.K., but I think that when you are a guy and you are real hot and with a girl and you are kissing and feeling and all that, I think your nose gets confused, and a vagina doesn't smell bad at all—in fact, it smells pretty cool in a kind of gross way. But

when you are just a guy and you are by yourself, your vagina reeks. They must all do that because there seems to be a lot of those antiperspirant deodorant sprays for females over by the Kotexes at the grocery store.

The other important thing about the vagina was that I located that "little thing." It is so small you can hardly see it! Which is ridiculous because, man, there's a lot of room down there for all kinds of stuff that doesn't even have anything to do with sex. This "little thing" was about as big as the pusher-inner thing on a ball-point pen—it's that tiny! So that may be why girls are not all that crazy about sex, not like guys are. But anyway, besides being so tiny, it's also buried in a wad of skin. I had to uncover it to get to the good part, and it's really good because it's so sensitive that when I touched it I got a huge shiver! It was a sex shiver, but I think it was also a go-to-the-bathroom shiver because I had to whizz like crazy!

"Holding it in" when you are a girl is hard because, where are the hold-it muscles? In a guy they are back near your rear end. So I had to get to the bathroom pretty fast since I didn't know how to use that thing. I was very glad that my mom and my dad and my sisters were gone, because my sister was in a figure skating thing so I didn't have to worry about anybody seeing me, which was one good thing so far.

By having two sisters and a mom, you know, I knew a little bit about how girls go to the bathroom and, I know, thank God, that you better sit down because you don't have anything to point. You just have a little hole, and if you stand up, believe me, it won't work very well; in fact, it will be a huge mess. Sitting down is the stupidest way in the world to take a leak. It's over so fast you don't have time to read or anything, and, like, what do you

do with your hands? Another thing about sitting down is that you get everything wet and you have to waste a lot of toilet paper.

Also a vagina makes a rude sound when you use it to go to the bathroom. It's like this-*fiiiiiiiisssssss, fiss, fiss, fiiiiiiiisssssss*. It's a typical girl's sound, real high and dainty and gross. Well, after getting the go-to-the-bathroom business out of the way, I decided to have a look at myself in the big mirror on the back of the door and look at my whole body. I took off my pajama bottoms and then my top and then I got more bad news!

I had two tits! Shit! What a fucking pain in the ass this whole thing was turning into—next thing I knew I would be down in the basement doing a load of laundry with my mom! Well, at least nobody in my family except my Grandma Jessie, who had torpedo tits but is dead now, has large tits, so I was flat like my mom and my sisters. But ... I had big brown nipples. I wouldn't have anything to do with the girls who had brown nipples myself. I personally consider that a deformity and if I ever found out that my wife had them I would get a divorce. Plus, they were huge and lopsided! So, not only did I get screwed by having tits in the first place, but I also got screwed by having gross ones. Just my luck!

I looked at myself and it was *weird*. I had muscular-type arms (with the kind of veins that stick out from working out with weights) and hairy pits like normal and good shoulders and neck, and then these smallish tits with big nipples, and a belly button and good stomach ripples and no hair on my chest or on my stomach or below my belly button, and then ... the vagina. My legs were slimmer than they used to be, I think. When I turned around and looked at my butt it was real neat. I kind of liked it. It was real round and, well, it was pink and cute and there wasn't any hair on it and it was just … cute. It was a girl's cute little butt.

Anyway, you know, that got boring real fast, just looking in the mirror, so I kind of walked back to my room and I looked around to see if I walked like a girl does and I did, sort of. Then I went into my room. Then what I did was … well, I think, but I'm not sure, what I think I did was what would still be considered "jacking off." It felt pretty good and I had an "orgasm," but I wasn't doing it just to jack off. It was more like an experiment that kind of turned into jacking off, only with a girl's vagina it's more like "rubbing off" because there's nothing to jack.

What I did at first was pretend my hand was me and my vagina was this girlfriend I used to have so I could sort of see what it was like for her what I did to her when we were on dates and once at her parents' cottage up north. I think it must have felt lousy because what I did seemed like it had been good, but it wasn't at all. It doesn't feel that great to have somebody shoving their finger in and out of you real fast, and it doesn't feel good at all to get your breasts squeezed and pinched. What does feel good is just old-fashioned rubbing down there. You don't have to fool around with the hole at all because it doesn't have hardly any nerves, so don't waste your time. I know, because later on I tried a lot of stuff, like carrots and candles and hot dogs and breakfast links and one of those toilet paper holder things and rolled up Cliff Notes (*Brave New World*) and bananas and a cucumber and a hairbrush handle and even an old GI Joe's head, and none of them made me have an orgasm. The hole is just for "intercourse" with men.

So, I was rubbing away and then, all of a sudden, I hit the jackpot, and my legs started jumping around and my hips started going back and forth automatically and there was this tremendous tickle feeling up my butt and then zing! It was over, but then another one started coming. *Zing! Zing! Zing! Zing!* More and more! Not like a guy's at all! Smaller, but tons and tons of them! Guys' are over right away and that's the end of it, and you don't ever want to do it again in your whole life and you feel like a slob and girls are revolting to think about and you want to just burn the magazine you were looking at, you know. But not with a vagina! You can keep going and going and going and there isn't even any mess to clean up. All the messy stuff goes on inside. Also no "hard-on" is required, you know. You're ready to do it any time of the day or the night—it's really pretty cool. And there is no way for anybody to tell that you did it because there's nothing to poke out of your pajamas. Finally, I had to stop because all that feeling good was starting to feel bad, and I was getting sort of afraid that I might have a heart attack or something. When I looked at the clock, I couldn't believe it! I had been masturbating that thing for almost three hours and, boy, was it sore!

Also, it was almost time to go to my swim meet, which was real important, and I would be in a lot of trouble if I missed it, and I'd let down all the guys on the team and they'd be pissed off. So I washed my hands about fifty times until they smelled like hands again, and then I got dressed. But my shirt scratched up my nipples and my underpants didn't fit because there wasn't a guy's "thing" to fill it up right. I figured I better wear a bra or I might make my tits bleed or something, or I could get cancer or who knows. I sure didn't!

It was really creepy and weird to be going through my sister's underpants and bras and boyfriends' letters drawer looking for a bra to wear. There were a whole bunch of them, so I picked out the lightest-weight one that wouldn't show the most, and it was one of those real thin ones and it was O.K. except, how do you put it on? They are real easy to fasten and unfasten when you are holding them in your hand, but when you put them on and put your bosoms in the holders you can't reach behind you far enough to fasten them, which I think is stupid unless women have longer arms and narrower backs. I tried and tried and it was no use, so finally I had to just fasten it, then lay it on the floor, and then step into it and pull it up over my legs and my hips and my stomach and then over my chest, and then stick my bosoms in. But that kind of stretched it out and tore it a little in the middle between the holders. Boy, what a pain!

I decided that I may as well take a pair of underpants as long as I was in her drawer and was feeling creepy anyway. At first, I didn't think I would wear any underpants at all, but if you have a vagina you have to wear underpants because those things leak all the time. I found a nice pair of red ones with a little kitten sewed on the butt. They were real soft and smooth and silky and cool, and they were much better than guys' underpants, and I thought it's too bad that guys don't get a chance to appreciate really nice underwear, except that I guess if guys wore this kind of underwear they'd just spend too much time thinking about how good their underpants felt and they wouldn't get their work done and they'd get fired. By the way, if I had had my regular guy's "thing," I would have gotten a hard-on when I looked at myself in my sister's mirror, because without my arms and my head and my feet I was a pretty cool-looking girl.

So I was all ready to go and I went out to the garage to get my motorcycle. I had a lot of trouble just holding it up, and kicking it over was almost impossible for me because I was just weaker, it seemed, than I was before, and I didn't know if it was because I spent so much time masturbating the vagina, or that I didn't eat breakfast, or that maybe I was losing my muscles as part of the deal of getting a vagina in the first place.

But after I got it going I had another problem. I was sitting right on top of my "little thing" and the motorcycle was vibrating. That made me have more orgasms, and I just sat there and revved the engine for about ten minutes enjoying it until I was afraid that it would blow up. Then I had to ride, and it's pretty dangerous to drive a motorcycle when you are having non-stop orgasms, especially making a left-hand turn when you are moaning and your hips are moving automatically. I almost creamed myself by running into a truck because I didn't want to let up on the gas since the vibrations were just perfect. It is no surprise to me why there aren't any girls motorcycle gangs or motorcycle cops. I made it to school, but almost not, and my bottom was soaking wet.

I had two problems with the swim meet. Actually, I had three, but number three was the problem of changing into my bathing suit in front of the other guys (and that problem went away because I was late because I went around the parking lot a couple of extra times to finish off my last orgasm). The other two problems were hiding my tits and not having a lump to make it look like I had my regular guy's "thing" when I put on my bathing suit. We wear little thin bathing suits and your thing shows a lot, so to not have your thing show would

make people suspicious, and the last thing I needed was to have the whole school know about my vagina, so I put a sock in there, took off my bra, and put my shirt back on and wore it into the pool area and didn't take it off—and that covered up my tits.

The coach was pissed, but I was in the next race they were just about to start so he couldn't be pissed for too long. Anyway, I walked over to the edge of the pool and bent over like I was going to dive in with my arms in front of me, and I took off the shirt and I sort of tossed it the side (but close enough so I could get it when the race was over), and I just stayed in that tucked position so that no one would see my tits or my brown nipples. Except that this dipshit guy from the other school took forever to get ready, and I must have looked like a real jerk being all tucked under and ready to begin the race three or four minutes before we started. Then when we started the race I was so stiff I could hardly keep up, but that was my smallest problem as it turned out.

When I hit that warm water something happened to my stomach and it started to hurt, and when I got to the end of the pool the coach was waving his arms like crazy, and when I finished going into my first turn I saw what he was waving at! It was red and it was a big cloud in the water and-guess what it was coming out of me. I had my period!

Holy shit! I wanted to drown! I was treading water with my period and my tits and my vagina, and about 100 people were all watching me! Somehow I had enough brains at the time to swim over to where my shirt was and I grabbed it and climbed out and covered my tits, and the coach came running over and he was real concerned. I

told him I had an infected pimple on my groin and that it was bleeding, and he got kind of mad at me for not telling him about it because of the dangers of spreading infection and all that crap. Then he said to go get dressed and go see my family doctor and not to get blood poisoning.

I was so glad to get out of there! But I wasn't that glad because I still had my period and I had a long way to go to get home. But after just a couple of minutes I knew I would never make it home unless I did something that was so horrible and embarrassing and terrible that I almost didn't do it.

Do you know what it's like to go into a girls bathroom when you are not a girl? It's awful, but where else can a guy get a Kotex? I hurried down the hall as fast as I could with a whole towel stuffed in my pants. I went across the hall and through the cafeteria to the girls' bathroom way over by the music room where there wouldn't be anybody, and there wasn't anybody so I was happy about that.

There were two machines in there. One was for Kotexes and the other was for Tampaxes. I didn't know anything about that stuff (my only experience with female hygiene equipment was filling up a sink and soaking them to see how big they get), and I didn't know what to do then, but I bought one of each. They were only ten cents a piece, which was pretty cheap. I am not a moron, it's just that when a guy gets his period he's really out of it because that period stuff isn't taught to guys, and girls don't talk about it. It's one of the "female mysteries." Even the fat, ugly girls don't tell you anything about it. But then, how many guys ever think they're going to get their period?

Anyway, I know that the object of a Kotex is to soak up stuff, and so it has to go into the hole. And that also is the object of a Tampax, which is much, much smaller than a Kotex and is shaped a little different but is made out of the same stuff and smells like toilet paper, too. So it was obvious that the Kotex must go in the vagina hole because that hole was the biggest of the holes down there, and the Tampax must go in the rear end because it was smaller. The third hole is for taking a leak, but it's so tiny that I don't know what you could shove up there, and I never saw a commercial for anything smaller than a Tampax so I just left it alone.

Now I know why there are couches in girls' bathrooms. You need them to lay down on to get the Kotex in your vagina and the Tampax in your butt. A Kotex, you know, is about as big as half a box of Kleenex, and it doesn't slide too well. But anyway, after shoving for about ten minutes I got most of it up there. Getting the Tampax in my ass was a little easier but it hurt more.

So there I was with this giant wad of stuff in my vagina and another wad in my rear end. I guessed it was all fixed up, but it sure was hard to walk normal with all that crap in my holes. No wonder women get so crabby when they get their periods. I was pretty crabby myself about having to go through all that, and I felt real sorry for all the girls and I also felt pissed off at the female period supply companies for making their products too big and too hard to put in and not slippery enough.

Anyway, I got home and everything, and by about 4:00 my period stopped and I took a bubble bath. My parents came home about 5:00. It was real weird being around my dad when I had a vagina. But it wasn't so weird around my mom and I helped her cook dinner, which was fun. I

made the frozen peas and mashed up the potatoes and I did really good, and it wasn't boring or anything, which was neat.

During dinner I got a phone call. It was my best friend, Dan. He asked about how my groin, which was bleeding at the swim meet, was and I said it was O.K. and it was just nothing and it was all gone away, and he asked if I was still going to go with him and Jeff and Steve and Steve's cousin, who goes to junior college, and I said no, and he got pissed off because before I said I would and I said no again, and he asked why not, but I couldn't tell him the real reason why so I said O.K. and he said, "Great! We're going to get high and look for girls."

I finished dinner, and my sister, Kristen, gave me a whole bunch of shit about hogging the bathroom and leaving hair in the sink, and I started to cry and my mom told Kristen to shut up, and I went upstairs to steal another pair of her underpants, because the other ones were buried in the backyard along with my pants. By the way, don't flush Kotexes down the toilet because they back it up, which is what happened in our downstairs bathroom, and there was a big fight between my dad and my younger sister, Mandy, who is thirteen, for flushing Kotex, and she got embarrassed and screamed, "I don't have my time of month, I don't have my time of month, it's Kristen!" And Kristen screamed back, but louder because she is nineteen and really an asshole, "I don't even use Kotex, you little shit!" That earned her no car for two weeks, and finally my old man got so embarrassed listening to his daughters fight about periods that he left and said he was going to the hardware store to buy some washers for his sailboat.

Boy, what would he have done if he knew it was *my* Kotex that caused the trouble?

I was not in love with the idea of going out with all those guys, but at about 8:00 they showed up, and while I took one last look at my face and hair and checked to see if there was anything up my nose, the guys joked around downstairs with my dad. Finally, my dad got sick of them and yelled at me to come down, and I did. I was the last guy to be picked up so I had to sit in the back seat in the middle, which is not a great place to sit. I had Steve on one side of me and Steve's cousin, who goes to junior college, Jim, on the other side. Up in front Dan was driving and Jeff was shotgunned, and there was a case of Stroh's beer in the middle. We smoked some joints and drank and talked and listened to Ace Frehley's solo album (he is the guy who plays lead for KISS), which I used to love but suddenly did not love anymore, and I think I would have rather listened to Fleetwood Mac or Chuck Mangione or the Bee Gees, but even though I didn't like the music, I still sort of sang along with it like my sisters do. Jim told me to shut up. It hurt my feelings real bad and I almost wanted to cry.

I was real quiet (except for singing that time) because my vagina was sort of pulsating and throbbing. I think it was doing that because of the Kotex being up there before, and also my butt was in pain. Everybody wanted to know why I was so quiet and I said I said I didn't feel too good. If you ever want a bunch of guys my age to leave you alone, don't tell them you don't feel too good, because if they know that something is wrong they will attack you and take advantage of you and try to make you feel worse, which is just what Jeff did when he turned around on the seat and look right at my face and said, "Ass Patrol on Alert!" "Alright!" Dan shouted. And I freaked out inside.

Ass Patrol is the same as mooning, and mooning is hanging your ass out of a car window, and I couldn't hang my ass out of the window because (a) I was wearing my sister's underpants, and (b) the vagina was right in front of my ass. "It's your turn, Larry," Dan said. "Flash flesh."

"I can't," I said. "I have a cold."

"Bullshit!"

"Fuck you!"

No matter how much I said no they said yes, and they would have pulled my pants down and shoved my ass out (they were so drunk and high), and the dangerous part about that is that when you are going sixty-five miles an hour and a bunch of drunk guys are trying to get your butt out the window, you can fall out and die or get into a crash and have to die with your pants down and have people laugh at you for the rest of your life—and even laugh louder if you have a vagina! So I said I would do it then. On top of everything terrible that had just happened, Steve's cousin said, "Why don't we moon the drive-in window at the Burger King?"

Everybody thought that was the coolest thing they ever heard, and we turned around and headed back for the Burger King. One good thing was that it gave me time to figure out how to put my ass out without revealing my sister's underpants or the vagina and also to get my pants ready so that I could do it quickly and get it over with. Except everything got fucked up because Dan was too busy trying to watch and not busy enough driving, and he crashed into the Burger King and I flew forward into the front seat and hit my head on the ashtray. I knew I was in big trouble because I could see four faces staring at the beaver I was flashing.

"It's a cunt!"

"Larry's got a cunt!"

"It's real!"

I didn't do anything except almost shit in my pants, which were down by my knees. And do you know what else?

All the people who worked at the Burger King were crowded in the window looking at my vagina. I think they must have thought I was a girl but still, shit, that's super embarrassing! Dan suddenly got smart and saw that he was going to get into trouble for hitting a Burger King, so he pulled out into the street and swerved to miss a car and we were gone.

"Far out!" Steve said.

"It's incredible, look at it!"

I just laid there, mainly because of the position I was in I couldn't do anything else. My head was down on the floor and my back was on the beer and my legs were hanging over the back seat, and there was a guy on either side of me and two guys in the back about a foot from my vagina, just staring like morons. Then the guy from junior college reached out and touched it.

"*Get out of there!*" I screamed!

"Where's your dork?" Jeff asked me.

"What's happened?" Dan said.

Then the guy from junior college tried to open my legs up, and I kicked him but he just started laughing like an animal and then he made me faint when he said, "Let's fuck Larry!"

Oh, God! I was in deep-shit trouble!

When I woke up, the car was parked at the golf course and my pants were completely off. I tried to get up but no one would help me.

"You can't fuck me!" I said. "I am a guy!"

That sort of slowed them down, and they were all quiet for a minute and then Dan said that I was right. But then Jeff said, "If he's a guy, what's he doing with that!"

"You know what?" Steve said, like he suddenly figured out what was

going on but he really didn't, "Larry's a girl who's pretending to be a guy and has always been a girl!"

"I have not," I said. "You guys have seen my..."

Nope, I never had gym with any of those guys and as far as I know they never saw my "thing" out in the open, and it didn't make any difference because they were so drunk and high that I could have been a zebra and they wouldn't have known it.

"I don't want to take any chances on being a homo," Dan said.

"It's a vagina, dumb shit!" Jeff said.

"You can't be a homo if it's a vagina."

"Yeah," Dan said. "I guess so."

"Let's do it," Steve said.

"Is it O.K. with you, Larry?"

"No!" I screamed!

I was scared as shit and I was struggling like crazy, and normally I could have whipped those guys in about one and a half minutes, but I just didn't have any muscles left. I have to admit this and it's really gross and disgusting and horrible and a nightmare but ... my friends all fucked me.

Everything worked out O.K., I guess. I never talked to those guys again and they never talked to me, either, and then my dad got transferred to California and we moved there in the summer, so I don't know what happened to them, except I heard Steve's cousin joined the navy and got thrown out for setting fire to a guy's bed. The vagina went away after a few months. The "little thing" just got bigger and bigger until one day it was my regular guy's thing again. It doesn't bother me any more that I had the vagina. I mean, it didn't make me insane or anything. I guess the worst thing that happened was that I had to use up most of my money I was saving for new skis and waste my Easter vacation having to get an abortion. □

CONDOMS THROUGH THE AGES

compiled by Steve Brykman

20,000 B.C., ICE

Sensitivity: Moderate
Failure Rate: 80-90% (depending on coital duration)
Advantages: Frictionless, See-Thru
Disadvantages: Chilly, Frostbite

2,000 B.C., WOOD

Sensitivity: Unpleasant
Failure Rate: 50%
Advantages: Easily Whittled, Biodegradable, Floats
Disadvantages: Splinters, Termites, Flammable, Sap

0 A.D., IRON

Sensitivity: Slight
Failure Rate: 2%
Advantages: Doubles as Goblet
Disadvantages: Rust, Magnetic

300 A.D., ALUMINUM

Sensitivity: Relatively High
Failure Rate: 15%
Advantages: May be Purchased by the Roll, Recyclable
Disadvantages: Noisy, Requires Tin Snips

500 A.D., LEATHER

Sensitivity: Adequate
Failure Rate: 14%
Advantages: Stylish
Disadvantages: Must be Kept Dry

1500 A.D., PAPYRUS

Sensitivity: Extremely High
Failure Rate: 98%
Advantages: Pliable, Festive Colors
Disadvantages: Paper Cuts, Combustible

1973 A.D., POLYESTER

Sensitivity: Excellent
Failure Rate: 5%
Advantages: Wearable Day-to-Day Stretchable, Machine Washable
Disadvantages: Flammable, Tacky

2010 A.D., KEVLAR

Sensitivity: Lacking
Failure Rate: 0%
Advantages: Bulletproof, Microwaveable, Camo Pattern Available
Disadvantages: Pricey, Rigid

5,000 B.C., STONE

Sensitivity: Nonexistent
Failure Rate: 1%
Advantages: Sturdy, Readily Available
Disadvantages: Weight, Abrasion Requires Custom Chiseling

500 B.C., BRONZE

Sensitivity: Reasonable
Failure Rate: 5%
Advantages: May be Buffed to High Sheen
Disadvantages: Easily Tarnished

250 A.D., STEEL

Sensitivity: Unimpressive
Failure Rate: 4%
Advantages: Reflective
Disadvantages: Rivets

350 A.D., GLASS

Sensitivity: Above Average
Failure Rate: 22%
Advantages: Dishwasher-Safe, Good Thermal Conductor
Disadvantages: Breakable, Spots

1350 A.D., ANIMAL INTESTINE

Sensitivity: Remarkably High
Failure Rate: 43%
Advantages: Realistic, Edible
Disadvantages: Disgusting

1600 A.D., WOOL

Sensitivity: Surprisingly High
Failure Rate: 80%
Advantages: Absorbent, Warm, Comfy-Cozy
Disadvantages: Itchy, Pilling, Dry Clean Only

1990 A.D., LATEX

Sensitivity: Glove-Like
Failure Rate: 5-7%
Advantages: Variety, Money-Back Guarantee
Disadvantages: Odor, Messy, Flavor

SEXUAL APTITUDE TEST

and Test of Standard Body Language

You will have three hours to work on the questions in this test. If you finish a question too soon, do not worry. It happens to everyone sometimes. If you are uncertain where to make an entry, do not guess. Go on to the next question. Science has established that the size of your number-two pencil is not a factor in your success. You will be graded on enthusiasm, imagination, and performance, not on the number of entries completed, or the size of your number-two pencil. When you have finished this test, be sure to fill in your name, room number, and the name of the motel where this test was taken.

DO NOT OPEN THIS BOOK—OR ANYTHING ELSE— UNTIL TOLD TO DO SO BY SOMEONE IN AUTHORITY.

3SA096

Z8-E-35

SECTION 1
VERBAL APTITUDE
20 QUESTIONS

For each question in this section, choose the best answer and blacken the corresponding space.

Vocabulary:
Choose the word or phrase that is most clearly the SAME in meaning as the word in capital letters.

1. FRIGID: (A) *Ur*-Maytag (B) a girl's name (Irish)
   (C) coked up (D) suffering from a yeast infection
   (E) a carpet-muncher

   (A) (B) (C) (D) (E)

2. DISCIPLINE: (A) between consenting disciples
   (B) West Point gang bang
   (C) nip-clipping to disco music
   (D) a girl's name (New England Puritan)
   (E) wearing spurs to bed

   (A) (B) (C) (D) (E)

3. JISM: (A) breach with the Church
   (B) a gymnasium for queers
   (C) American Negro slang for "Yes, ma'am."
   (D) the poor man's ambrosia
   (E) the poor woman's ambrosia

   (A) (B) (C) (D) (E)

Choose the word or phrase that is most clearly the OPPOSITE in meaning as the word in capital letters.

4. SPANISH FLY: (A) Julie Andrews
   (B) Canadian goose (C) marriage
   (D) Japanese ground ball (E) Tabasco douche

   (A) (B) (C) (D) (E)

5. NECROPHILIA: (A) live TV (B) necropittsburgh
   (C) a girl's name (rural black American)
   (D) blowjob from Karen Anne Quinlan
   (E) curing a chicken hawk of cancer

   (A) (B) (C) (D) (E)

Analogies:
Select the lettered pair that best expresses a relationship similar to that expressed in the original pair.

6. COALS : NEWCASTLE ::
   (A) masturbation : cerebral palsy
   (B) condom : homosexual
   (C) barbecue : Yorkshire pudding
   (D) meaningful relationship : California
   (E) cinder blocks : Vladivostok

   (A) (B) (C) (D) (E)

7. PEDERASTY : ENGLISH LITERATURE ::
   (A) alcohol : party (B) feet : adult bookstore
   (C) shame : ecstasy (D) Ben-Wa balls : convent
   (E) gerrymandering : E. M. Forster

   (A) (B) (C) (D) (E)

8. FRENCH TICKLER : TIED FLIES ::
   (A) artificial heart : sump pump
   (B) feather boa : vying gnats
   (C) Koo Stark : Elizabeth II
   (D) Häagen-Dazs Chocolate Chocolate Chip Ice
       Cream : ground glass
   (E) Le Pétomane : insect bondage

   (A) (B) (C) (D) (E)

9. MAMMARIES : MASTECTOMY ::
   (A) Al Jolson : chewing gum
   (B) Dolly Parton : Mount St. Helens
   (C) reminiscence : Egyptian pharaoh
   (D) satin sheets : white sale
   (E) whales : Sherman's march through Georgia

   (A) (B) (C) (D) (E)

10. FELLATIO : BUGGERY :: (A) czar : proletariat
    (B) Hamlet : Watergate (C) Sausalito : San Quentin
    (D) Italian ice : mosquitoes
    (E) Don Knotts : William the Conqueror

    (A) (B) (C) (D) (E)

Sentence Completion:
Choose the one word or set of words that, when inserted in the sentence, best fit the meaning of the sentence as a whole.

11. His ---- was so enormous that she despaired of its ever fitting in her ----.

    (A) vasectomy scar...viewfinder (B) nose...tent
    (C) cucumber...bumhunkie (D) inheritance...IRA
    (E) testicle...vise

    (A) (B) (C) (D) (E)

12. The number of ---- in the place was unbelievable; it was difficult to realize that a ---- could be so crowded.

    (A) crabs...merkin
    (B) television cameras...vagina (C) tits...brassiere
    (D) dildos...chief executive's desk drawer
    (E) digits...rectum

    (A) (B) (C) (D) (E)

13. The ---- that gleamed from the two vibrating bodies gave the distinct impression that they had been ---- for a long time.

    (A) sleigh bells…ringtingtingaling, too
    (B) lubricant…voyeurs   (C) urine…showering
    (D) Béarnaise sauce…sterile
    (E) twilight…gallantly streaming

    (A) (B) (C) (D) (E)

14. Such a ---- encounter might be ----.

    (A) lewd…tax-deductible
    (B) close…of the third kind
    (C) perfect…sodium nitrate
    (D) homosexual…politically beneficial
    (E) brief…easy to lie about

    (A) (B) (C) (D) (E)

15. What we consider a luxury at one time frequently becomes a ----; many people find that solitude encourages ----.

    (A) lust…Bible reading
    (B) nuisance…self-immolation
    (C) sick perversion…philately
    (D) necessity…choking the chicken
    (E) chore…making it with your dog

    (A) (B) (C) (D) (E)

Reading Comprehension:
After reading the following passage, choose the best answer to the following questions.

Upon retiring from the presidency of the United States, George Washington embarked on a life far removed from that of idle gentleman farmer. In fact, scholars have collected substantial evidence that the Father of Our Country pursued many interesting hobbies on his Mount Vernon plantation, the chief among these being cunnilingus. Practicing on his slaves, for this was before the Emancipation Proclamation of 1863, Washington became a highly skilled genitophage who eventually was competing successfully, despite his advanced age, in the great labiamangerant fairs of western Virginia and southern Delaware—immortalized later by Walt Whitman in his epic poem, *Munching Leaves of Grass*.

Although revisionist historians have proposed that Washington derived personal satisfaction from his consistently high scores at these "cuntry fairs," most Washington biographers insist that he practiced his craft out of a highly developed sense of duty.

It was noted that Washington's mahogany teeth, false, of course, were of particular value to him in the field, enabling him to finish off 10 percent more females than his nearest competitor, Thomas Jefferson.

In his memoirs, Washington fondly recalls his early pubicmastication training with the legendary Cherokee snatchophile, Lukmahno Hands, who gave young Washington his first lozenge. Somewhat tongue-in-cheek, Washington once reminisced to Virginia Commonwealth newspaper editors about the time when, practicing "la joiebuzzerie" on a young slave girl, he mistakenly bit down upon the slave's privates when a hornet maliciously stung him from behind. Admittedly unable to lie, plan, or form complex thoughts, Washington was at first afraid to tell his father what had happened. But eventually, true to American form, the young Washington admitted to his stern, uncompromising father—himself an accomplished clitoridominus—that he had, indeed, chopped down his father's favorite cherry.

16. The title below that best expresses the ideas of this passage is

    (A) George Washington, Master Cocksman, Ha-Ha
    (B) Folk Dentistry of Central Virginia
    (C) How to Say "Eat Pussy" in the Queen's English
    (D) Why Virginia Slaves Did Not Try to Escape
    (E) Mein Kampf

    (A) (B) (C) (D) (E)

17. When Washington left the presidency he led a life of

    (A) idleness and sloth   (B) Riley
    (C) duty to his country (D) childlessness
    (E) incredible bad breath

    (A) (B) (C) (D) (E)

18. Washington practiced cunnilingus because

    (A) he grew up near coal-mining country
    (B) "it's there"
    (C) he liked chocolate-covered cherries
    (D) "Little George" wouldn't stand up straight
    (E) his mother made him

    (A) (B) (C) (D) (E)

19. The great American poet Walt Whitman wrote an epic poem about

    (A) fruit
    (B) coming of age in Samoa
    (C) the first Michelin guide to eating out in America
    (D) orgasm among livestock
    (E) American Presidents and Sappho: Magic Carpet in the New World

    (A) (B) (C) (D) (E)

20. What do George Washington and this section of the SAT have in common?

    (A) They both suck
    (B) One sucks, the other doesn't
    (C) Lukmahno Hands
    (D) slavery
    (E) Mein Kampf

    (A) (B) (C) (D) (E)

GO ON TO THE NEXT PAGE >

SECTION 2
MATHEMATICAL APTITUDE
9 QUESTIONS

In this section solve each problem, using any available space on the page for scratchwork, then indicate the correct answer in the corresponding space.

Standard Multiple-Orgasm Questions

1. If $x < y$, which position will be satisfying to both partners?

   (A) $\frac{y}{x}$ (B) $\frac{x}{y}$ (C) $\frac{x+2}{y}$ (D) $\frac{x+y}{\pi}$ (E) $\frac{x+y}{0 \quad 0}$

   Ⓐ Ⓑ Ⓒ Ⓓ Ⓔ

2. a is a female, age 80, and b is a male, age 80. c is a female, age 20, and d is a male, age 20.

   If $\frac{a}{d}$ and $\frac{c}{b}$, which of the following is true?

   (A) d goes into a more times than b goes into c.
   (B) b goes into c more times than d goes into a.
   (C) b does not go into c.
   (D) c gets mad and leaves b.
   (E) a dies and d and c get together.

   Ⓐ Ⓑ Ⓒ Ⓓ Ⓔ

3. If three boys can frost a cookie in two minutes, what part of the job can be completed by two boys in one minute?

   (A) $\frac{1}{3}$ (B) $\frac{2}{3}$ (C) $\frac{3}{4}$ (D) $\frac{19}{20}$ (E) the raisins

   Ⓐ Ⓑ Ⓒ Ⓓ Ⓔ

4. Mrs. Crocker can give a blowjob as fast as her two daughters working together. If one daughter does the job alone in three minutes and the other does it alone in six minutes, how many minutes does it take the mother to do the job alone?

   (A) 1   (B) 2   (C) 3   (D) 4
   (E) 6 hours, because Mr. Crocker has to recover from what the daughters did

   Ⓐ Ⓑ Ⓒ Ⓓ Ⓔ

5. x is a Catholic male; y is a Catholic female; z is a prostitute. If $x + z = 69$, what is $x + y$?

   (A) 66 (B) 99 (C) 34½ (D) 0 (E) Oct. 6, 1982

   Ⓐ Ⓑ Ⓒ Ⓓ Ⓔ

Comparative Geometry

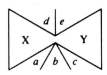

6. Which angle has the most direct view of X?

   (A) a
   (B) b
   (C) c
   (D) d
   (E) e

   Ⓐ Ⓑ Ⓒ Ⓓ Ⓔ

7. Which relationship is least likely to result in *$%&!!!#$%¢!!!¢$%#&@*?

   (A) ◯ ← (B) ◯◯ (C) ← ← (D) → ← (E) ◯ⁿ

   Ⓐ Ⓑ Ⓒ Ⓓ Ⓔ

8. If ⊙ ⊙ is great, which is greater?

   (A) (large circle with dot)   (B) ⊙⊙⊙⊙

   Ⓐ Ⓑ

9. If X and Y are two sides of a bikini, then which angle is the greatest?

   (A) "Hi, my name's Brad, and I'd like to invite you to my parents' pool party this afternoon."
   (B) "With knockers like those you make a guy come in his pants."
   (C) "I'm a professional photographer, and I was hoping you might agree to pose for some photos for my new book about Cape Cod."
   (D) "Would you mind putting a little sunburn lotion on my back?"
   (E) *"Uta, la chingao! Ai-yai-yai, qué caramba! Hijo! Muchacha, qué quiero te chingar! Bese, bese, bese!!!!!"* (SMACKING NOISES)

   Ⓐ Ⓑ Ⓒ Ⓓ Ⓔ

S T O P

IF YOU FINISH BEFORE TIME IS CALLED, CHECK YOUR WORK ON THIS SECTION ONLY.
DO NOT WORK ON ANY OTHER SECTION IN THE TEST.

WHAT EVERY YOUNG WOMAN SHOULD KNOW

A guide to the facts of life and love for high school girls, published as a public service with the compliments of the editors of the *National Lampoon*.

YOU'VE PROBABLY BEEN WONDERING...

About those curious sensations in your body ... about those warm, "ticklish" feelings you've been having the last couple of years ... about all those things your parents told you they'd talk to you about "when you're a little older."

Well, we want you to know that, as far as we're concerned, *you're old enough now!* Old enough to know what your body wants you to do ... and how to do it. Old enough to be a fully knowledgeable, skilled young woman.

It's important that you get this information candidly, clearly, fully. So first of all—and this is important—don't ask your parents. In fact, don't even show them this booklet! It's not that they don't want the best for you. But they grew up in a earlier age, when the facts of life and love were considered shameful ... something to keep secret. Well, we don't think it's shameful at all. We think it's *terrific*. And we want you to get the best out of all the wonderful experiences soon to come your way. So listen—look—and then, welcome to the wonderful world of fulfillment.

WHAT KIND OF MAN MAKES THE BEST LOVER?

Unfortunately, many men who seem attractive on the surface are actually strongly homosexual—often without even knowing it. Men with lean waists, overdeveloped chests, arms, and shoulders, and clean skin are actually unconsciously obsessed by male bodies.

You should stay far away from men who are athletes or rock stars, and men who feel compelled to dress in fancy suits with clean shirts and polished shoes. These "men" often have a compulsion to spend money on sumptuous meals, taxicabs, and expensive trinkets to compensate for their affliction. Experienced, self-confident lovers—the kind you want—don't need to alter the natural contours of their bodies. They are content with slender arms, relaxed chests, and waists with a comfortable amount of flesh—which can come in handy during moments of intimacy (why do you think they call them "love handles"?) Introspective, thoughtful men with a sense of humor are especially valuable; men who write humorous magazine material, for example.

One other tip: Married men can be depended on *not* to cause embarrassing rumors about you at home or school. Men on short business trips are discreet, grateful, and particularly driven by passion. Look for them!

HOW ... "BIG" ... SHOULD A MAN BE?

Don't by shy. It's an important question, and one surrounded by confusion.

The average man's penis is 2 1/2 to 3 inches long. Men substantially larger than this must often undergo painful surgery to cure their condition. In thickness, the average man is somewhat larger than a ball-point pen.

HOW ... "LONG" ... SHOULD A MAN LAST?

Some men can prolong the sex act beyond the once-impenetrable thirty-second barrier; intercourse with an experienced man can go for up to forty-five seconds. Once in a long while, you'll find a man who can "last" as long as a minute. Whatever you do, don't let your girlfriends know you've landed owe of these desirable "sixty second wonders."

HOW DO I KNOW IF I'M HAVING AN ORGASM?

The female orgasm is a sensation that's very hard to put into words, but most fulfilled, experienced women agrees that it "feels like something inside of you." When a man's penis is inside your vagina, or mouth or buttocks, that is an orgasm. You'll find that a really skilled lover applies the same technique to love as a gourmet does to a meal: he "leaves a little something on your plate." When, after intercourse, you feel a vague sensation that there could be "more to come," that "vaguely unsatisfied" feeling, then you can be sure you've experienced a sexually memorable adventure.

WHAT IS A MULTIPLE ORGASM?

There is no such thing.

WHAT ABOUT ORAL SEX?

This is one of the most significant differences between the sexes. If you look at pictures of a man and a woman, you'll see the a man's penis fits naturally into a woman's mouth. On the other hand, a man's mouth does *not* naturally fit into a woman's vagina. Thus, a woman orally stimulating a man is performing a "natural" act. But a man seeking to put his mouth on or near a vagina is committing an "unnatural" act (why do you think they call the vagina your "private parts"?)

WHAT IS AFTERPLAY?

Men have ways of expressing their satisfaction. His satisfied sigh, followed by a deep, consuming sleep, is a sure sign that he, and you, are "GIB." Another example of male "afterplay" is his turning on a football or basketball game immediately after climax.

Many women find a particularly satisfying postcoital experience in going into the kitchen and bringing a nice, cold beer back for the man, along with a light snack—sandwich, potato chips and dip—to help her love put back depleted calories.

WHAT IS IMPOTENCE?

Impotence is what happens when a girl fails to stimulate her man properly. This can happen when her figure is not perfect, or when she tries to talk with him for too long before getting into bed with him.

When this happens, you can help by turning on a sports event on TV or getting your man a sandwich. Another really good "foreplay" technique is to invite a really good-looking girl friend over, and do whatever he asks, to him or to each other, while he watches.

HOW CAN I KEEP THE MYSTERY ALIVE?

One good way to keep things from getting routine is to vary your dress. Garter belts, black mesh stocking, leather or rubber suits will all help get your man's attention. Also, don't keep playing "one on one." Invite your more attractive and energetic girl friends over to take part.

Another technique—and we think the best—is to *use anonymous names*. Have your lover call himself "Mr. Smith." Don't let him tell you where he lives, or his home telephone number. You'll find it lends an air of real "mystery" to the affair.

HOW CAN I MEET *REAL* MEN?

When looking for the ideal man about—twenty-five to forty, married, on a business trip, with enough flab to assure you of his masculinity—go over to a Ramada Inn or Holiday Inn cocktail lounge about 8:30 at night. Look around the room: then, when you've found your man, unbutton the top three or four buttons on your blouse, wink at him, walk over, and whisper in his ear, "You're cute—can I buy you a drink?" This is a real conversation icebreaker and things will naturally progress from there.

SOME OTHER IMPORTANT QUESTIONS:

"If I get pregnant, how do I know who the father is?"
There is absolutely know way to tell.

"Where should a man take me?"
Because so many homosexual men like to take their "dates" out for fancy meals, look for the man who will send you out to a local Arby's or Carl's, Jr., for a sandwich. That means his mind's not on food—so you *know* what he's thinking about.

"What happens if he doesn't call?"
He may be trying to keep the romance alive; go out every few weeks to your local Ramada Inn or Holiday Inn cocktail lounge and look to see if he's come back. If he hasn't, find another person who sort of looks like him and maybe writes for or works for a humor magazine, and try the "Can I buy you a drink?" technique with *him*. You may find you've met a *new*, exciting lover.

IF YOU STILL NEED HELP, WE'RE HERE...

Call the *National Lampoon* Hotline; we can answer all your questions. If you send them along with a photo of yourself, we can send an editor to your hometown to provide personal counseling. You pay only for is air fare, hotel bills, cab fares and a small consulting fee. □

First Blowjob

*A Young Girl's Senior Prom Can Mean Many Things:
A Bouquet Of Memories . . . Or a Pillow Full of Tears . . .*

by Doug Kenney

*"Connie! Connie Phillips! You'd better hurry,
Jeff will be here any minute!"*

Mrs. Phillips's call from downstairs found Connie, still in her freshly ironed slip, sitting crosslegged on the bedspread to put the finishing touches on her nails. A startled glance at the clock on the bureau reaffirmed her mother's warning—it was almost half past seven. Fanning the air with her hands to dry the polish, Connie gulped and hurried to dress.

Carefully, she drew the sheer nylons over her tan, athletic legs and slipped on the white organdy gown that hung in its plastic bag on her closet door. (Thank heaven Mrs. Phillips had relented at the store in her preference for the green taffeta—a high-necked confusion of bows, flounces, and spaghetti straps that looked more like a circus tent than a party frock.) Connie fastened the three simple strands of cultured pearls around her neck and took the rhinestone bracelet Mrs. Phillips had lent her especially for tonight from the dressing table. Blotting her cherry-frost lipstick on a tissue and giving her pert, blonde curls one last flick with her brush, Connie sighed and stepped back from the mirror for final inspection.

Looking at the unfamiliar figure who peered back from the glass with equally wide-eyed astonishment, Connie suddenly felt a curious sense of elation. What this afternoon was only a gum-snapping, floppy-shirted teen with one ear glued to the telephone and the other permanently cocked toward the hi-fi had been miraculously transformed somewhere between this afternoon's bubble bath and that teetering test-walk in her new yellow satin pumps—into an undeniably attractive, grown-up woman.

Good looks aren't a passport to a happy and productive life, Connie reminded herself as she lingered another moment before the mirror, *but is it wrong to know you're pretty and be glad of of it . . . at least for one special night?*

"Hey, nobody told me *Grace Kelly* was in here! I wonder where that dumb old Connie is?"

Connie started from her reverie and quickly flushed with embarrassment as she saw Didi's reflection behind her. Didi Phillips was a pesky, pug-nosed, freckle-faced imp who Connie's parents persisted in maintaining was her own little sister.

"And I suppose no one told you it's impolite to barge into other people's rooms without knocking either?" retorted Connie, whirling around to confront her impudent sibling.

"No-o, but I hear you can get stuck-up from looking at mirrors too long," Didi returned airily. "Anyway, Prince Charming's in the living room getting the Third Degree from Mom an' Pop, so you'd better trot on down before he shrivels up like a raisin."

Snatching her handbag from the bureau, Connie brushed by Didi and, pausing at the top of the stairs to take a deep breath, descended in a slow, "ladylike" manner to the living room where she found Jeff sitting on the couch chatting amiably with her parents. Everyone turned toward Connie as she appeared and Jeff, rising to stand, stared at her with an appreciative grin.

"Ho-ly Bananas," exclaimed Jeff, making a comical bow, "I didn't know I had a date with a *movie star*!"

"And *I* didn't know I had a date with such a *smoothie*!" laughed Connie, joining in the general amusement.

"Oh yes," chuckled Mr. Phillips as he lit his pipe, "Jeff and I have just been discussing that forty-yard pass he made against Hillcrest last season, and now I see why you think he's such a 'dreamboat'!"

For the second time that evening, Connie blushed, then joined Jeff, whose tan, athletic good looks were set off by merry blue eyes and a bow tie in a smart green plaid.

"Now, Wayne," said Mrs. Phillips, "leave the jokes to Jack Benny and let the children go—they don't want to sit around listening to *us*."

"You're right, Ruth," said Mr. Phillips sheepishly as he knocked the ashes from his pipe and slipped it into the pocket of his cardigan sweater. "You know, it wasn't until you came down those stairs that I realized what a beautiful young woman my little Connie has become."

"Oh Daddy, don't be silly," chided Connie affectionately, as she kissed her father's cheek. "You know I'll *always* be 'your little girl.'"

"I know you will," said Mr. Phillips, "and I also know that Jeff is a fine boy—but there'll be other fine lads around when you go to State in the fall, so I'd like you to promise a prehistoric old dad one thing...."

"Sure Daddy," said Connie, giving a mock conspiratorial wink to Jeff over her father's shoulder, "what is it?"

"Just promise me," said Mr. Phillips, fumbling for his pipe cleaners, "that no matter how wonderful the dance may be tonight, and no matter what Jeff and you may be feeling ... promise me that you won't give him a blowjob."

"A w-what?" stammered Connie, backing away slightly.

"A blowjob," Mr. Phillips repeated. "You know, when a fellow forces his dork down your throat and makes you suck on it until he eventually shoots his pecker-snot all over your tonsils."

In the silence that followed, Connie, suddenly quite pale, looked beseechingly from Mrs. Phillips to Jeff, both of whom could only avert their eyes to the carpet.

"Oh my God," gasped Connie, "th-that's ... horrible ... *sickening*...."

"You bet it is," replied Mr. Phillips, puffing his pipe alight, "just ask your mother."

Once in Jeff's convertible, Connie tactfully passed over Mr. Phillips's unusual behavior and admired the single, perfect white gardenia Jeff had brought. "What a gorgeous flower," she said as she admired the blossom in Jeff's rear view mirror, "but you shouldn't have spent so much!"

"Oh, a couple of weekends at hard labor on my pop's lawn mower," Jeff admitted, "but seeing how fabulous you look tonight wearing it makes it a bargain."

"It *is* a grand evening, isn't it?" Connie said, inhaling the fresh late spring greenery as they sped along Lakeshore Drive to the prom.

"And a grand date for me," Jeff returned. "I feel like the luckiest senior in the history of Parkdale High."

"And *I'm* the luckiest girl," Connie smiled. "After all, it isn't *everybody* who goes to the Spring Bounce with Jeff Madison—co-captain of the Varsity Football Team, chairman of the Student Senate, *and* Hi-Tri-Y activities coordinator!"

"Aw, cut the softsoap," Jeff laughed. "Let's just say that we're *both* lucky before we get swelled heads!"

"Fun ahoy!" Jeff sang as he turned off Glenview Boulevard into the already crowded parking lot. "Last one on the dance floor is a wallflower!"

"Not me!" cried Connie excitedly, "and you'd better've eaten your Cheerios because I'm not going to sit out a single dance!"

The Senior Bounce was everything Connie hoped it would be, and together with Jeff she floated and swayed to the lilting rhythms of fox trots, sambas, and polkas until Connie thought her heart would burst.

"I have to powder my nose," said Connie, excusing herself at the break as the crowd eagerly gathered at the tempting tables of Hawaiian Punch and gingersnaps. For Connie it was a perfect evening, or almost perfect, for when Connie went to the coat rack to get a handkerchief from her wrap, she overheard Mary Ellen Peterson and Doris Wilkins whispering by the drinking fountain.

"Doesn't Connie Phillips look ... *sophisticated* tonight?" said Mary Ellen archly.

"Who wouldn't," Doris sniffed, "with that swanky rhinestone bracelet of her mother's?"

"Well," said Mary Ellen, "she certainly seems to have Jeff Madison on a string. Do you think they'll get engaged?"

"Maybe," said Doris vaguely, "although I can't *imagine* Connie not minding Jeff's personality problems...."

At that point Connie "accidentally" dropped her compact and the two gossips, both red-faced, ended their discussion in mid-meow.

"Hel-lo girls," said Connie. "Did I hear you mention Jeff?"

"W-well, as a matter of fact," began a flustered Mary Ellen, "I was just this minute telling Doris that ... with a *personality* like Jeff's he certainly has no *problem* snagging the most popular girl in Parkdale!"

"Oh," said Connie uncertainly.

The band tuned up again, but this time as Connie whirled around the floor in Jeff's appreciative arms, her happiness was clouded by the snatch of conversation she had overheard in the Ladies Room. Even the intoxicating, quicksilver arpeggios of the accordian could not drown out the two false notes in the evening. *Personality problems . . . blowjob . . . personality problems . . . blowjob,* a small, nagging voice kept repeating.

Too soon, the band struck up "Good Night Ladies" and it was time to go. Connie and Jeff were invited to join some of the crowd at the Snak Shoppe for post-prom munchables and, it was darkly hinted, some good-natured hijinx. But Jeff begged off and, as he held Connie's hand, shyly murmured that there was something he wished to ask her alone.

As they drove away under a sky pin-pointed with stars, Connie noticed that he was strangely silent. Finally, she asked Jeff if something was troubling him.

"Yes, Connie, there *is* something," Jeff replied as he turned off Lakeshore Drive onto Clinton Avenue. Without a word, he reached into his breast pocket and offered Connie a tiny, velvet-covered box.

She still was staring at the unopened box in her hand when Jeff pulled off Clinton Avenue into a deserted alley next to the Apex Dry Cleaners.

"Oh Jeff, I don't know what to say," Connie began. "I know we've *talked* about marriage, but I really feel we both should complete our college education at State before I could even *think* of accepting your ring."

Jeff shut off the motor and turned questioningly to Connie. "State . . . marriage . . . ring?" Jeff said puzzledly. "*I'm* not going to the State *College*. My folks are sending me to the State *Mental Hospital*—that box I gave you has a couple of Dramamines in it so you don't gag too much when you give me my blowjob."

"Y-your what?" said Connie tonelessly.

"My blowjob," Jeff explained. "You know, where a guy crams his meat into your gullet and you eat on it until he goes spooey all over your uvula."

"Aaah!" Connie screamed, fumbling at the door handle, "No! Jeff, no!" But before she could escape, Connie felt inhumanly powerful hands seize her by the neck and force her head down below the dashboard. There, plainly revealed in the green flourescent glow of the "Apex" sign, Connie saw Jeff's tan, athletic penis straining toward her.

"Oh God, please *no!*" Connie pleaded a last time before Jeff pried her clenching jaws apart with his powerful thumbs and began by inches, to introduce his swollen flesh past her cherry-frost lipstick. As Jeff plunged and withdrew with pistonlike insistence, Connie felt her glottis constrict involuntarily, seizing the intrusive column.

"Atta girl, Connie," encouraged Jeff, "shake hands with it!"

At last Jeff rose to his final, shuddering spasm and Connie felt a wad of viscous fluid splatter off her palate and slowly begin to trickle through her vitals.

"Not bad for a beginner," reassured Jeff as he tied Connie's wrists and ankles to the steering wheel with his matching plaid suspenders. "You should learn to breathe through your nose, though," he added thoughtfully.

When Connie was firmly trussed and secured to the wheel, Jeff excused himself and returned a few moments later wearing a makeshift Nazi uniform, a snapped-off car aerial clutched in his hand.

"Gee," exclaimed Jeff as he began to lash out viciously at her unprotected body, "I've been wanting to try this ever since I first heard Negro music!"

It was many minutes past midnight when a blue convertible screeched to a stop in front of the Phillips's home. A car door could be heard opening, and, under the yellow radiance of the streetlight, a limp weight was kicked from the automobile on to the sidewalk before it roared off with a muffled growl.

Slowly, the girl began to stir. Connie, still only semi-conscious, opened her eyes to a brilliant starscape. This puzzled her because she had landed face first. *Sky up, not down*—Connie reminded herself with the characteristic common sense that had made her one of the most popular seniors at Parkdale, *why stars on ground?* Then, as her eyes began to focus, Connie realized that the twinkling array before her was not stars, but a scattering of precious rhinestones on the pavement.

"Uh-oh, gonna get it now, . . ." Connie sang to herself sadly as she crawled across the moist green lawn to her door. Hauling herself to her feet with the aid of a pair of lawn flamingos, Connie used them as simple crutches to stagger the last few steps to the front porch. There, she collapsed and began to scratch feebly at the screen.

Answering the door, Mr. Phillips was surprised to find Connie's crumpled form on the steps, her half-naked body crisscrossed with red welts and her tattered nylons seamed with thin rivulets of dried blood.

"Well, it certainly looks like you've had *your* fun," said Mr. Phillips, "do you have any idea what time it is, young lady?"

Connie remained motionless on the steps as Mr. Phillips puffed his pipe angrily. Finally, Mr. Phillips sighed and lifted the dazed girl to her feet and leaned her against the screen door.

"I suppose you think your old Dad's an ancient old stick-in-the-mud," said Mr. Phillips. "But I *can* sympathize with the problems facing young people today . . . heck, you may not believe it, but I'm even 'hep' to a lot of your kookie teen lingo."

With that, Mr. Phillips's fist struck Connie in the face and sent her somersaulting through the screen door back out onto the lawn, the force of his blow immediately closing her right eye.

"Padiddle, for example," chuckled Mr. Phillips. □

TWO-WAY COMICS!

A CLEAN COMIC AND A DIRTY COMIC IN ONE   by ED SUBITZKY

FOR THOSE CLEAN-MINDED READERS WHO WANT TO READ AN INNOCENT STORY ABOUT A BOY AND HIS SISTER TRYING TO PIN A PRETTY PAINTING ON THE WALL OF THEIR HAPPY HOME, READ ACROSS IN THE NORMAL WAY, LIKE THIS:

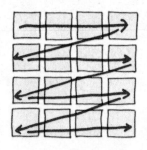

FOR THOSE FILTHY-MINDED READERS WHO WANT TO GET THEIR ROCKS OFF AND READ AN EXPLICIT SEX STORY THAT TAKES PLACE IN A CHEAP HOTEL, READ DOWN INSTEAD, LIKE THIS:

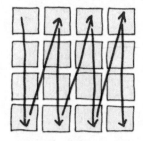

How t-- Tell What Girls Are Like Under Their Clothes by John Hughes

The Breasts

Shape

Breast shape mimics nose shape.

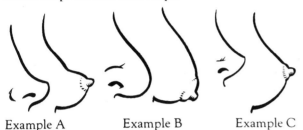

Example A   Example B   Example C

Size

Tits come in three sizes: Not Enough, Plenty, and Too Much. The best method for determining the knocker size is to look at the amount of "pull" on the fabric between the bosoms, roughly estimate the distance between mid-breast and shoulder, observe the breasts in motion, and then compare your results with the identification chart below.

Stationary   *In Motion*

Not Enough

7″

No stretch—no gap.

Breasts jiggle rapidly up and down, independently of one another.

At dead run, max. movement 3″ vert., 1″ lat.

Plenty

11″

Moderate stretch—½″ gap.

Breasts bounce rhythmically in unison, up and down with slight lateral sway.

At dead run, max. movement 8″ vert., 4″ lat.

Too Much

17″

Ripping—3″ gap.

Breasts slosh and roll up and down and from side to side with no apparent pattern.

At dead run, max. movement 18″ vert. 12″ lat.

The Principal Nipple Classifications

The Pygmy Gumdrop

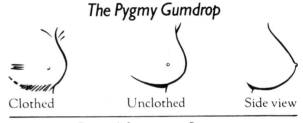

Clothed   Unclothed   Side view

Raised American Beauty

Clothed   Unclothed   Side view

All-Night Salute

Clothed   Unclothed   Side view

Flapjack

Clothed   Unclothed   Side view

Detecting Vaginal Tightness

Look for vaginal tightness in a woman's face. The tightest vaginas belong to the "lemon suckers," the sour-faced girls with the tiny mouths, pursed lips, miniature features, troubled looks, and pointy chins (i.e., the First Lady). The large, open pit variety vaginas are to be found in the women with big mouths, big teeth, lots of hair, and sparkling personalities (i.e., Carly Simon). How close to either of those extremes a gal is will let you know her vaginal size, give or take a thumb or two.

Note: Girls under the age of consent, women under five feet tall, and all Hawaiian females have extremely tight vaginas.

Basic Bush Designs

With the exception of redheads and raven-haired women, all feminine hair is mouse brown. Texture follows the general texture of the head hair. Since pubic hair shape and character is controlled by grooming, the way to figure out what a woman has is to look at her lifestyle indicators.

Secretary

All-American beaver shape, clean, well-scrubbed. Still a year or two away from hairy leg spread and pubis to navel fur bridge.

Cocktail Waitress

Boyfriend clip, keeps the lips shaved for easy access, smells like lilacs, on weekends uses special genital makeup.

Lady Businessman

Natural over-thirties muff, untouched except for leg trim and occasional yeast-related trailblazing.

Housewife

Convenient utility cut, kept close after second child, turns on otherwise sleepy husband, is a snap to keep clean.

Fashion Model

Doesn't stick out of bathing suit, emphasizes height.

Philosophy Major

Wilderness designation, uncut, unclean, more hair than a Turk.

Unwanted Hair

Unwanted hair is hair that appears anywhere on the body, with the exception of the head and the pubis. Unwanted hair that appears on the arms and face will tip you off to hidden unwanted hair.

If She Has	She Will Also Have → Armpit hair	Rectal hair	Nipple hair	Back hair	Buttock hair	Chest hair	Navel hair
Arm hair	X			X			
Hairy moles			X				
Moustache	X			X	X		
Sideburns	X			X	X		X
Eyebrow bridge	X	X		X	X		X
Chin hairs	X	X	X			X	
Knuckle hairs	X	X	X	X	X	X	X

The Ass

A great rear end can elevate a homely face, stupidity, bad skin, buck teeth, filth, and sloth to regal status. Most guys can live with a pair of infantile teats, but not too many good men linger around an ugly ass. When the ass goes, as they say, so does the man.

The Perfect Ass

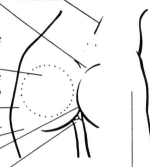

Cheeks separate, forming cute triangular indentation or "chin rest."

Charming dimples.

Cheeks form complete circle.

Skin is clear and white and smooth and cool to the touch.

Cheeks meet thigh without creating line.

Pink and hairless.

High cheeks allow view of genitals.

Feathery stroke of blond down continues to neck.

Lots and lots of adorable goosebumps when it's cold.

How to Tell a Good Big Ass from a Bad Big Ass

 The Good Big Ass The Bad Big Ass

The Good Big Ass	The Bad Big Ass
Expensive designer jeans	Penney's denim slacks
Buttock definition	One cheeks hangs lower
Light between legs	Thighs rub
Hips jog up and down when in motion	Buttocks vibrate when in motion

The Bag Over the Head Principle

Don't be dope! Just because her mug could spook a horse doesn't mean she can't have a great set of cans. We're all God's children and we each get our fair share of good and bad. For instance, those broads in *Vogue* look pretty sharp, but they can't remember their own phone numbers. So, if you're looking for the best individual parts, they're down on the bargain floor.

BEST TITS—Ugly Jewish girls studying law or medicine

Best Nipples—Fat white girls with freckles

Best Legs—Women over 6′ 6″

Best Asses—Short black women

Best Bushes—Girls with acne

Best Overall Genitals—Horse-faced girl athletes

The Four Basic Feminine Odor Groups

Smells But Doesn't Notice

Bless her heart, this little pie-faced sweetie works hard and tries her very best, but she stinks and she's not smart enough to know. She makes the best secretary, but on a hot day, she'll bring your lunch up.

Smells, Knows It, Covers It Up

She's the gal with the false eyelashes, the frosted hair, the blood-red lip gloss, and the skin that looks like flesh-colored paint. Downstairs, she smells like a sewer with an Airwick in it.

Smells And Loves It

You'll recognize her Swiss khaki hiking shorts, wool socks, waffle stompers, and flannel shirt. On the outside she smells like you, but unpeel her and you'll get a hint of what our evolutionary predecessors smelled like. She doesn't believe in covering up what is natural and beautiful and woman.

Doesn't Smell

Best that can be hoped for in real life. Very clean. Smells like soap and shampoo and baby powder and, sometimes, suntan lotion. These are the kind you marry.

Ethnic Considerations

The basic racial and ethnic types have distinct anatomical characteristics.

Black: Large brown nipples, chin-chapping corkscrews of wiry black pubic hair, protruding buttocks.

Oriental: Sparse black pubic hair, very fine texture, small brown nipples, small breasts, flat rear end.

Slavic: Woolly brown pubic hair in great abundance, large pink off-center nipples, big thighs, brownish to liver colored vaginal lips, low-slung butt.

Nordic: Pink nipples well-placed on large breasts, fine wispy light brown pubic hair, firm high buttocks, long legs, no brains.

English/Irish: Pure white skin, red nipples on large milky breasts, red pubic hair, large firm buttocks, short legs, thick ankles, thin waist.

Mediterranean: Huge full breasts, brown nipples, chubby stomach, big round buttocks.

Danger Signs

Women are very adept at concealing their shortcomings, but there are a number of clues and hints that will alert you to major structural, cosmetic, and hygienic flaws.

She's Old

High collar (to hide stringy chicken neck)
Thick yellow toenails
Nice ass but hunched back
Funny spots on hands
Bad breath
Nose veins
Perfect teeth; *too* perfect

She's Fat

Deep laugh
Long hair parted down the middle
Caftans
Clothing mostly black and twelve to eighteen months out of style
Peasant tops
Unusual wear patterns between upper trouser legs
Stretch waist skirts
Puffy fingers
Looks good standing but bulges when she walks
Goes to the beach in street clothes
Resewn seams on pants' seats

She's Dirty

Makeup line on jawbone
More than three runs per nylon
Crotch stains
Baggy knees on pants
Salt stains on blouse underarms
Open-toe shoes with dirt visible at base of toes
Neck pimples
Wearing scarf on head (to hide greasy hair)
Pubic hair hanging out of bathing suit
Caste mark

She's Crazy

More than three earrings
More than five rings
Black woman with white eye shadow
White woman with black eye shadow
Shorts and heels
Bathing suit in public
Burgundy, blue, or pink hair
Safety pin in cheek
Under 100 lbs.

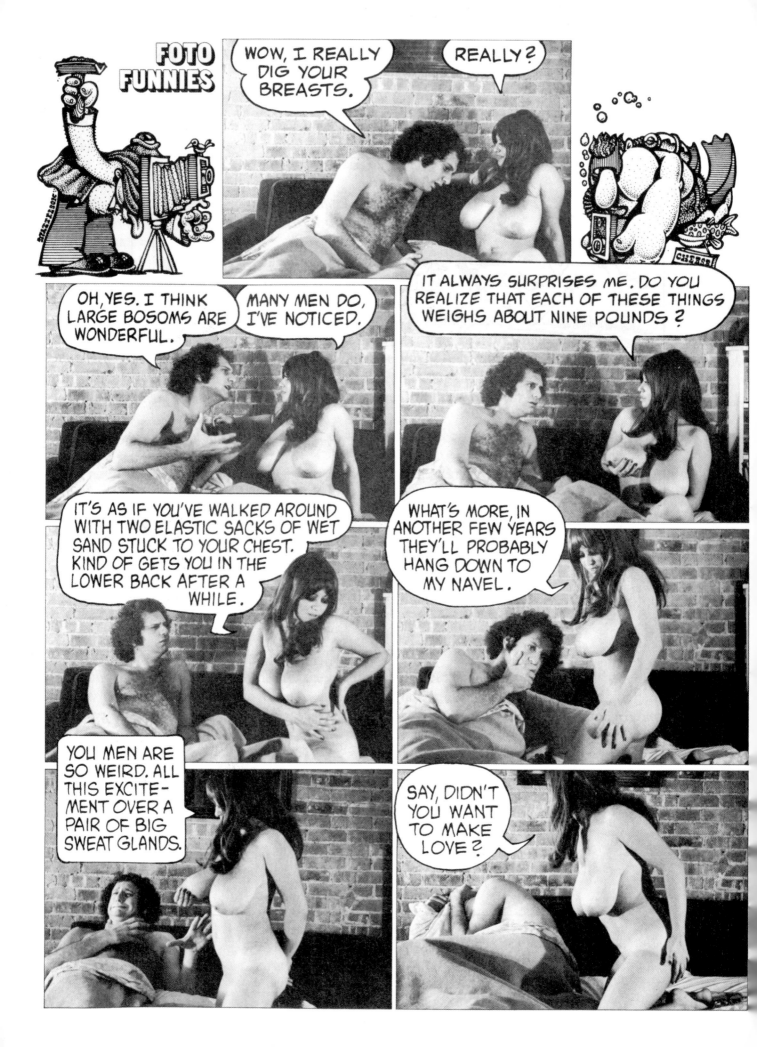

For God's sake, if you have never before
used a **CLAMPAX**© menstrual poonton

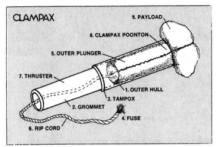

...WORLD'S FOREMOST MENSTRUAL POONTON

COMMIT THIS SIMPLE HANDBOOK TO MEMORY BEFORE YOU EVEN TRY

Like everything else you learned to do, from re-wiring your waffle iron to parallel parking a camper-trailer, doing it yourself with Clampax menstrual poontons is just as easy once you get the knack.

We suggest you get acquainted with your Clampax poonton and see how it works. Introduce yourself to it before you introduce it into yourself! First, re-move the hermetically-sealed and discreetly designed paper wrapper by placing your fingers at both ends and pulling vigorously just as you would a birthday cracker. It will pop right open, revealing the highly absorbent poonton enclosed in its safety-tested outer immersion tube which encloses the inner pumper tube which encloses the decorative braided ejection string or rip cord (see diagram).

Stand up, grasp the poonton vertically, and pretend for the moment the room you are in is a huge vagina. Good. Now, with the thumb and index finger touching, make a bunny rabbit of your right hand. Gently slide the bunny's head over units 1, 8, 5, 4, and choke it until it fits slide piston snugly. Hook your pinky, just as in crocheting, around unit 6 and hold, resting your solitaire finger on main thrusters. Now, pointing the Clampax away from your eyes and keeping hold of 6, push plunger and 2 up through 3, 4, 5, and out 8, letting go of 6 just at the last moment. If you followed the directions properly, the poonton should now be lying on the carpet.

You'll be relieved to know that because the outer immersion tube and inner pumper tube are generously prelubricated, the poonton's business end will glide easily into yours, without your ever having to look at it, touch it, or anything.

Now you are ready to embark on a maiden voyage with your Clampax poonton. Turn the page and follow the explicit directions.

Welcome to the millions who delight in the companionship of Clampax menstrual poontons.

HOW TO USE CLAMPAX© POONTONS

Get hold of yourself . . .

The clue to proper insertion is to *get hold of yourself*. Make sure you are calm and relaxed. If you are tense, the muscles of your vaginal opening will snap shut like the valves of a scared mollusk and insertion will be unnecessarily difficult. No need to worry, millions of girls just like you had their "first time" and most are already walking normally!

So pop open a fresh poonton . . . *get hold of yourself* . . . and follow these five easy steps.

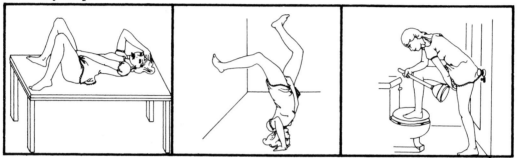

1. Lie flat on back on kitchen table. Bite bullet   *OR*   Stand on head to avoid leakage   *OR*   Forget the whole thing, lock door, and think dirty things

. . . whichever seems most natural and comfortable for you.

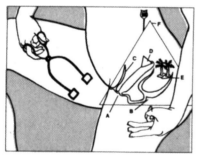

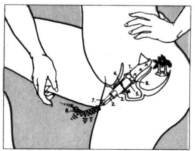

2. Inserting your fist and giving the Girl Scout Salute, or, if you prefer not to touch it, using spaghetti tongs, spread the sides of your vaginal canal A (somewhere near the rectal canal B, the urinary canal C, the Bermuda Triangle D, the Islets of Langerhans E, and Interstate 90).

3. Set the poonton end 3, 4, 5, 8, and 1 into the vaginal opening. Now wrap the ejection string 6 around and around 7 and '2 as tautly and as rapidly as you can until you are holding only the tiniest end and then *yank!* The poonton will spin upward, inserting itself into your vagina, pleasantly but firmly coming to a stop only when it is satisfied it's properly placed and feels at home. NOTE: *The Clampax poonton must*

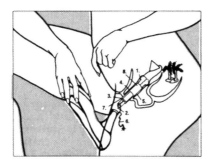

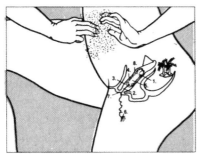

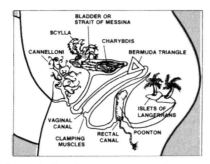

be aimed in the right direction. This is important in order to avoid internal hemorrhaging and the remote possibility you may never be able to have children.

4. Now, with the tip of your forefinger or the heel of one of your pumps, *gently* plunge 7 and 2 into your body. When you can feel (and you will) 1, 2, 3, 4, 5, 7, and 8 up inside you and the cheerful tickle of 6 against your inner thigh, the poonton is on the job.

5. Wait! *You must remove all units except 1, 2, and 6 before you can leave* the area. So select from your hands the three fingers you like least, reach all the way up there, and take out 7, 3, 5, 4, and 8. This may be difficult as they will be damp and slippery as eels. Try powdering your hands with cornstarch or Shake 'n Bake or rub them in kitty litter to give them sufficient traction for removal.

If you followed these directions with care the poonton will be bobbing happily, tossed on the ebb and flow of your vaginal canal's monthly tides and tidal waves. You should not even feel the poonton is there. If you do, it's in the wrong orifice (see anatomical diagram, stupid) and you must take your compact mirror, penlight, and plug wrench, locate your mistake, and remove it without delay. Don't be discouraged. There are so many openings down there that even doctors refer to it as the "miraculous maze of womanhood," and you're just a weekend spelunker. So think of it as a puzzle, relax, and begin again. Your life depends on it.

IF THE POONTON FITS, WEAR IT

No matter if your flow is mercifully light or rich and full-bodied, Clampax has a poonton of sufficient strength to accomodate you. Many use Aswan or Grand Coulee during the days of heavy flooding and taper off to Beaver when less sandbagging is needed. On those flood tide days when you can't change your poonton readily, try using from two to ten at the same time. Insert them one by one, and should you use an entire box, remove box first. Arrange them inside in a pyramidal fashion like bowling pins up your alley.

ANSWERS TO QUESTIONS
NEW USERS OFTEN ASK

"How old must I be to start using Clampax poontons?"

It is not true that your eyes are bigger than your vagina. The Clampax poonton is inserted into the same opening from which quarts of menstrual fluid and 11-pound screaming infants have been known to emerge. This opening is sufficiently large to accomodate a casaba melon, as field researchers in Tijuana have testified, and any normal girl should be able to use them with complete confidence. *If you are over 40, however, you're probably fooling yourself and may wish first to seek the advice of your family physician.*

"I can't get the poonton in. It feels dry. What should I do?"

Clampax poontons are, of course, prelubricated, but should insertion prove difficult, run out to your local bookstore, purchase a copy of Guillaume Apollinaire's *The Debauched Hospodar*, read pages 26 to 34, and try again. You should have no trouble whatsoever.

"May I swim and exercise during my menstrual period?"

Certainly. Clampax poontons are designed so that you can lead a normal life during menstruation. Most girls, however, find it easier to erect a small tent in the backyard for the duration.

"Can the poonton get lost or drop out?"

Not bloody likely, but *don't wear white.*

"How will I know when to change a poonton?"

A Clampax poonton should be changed at least as often as you change your mind. With a little experience, you'll know only too well when. There is no need to change for urination, tub, or shower, depending, of course, on what kind of girl you are.

"Will anyone be able to tell that I'm menstruating and wearing Clampax?"

In addition to you, only clairvoyants, bloodhounds, and most men and little brothers will know for sure. Don't be embarrassed. Threaten to make him eat one.

IT'S AFTER YOUR PERIOD—

DO YOU KNOW WHERE YOUR POONTON IS?

A Clampax poonton feels so pleasant and fulfilling you may forget about it entirely. Please, always remove the last poonton you use each period. If you don't, monilia, nonspecific urethritis, herpes simplex, yeasts, mastectomy, yaws, ectopic pregnancy, senile caritosis, stretch marks, plantar's warts, nymphomania, varicose veins, elephantiasis, cellulite jungle rot, or a trip to the Schlimm-Katze Clinic in Zermatt, Switzerland, at $475 per day can result.

CLAMPAX INCORPORATED • GOOSE BAY 00069 • ALASKA • U.S.A.

PLAYBORE'S DIRTY JOKES

Legend has it that one day J. S. Bach appeared at the door of the local organ-maker in quite a dither. "Hans," said Bach to the deaf craftsman, "der King ist coming today to hear my latest masterpiece and my organ has just gone on der fritz. Can you come right over und fix it for me?"

"You say your *organ* ist on der fritz?" replied the old man, cupping a hand to his ear.

"Ja," replied Bach impatiently, "my organ ist on der fritz und I vant you to *macht schnell* und fix it before der King comes!"

"Your *organ*, ja?" cackled the wizened tradesman.

"Ja, ja, my organ," pressed Bach, "How much will you charge me?"

"Vell, normally I vould charge fifteen marks," began the old man with a twinkle in his eye, "but since you are such a good customer, *I'll make it ten!*"

Our Unabashed Dictionary defines *pornography* as obscene or licentious literature or pictures.

Two pot-puffing hippies were staggering down Fifth Avenue one afternoon when they were suddenly confronted with a parade of sixteen-thousand naked lovelies marching toward them accompanied by a fifty-piece naked brass band and all the national leaders of the western hemisphere, each as bare as the day they were born. "Oh wow," exclaimed one of the hippies to his companion.

"Yeah," quipped the other stoned freak slyly, "wow!"

Our Unabashed Dictionary defines *fetish* as a part of the body, article of clothing or simply any object which arouses abnormal erotic desires.

A man walked into the local pub with a fat penguin perched atop his head. The startled bartender looked up in disbelief, but attempting to hide his astonishment, the bewildered barkeep casually asked the man what he wanted to drink. "A whiskey and soda, please," was the man's straight-faced reply.

Then there was the topless pianist who played so badly that her pathetic gimmick failed to attract any publicity, much less an audience.

A swinging young executive had been listening to his cronies at lunch discuss the supposedly superior love-making techniques of married women. Intrigued with the idea, he ran to a booth and called his boss's wife and asked if he could come over right away and "discuss an important matter." Soon after his arrival and a couple of double martinis, he managed to coax the apprehensive young lady into bed. But, as is usually the case with such stories, her irate husband came in early from the office and found the guilty couple still locked in the primal embrace. "What's going one here?" he demanded.

"W-why, I'm commiting adultery with your wife," came the stammered reply.

"That's what I thought," snapped the angry husband as he slammed the door behind him and left.

The next day the boss fired the young exec, filed divorce proceedings against his distraught wife, and moved into a motel, looking forward to many years of loneliness and unhappiness.

We know an airline stewardess who told every ardent pilot she dated that she wanted to save her favors for her husband, should she ever marry. Finally she met the right man, married him and settled down to make a wonderful wife and a devoted mother to their four children.

Our Unabashed Dictionary defines *rape* as the illicit carnal knowledge of a woman without her consent.

An obviously newlywed couple sat cooing at each other in a vacation resort bar when a rather greasy-looking smoothie in a shiny suit glided up to them. "Gotta match?" he asked, eyeing the zestful little breastful coolly.

"No," smiled the unruffled groom, "but I have a lighter."

Our Unabashed Dictionary defines *breast* as the milk-producing gland found on the ventral areas of most female mammals. ∎

Heard any hot ones lately? Send it in a plain brown paper envelope to Dirty Jokes Editor, PLAYBORE, Room 1301, 1790 Broadway, New York, N.Y. 10019. Theoretically, contributors would be paid $50 for each joke, but you know as well as we do that we get 'em all from out-of-print Spicy Story anthologies. Won't you kiss me in the dark, baby? □

How to Drive Fast on Wing-Wang Squeezed

When it comes to taking chances, some people like to play poker or shoot dice; other people prefer to parachute jump, go rhino hunting, or climb ice floes, while still others engage in crime or marriage. But I like to get drunk and drive like a fool. Name me, if you can, a better feeling than the one you get when you're half a bottle of Chivas in the bag with a gram of coke up your nose, and a teenage lovely pulling off her tube top in the next seat over while you're going a hundred miles an hour down a suburban side street. You'd have to watch the entire Mexican air force crash-land in a liquid petroleum gas storage facility to match this kind of thrill. If you ever have much more fun than that, you'll die of pure sensory overload, I'm here to tell you.

But wait. Let's pause and analyze *why* this particular matrix of activities is perceived as so highly enjoyable. I mean, aside from the teenage lovely pulling off her tube top in the next seat over. Ignoring that for a moment (despite these perfect little cone-shaped breasts that stand right up from her chest and end in a pair of eager hot pink lust-hardened nipples as thick as your thumbs), let's look at the psychological factors conducive to placing positive emotional values on the sensory end product of experientially produced excitation of the central nervous system and smacking into a lamppost. Is that any way to have fun? How would your mother feel if she knew you were doing this? She'd cry. She really would. And that's how you know it's fun. Anything that makes your mother cry is fun. Sigmund Freud wrote all about this. It's a well-known fact.

Of course, it's a shame to risk young lives behaving this way—speeding around all tanked up with your feet hooked in the steering wheel while your date crawls around on the floor mats opening zippers with her teeth and pounding on the accelerator with an empty liquor bottle. But it wouldn't be taking a chance if you weren't risking *something*. And even if it is a shame to risk young lives behaving this way, it is definitely cooler than risking *old* lives behaving this way. I mean, so what if some fifty-eight-year-old butt-head gets a load on and starts playing Death Race 2000 in the rush-hour traffic jam? What kind of chance is he taking? He's just waiting around to see what kind of cancer he gets anyway. But if young, talented *you*, with all of life's possibilities at your fingertips, you and the future Cheryl Tiegs there, so fresh, so beautiful—if the two of *you* stake your handsome heads on a single roll of the dice in life's game of stop-the-semi— now *that's* taking chances! Which is why old people rarely risk their lives. It's not because they're chicken—they just have too much dignity to play for small stakes.

Drugs While Getting You and Not Spill Your Drink

by P.J. O'Rourke, Technical Consultant: Joe Schenkman

Now a lot of people say to me, "Hey, P.J., you like to drive fast. Why not join a responsible organization, such as the Sports Car Club of America, and enjoy participation in sports car racing? That way you could drive as fast as you wish while still engaging in a well-regulated spectator sport that is becoming more popular each year." No thanks. In the first place, if you ask me, those guys are a bunch of tweedy old barf mats who like to talk about things like what necktie they wore to Alberto Ascari's funeral. And in the second place, they won't let me drive drunk. They expect me to go out there and smash into things and roll over on the roof and catch fire and burn to death when I'm sober. They must think I'm crazy. That stuff scares me. I have to get completely fuck-faced to even think about driving fast. How can you have a lot of exciting thrills when you're so terrified that you wet yourself all the time? That's not fun. It's just *not fun* to have exciting thrills

when you're scared. Take the heroes of the *Iliad*, for instance—they really had some exciting thrills, and were they scared? No. They were drunk. Every chance they could get. And so am I, and I'm not going out there and have a horrible car wreck until somebody brings me a cocktail.

Also, it's important to be drunk because being drunk keeps your body all loose, and that way, if you have an accident or anything, you'll sort of roll with the punches and not get banged up so bad. For example, there was this guy I heard about who was really drunk and was driving through the Adirondacks. He got sideswiped by a bus and went head-on into another car, which knocked him off a bridge, and he plummeted 150 feet into a ravine. I mean, it killed him and everything, but if he hadn't been so drunk and loose, his body probably would have been banged up a lot worse—and you can imagine how much more upset his wife

would have been when she went down to the morgue to identify him if he'd been twisted up and smashed to pieces and covered in bloody gore.

Even more important than being drunk, however, is having the right car. You have to get a car that handles really well. This is extremely important, and there's a lot of debate on this subject—about what kind of car handles best. Some say a front-engined car; some say a rear-engined car. I say a *rented* car. Nothing handles better than a rented car. You can go faster, turn corners sharper, and put the transmission into reverse while going forward at a higher rate of speed in a rented car than in any other kind. You can also park without looking, and can use the trunk as an ice chest. Another thing about a rented car is that it's an all-terrain vehicle. Mud, snow, water, woods—you can take a rented car anywhere. True, you can't always get it back—but that's not your problem, is it?

Yet there's more to a really good-handling car than just making sure it doesn't belong to you. It has to be big. It's really hard for a girl to get her clothes off inside a small car, and this is one of the most important features of car handling. Also, what kind of drugs does it have in it? Most people like to drive on speed or cocaine with plenty of whiskey mixed in. This gives you the confidence you want and need for plowing through red lights and passing trucks on the right. But don't neglect downs and 'ludes and codeine cough syrup either. It's hard to beat the heavy depressants for high speed spin-outs, backing into trees, and a general feeling of not giving two fucks about man and his universe. Try a little heroin. Sometimes it makes you throw up, but if you haven't used all the ice in the trunk, you can spread some around on the back seat floor and that way when you forget whether you're in England or not and can't remember which side of the car you're on, you can just puke over your shoulder and the ice will keep the smell down, if you still care. Plus, some of the cubes will slide under the front seat and you can grab them and use them on the girl (which is really a kick in case you've never tried it).

Over all, though, it's the bigness of the car that counts the most. Because when something bad happens in a really big car—accidentally speeding through the middle of a gang of unruly young people who have been taunting you in a drive-in restaurant, for instance—it happens very far away—way out at the end of your fenders. It's like a civil war in Africa; you know, it doesn't really concern you too much. On the other hand, when something happens in a little bitty car it happens all over you. You get all involved in it and have to give everything a lot of thought. Driving around in a little bitty car is like being one of those sensitive girls who writes poetry. Life is just too much to bear. You end up staying at home in your bedroom and thinking up sonnets that don't get published till you die, which will be real soon if you keep driving around in little bitty cars like that.

Let's inspect some of the basic maneuvers of drunken driving while you've got crazy girls who are on drugs with you. Look for these signs when picking up crazy girls: pierced ears with five or six earrings in them, unusual shoes, white lipstick, extreme thinness, hair that's less than an inch long, or clothing made of chrome and leather. Stay away from girls who cry a lot or who look like they get pregnant easily or have careers. They may want to do weird stuff in cars, but only in the back seat, and that's already filled with ice and has throw-up all over it and, anyway, it's really hard to

steer from back there. Besides, they'll want to get engaged right away afterwards. But the other kind of girls—there's no telling what they'll do. I used to know this girl who weighed about eighty pounds and dressed in skirts that didn't even cover her underwear, when she wore any. I had this beat-up old Mercedes, and we were off someplace about fifty miles from nowhere on Christmas Eve in a horrible sleet storm. The road was really a mess, all curves and big ditches, and I was blotto, and the car kept slipping off the pavement and sliding sideways. And just when I'd hit a big patch of glare ice and was frantically spinning the wheel trying to stay out of the oncoming traffic, she said, "I shaved my pussy today—wanna feel?"

That's really true. And then, about half an hour later the head gasket blew up, and we had to spend I don't know how long in this dirtball motel, although the girl walked all the way to the liquor store through about a mile of slush and got all kinds of wine and did weird stuff with the bottle necks later. So it was sort of O.K., except that the garage where I left the Mercedes burned down and I used the insurance money to buy a motorcycle.

Now girls who like motorcycles really will do *anything*. I mean, really, *anything you can think of*. But it's just not the same. For one thing, it's hard to drink while you're riding a motorcycle—there's no place to set your glass. And cocaine's out of the question. And personally, I find that grass makes me too sensitive. You smoke some grass and the first thing you know you're pulling over to the side of the road and taking a break to dig the gentle beauty of the sky's vast panorama, the slow, luxurious interplay of sun and clouds, the lulling trill of breezes midst leafy tree branches—and what kind of fun is that? Besides, it's rough to "get it on" with a chick (I mean in the biblical sense) and still make all the fast curves unless you let her take the handlebars with her pants off and come on Greek style or something, which is harder than it sounds; and pantless girls on motorcycles attract the highway patrol, so usually you don't end up doing anything until you're both off the bike, and by then you may be in the hospital. Like I was after this old lady who pulled out in front of me in an Oldsmobile, and the girl I was with still wanted to do anything you can think of, but there was a doctor there and he was squirting pHisoHex all over me and combing little bits of gravel out of my face with a wire brush, and I just couldn't get into it. So, take it from me and don't get a motorcycle. Get a big car.

Usually, most fast driving maneuvers that don't require crazy girls call for use of

the steering wheel, so be sure your car is equipped with power steering. Without power steering, turning the wheel is a lot like work, and if you wanted work you'd get a job. All steering should be done with the index finger. Then, when you're done doing all the steering that you want to do, just pull your finger out of there and the wheel will come right back to wherever it wants to. It's that simple. Be sure to do an extra lot of steering when going into a driveway or turning sharp corners. And here's another important tip: Always roll the window down before throwing bottles out, and don't try to throw them through the windshield unless the car is parked.

O.K., now say you've been on a six-day drunk and you've just made a bet that you can back up all the way to Cleveland, plus you've got a buddy who's getting a blowjob on the trunk lid. Well, let's face it—if that's the way you're going to act, sooner or later you'll have an accident. This much is true. But that doesn't mean that you should sit back and just let accidents happen to you. No, you have to go out and cause them yourself. That way you're in control of the situation.

You know, it's a shame, but a lot of people have the wrong idea about accidents. For one thing, they don't hurt nearly as much as you'd think. That's because you're in shock and can't feel pain or, if you aren't in shock, you're dead, and that doesn't hurt at all so far as we know. Another thing is that they make great stories. I've got this friend—a prominent man in the automotive industry—who flipped his MG TF back in the fifties and slid on his head for a couple hundred yards, and had to spend a year with no eyelids and a steel pin through his cheekbones while his face was being rebuilt. Sure, it wasn't much fun at the time, but you should hear him tell about it now—what a fabulous tale, especially at dinner. Besides, it's not all smashing glass and spurting blood, you understand. Why, a good sideswipe can be an almost religious experience. The sheet metal doesn't break or crunch or anything—it flexes and gives way as the two vehicles come together, with a rushing liquid pulse as if two giant sharks of steel were mating in the perpetual night of the sea primordial. I mean, if you're on enough drugs. Also, sometimes you see a lot of really pretty lights in your head.

One sure way to cause an accident is with your basic "moonshiner's" or "bootlegger's" turn. Whiz down the road at about sixty or seventy, throw the gearshift into neutral, cut the wheel to the left, and hit the emergency brake with one good wallop while holding the brake release out with your left hand. This'll send you spinning around in a perfect 180° turn right into a culvert or a fast-moving tractor-trailer rig. (The bootlegger's turn can be done on dry pavement, but it works best on loose gravel or small children.) Or, when you've moved around backwards, you can then spin the wheel to the right and keep on going until you've come around a full 360° and are headed back the same way you were going; though it probably would have been easier to have just kept going that way in the first place and not have done anything at all, unless you were with somebody you really wanted to impress—your probation officer, for instance.

An old friend of mine named Joe Schenkman happens to have just written me a letter about another thing you can do to wreck a car. Joe's on a little vacation up in Vermont and will be until he finds out what the statute of limitations on attempted vehicular homicide is. And he was writing to tell me about a fellow he met up there, saying:

...This guy has rolled (deliberately) over thirty cars (and not just by his own account—the townfolks back him up on this story), inheriting only a broken nose (three times) and a slightly black-and-blue shoulder for all this. What you do, see, is you go into a moonshiner's turn, but you get on the brakes and stay on them. Depending on how fast you're going, you roll proportionately: four or five rolls is decent. Going into the spin, you have one hand on the seat and the other firmly on the roof so you're sprung in tight. As you feel the roof give on the first roll, you slip your seat hand under the dash (of the passenger side, as you're thrown hard over in that direction to begin with), and pull yourself under it. And here you simply sit it out, springing yourself tight with your whole body, waiting for the thunder to die. Naturally, it helps to be drunk, and if you have a split second's doubt or hesitation through any of this, you die.

This Schenkman himself is no slouch of a driver, I may say. Unfortunately, his strong suit is driving in New York City, an area that has a great number of unusual special conditions, which we just don't have the time or the space to get into right here (except to note that the good part is how it's real easy to scare old Jewish ladies in new Cadillacs and the bad part is that Negroes actually *do* carry knives, not to mention Puerto Ricans; and everybody else you hit turns out to be a lawyer or married to somebody in the mob). However, Joe is originally from the South, and it was down there that he discovered huffing glue and sniffing industrial solvents and such. These

give you a really spectacular hallucinatory type of a high where you think, for instance, that you're driving through an overpass guardrail and landing on a freight train flatcar and being hauled to Shreveport and loaded into a container ship headed for Liberia with a crew full of homosexual Lebanese, only to come to and find out that it's true. Joe is a commercial artist who enjoys jazz music and horse racing. His favorite color is blue.

There's been a lot of discussion about what kind of music to listen to while staring doom square in the eye and not blinking unless you get some grit under your contacts. Watch out for the fellow who tunes his FM to the classical station. He thinks a little Rimsky-Korsakov makes things more dramatic—like in a foreign movie. That's pussy style. This kind of guy's idea of a fast drive is a 75-mph cruise up to the summer cottage after one brandy and soda. The true skidmark artist prefers something cheery and upbeat—"Night on Disco Mountain" or "Boogie Oogie Oogie" or whatever it is that the teenage lovely with nipples as thick as your thumbs wants to shake her buns to. Remember her? So what do *you* care what's on the fucking tape deck? The high, hot whine of the engine, the throaty pitch of the exhaust, the wind in your beer can, the gentle slurping noises from her little bud-red lips—that's all the music your ears need, although side two of the first Velvet Underground album is nice if you absolutely insist. And no short jaunts either. For the maniacal high-speed driver, endurance is everything. Especially if you've used that ever-

popular pickup line, "Wanna go to Mexico?" Especially if you've used it somewhere like Boston. Besides teenage girls can go a long, long time without sleep and, believe me, so can the police and their parents. So just keep your foot in it. There's no reason not to. There's no reason not to keep going forever, really. I had this friend who drove a whole shitload of people up from Oaxaca to Cincinnati one time, nonstop. I mean, he stopped for gas but he wouldn't even let anybody get out then. He made them all piss out the windows, and he says that it was worth the entire drive just to *see* a girl try to piss out the window of a moving car.

Get a fat girl friend so you'll have plenty of amphetamines and you'll never have to stop at all. The only problem you'll run into is that after you've been driving for two or three days you start to see things in the road—great big scaly things twenty feet high with nine legs. But there are very few great big scaly things with nine legs in America anymore, so you can just drive right through them because they probably aren't really there, and if they *are* really there you'll be doing the country a favor by running them over.

Yes, but where does it all end? Where does a crazy life like this lead? To death, you say. Look at all the people who've died in car wrecks: Albert Camus, Jayne Mansfield, Jackson Pollack, Tom Paine. Well, Tom Paine didn't *really* die in a car wreck, but he probably would have if he'd lived a little later. He was that kind of guy. Anyway, death is always the first thing that leaps into everybody's mind—sudden violent death at an early age. If only it were that simple. God, we could all go out in a blaze of flaming aluminum alloys formulated specially for the Porsche factory race effort like James Dean did! No ulcers, no hemorrhoids, no bulging waistlines, soft dicks, or false teeth...*bash!! kaboom!! Watch this space for paperback reprint rights, auction, and movie option sale!* But that's not the way it goes. No. What actually happens is you fall for that teenage lovely in the next seat over, fall for her like a ton of condoms, and before you know it you're married and have teenage lovelies of your own—getting gang-fucked on a Pontiac Trans-Am's shaker hood at this very minute, no doubt—plus a six-figure mortgage, a liver the size of the Bronx, and a Country Squire that's never seen the sweet side of sixty.

I guess it's hard to face the truth, but I suppose you yourself realize that if you'd had just a little more courage, just a little more strength of character, you could have been dead by now. No such luck. □

UNDERWEAR for the DEAF

BY MICHAEL O'DONOGHUE

Beware questionable salesmen who promise the moon.

an excerpt from:

The
WORST-CASE SCENARIO
Survival Handbook
MASTURBATION

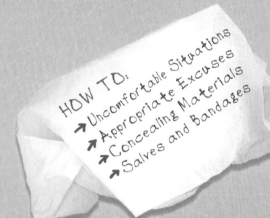

HOW TO:
→ Uncomfortable Situations
→ Appropriate Excuses
→ Concealing Materials
→ Salves and Bandages

By Pete Cummin

UNCOMFORTABLE SITUATIONS

HOW TO MASTURBATE IN YOUR GRAND-MOTHER'S HOUSE

You're visiting Nana for a whole week. Day one, you spend the afternoon looking through scrapbooks and sipping tea. Day two, you go antiquing while she tells you about the summer camp she went to as a little girl. Day three, you go through some items in the attic, marveling at how your grandfather's old sweaters fit you perfectly. By day four, you need to masturbate.

1 Don't panic.
Although you are surrounded by doilies, figurines and that weird old person odor, there are still options. Masturbating is about state of mind.

2 Find some material.
Unless it's Holiday catalogue season your pickings are going to be limited. Try to locate old photos of your lesser known aunts and cousins. Do any of them do it for you? Try to take into account the homemade nature of the pictures, leading one to think of innocence lost. Now get to work.

3 Ignore your dead grandfather.
He's been dead for years. He has better things to do than look down at you shining your skin soldier. If he is looking down at you, however, doesn't that kind of make him a freak too? Does that do anything for you? No one is judging.

4 Cleanup.
A good masturbator always leaves his masturbation site better than when he found it. And don't forget to put the pictures of your aunts back in their proper place and proper order! Remember, your grandmother is an expert at organizing her old memories. You don't need to be caught off-guard later on with uncomfortable questions.

HOW TO MASTURBATE AT THE OFFICE

1 Don't panic.
Remember, it only takes 10 minutes to masturbate. No more than a game of minesweeper. You have time.

2 Don't use the Internet.
Every time you use the Internet you leave a Website history. You don't need everyone knowing what a pervert you are… even though you are not. You only look at "normal" sex sites—if by normal you mean hentai videos of trampy schoolgirls sodomizing Japanese farm animals. No one is judging.

3 All right, fine—use the Internet, but be quick about it. After you've memorized your manga fantasy, try to close the window. When the endless series of pop-ups begin, unplug the computer and begin the rebooting process. Complain loudly about your piece of shit computer and how you might as well take a break for 10 minutes.

4 Go to the men's room.
Take the last stall. Lock it. If you can, take a dump; the smell will make it more realistic.

5 Avoid thoughts of being molested.
Block out the sound of men's dress shoes cracking with authority over the hard linoleum floor. Even though you have your pants down, masturbating like a British school lad, no one but you can touch you funny. So focus on the Internet.

Tell everyone about your awesome shit.
That's right — the best defense is a good offense. When you finally leave the bathroom, make sure everyone knows how "underrated a good shit really is."

HOW TO MASTURBATE IN THE LINE OF GUNFIRE

1 Don't panic.
Thinking about how at any second you could be shot only makes masturbating worse. And you don't want to be killed with your pants down by your ankles, because that makes for a really awkward eulogy.

2 Get down, and stay down.
If you are not the intended target, get flat on your stomach and stay there.

Imagine Halle Berry.
In most circumstances Halle Berry is so far beyond the realm of possibility that even fantasies involving her are considered too implausible to work. But that is the one advantage of being shot at. It's like you are the star of a big-budget action movie. And lying under the protection of your body is a quaking, helpless Halle Berry.

DON'T DIE TODAY
STARRING HALLE BERRY AND ME

3 Dry-hump the ground.
Use the friction of the ground to imagine Halle lying on her stomach pushing her wanton ass to your pelvis.

If there is mud or a puddle nearby, crawl into it.
Now finish.

4 Shit in your pants.
It is perfectly acceptable for a person who is being shot at to shit in their pants. It is not, however, acceptable to cum in them. Fortunately, once you shit in them, no one will want to examine your pants any closer and the cum will be overlooked.

HOW TO MASSAGE THE MEAT DURING A SHARK ATTACK

A shark is rushing forward to consume you, but you and your member haven't had a moment alone all day. It's not too late.

1 Don't panic.
Sharks can smell fear. They cannot however smell self-gratification. Your enjoyment will also serve to confuse it. "That must be one strong creature to be so disdainful of a shark's murderous frenzy and its three rows of razor sharp teeth," the shark will think. (Note: Sharks do not actually speak or think in English. Do not try reasoning with them.)

2 Remember "Splash."
Pretend any floating seaweed or passing fish are sexy, half Darryl Hannah, half fish stroking you from beneath. You should be hard soon. If not, think of mermen. No one is judging.

3 Dive feet first into the jaws.
If you fight a shark during an attack, it will most likely just tear off a piece, and leave you to bleed to death.

By maneuvering yourself to be engulfed bottom-half-first, it leaves your lower arms (and groin area) free to do their jobs.

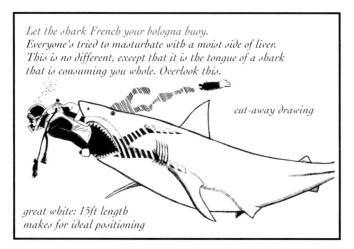

Let the shark French your bologna buoy.
Everyone's tried to masturbate with a moist side of liver.
This is no different, except that it is the tongue of a shark
that is consuming you whole. Overlook this.

cut-away drawing

great white: 15ft length
makes for ideal positioning

4 Use the loss of blood to your advantage.
The light-headed feelings associated with the massive blood loss from shark bites will diminish your inhibitions and let you just "have fun with it." Enhance the experience further by using a mix of your own blood and shark bile as lubricant.

5 Pop your cork inside the shark's mouth.
Hopefully, your shark is a heterosexual male shark. If not, your shark may enjoy what you've done and later force you into an undersea relationship. If your shark is straight, though, it should only take a moment before ejaculation before the realization of what has just happened induces a state of shock in the beast, at which point his jaw will drop, leaving you to swim free. There is no cleanup.

HOW TO SELF-INDUCE THE EJACULATION OF SEMEN FROM YOUR URETHRA IN THE VACUUM OF SPACE

The international space station you're on is struck by a micrometeor traveling at enormous speeds. The ship is blown apart, flinging you unprotected into the vacuum of space. Before the darkness engulfs you, the glowing image of an attractive female cosmonaut already burning up in Earth's atmosphere leaves you a little stiff.

1 Don't panic.
You can only survive a maximum of 40 seconds in space before your organs implode, so don't waste your breath on panic or last minute reflections about how good a life you may or may not have led. It's time for a little extra-vehicular activity.

2 Use other survivors.
To add to your own masturbation time, grab nearby surviving astronauts and suck the remaining air out of their lungs. Then kick them away. You don't need them watching you bump one off, unless you're into that, in which case, no one is judging.

3 Try to stay on the dark side of ship debris.
Not only is it harder for your dying shipmates to see you, the dark is just sexier. Imagine the stars are scented candles, that your weightlessness is because you're in a hot tub, and that the moon is something sexy and romantic, like the moon.

4 Pretend the Earth below is a pornographic movie.
Blinking quickly to avoid the popping out of your eyes, get a few good looks at Florida (Italy will suffice if the U.S. is not in view). Imagine it's having a threesome with the Gulf of Mexico and one of the Great Lakes. You should be about done.

Grab any squeeze packets floating by.
Space is notoriously dry. If you are floating near any NASA food tubes, grope around for the one with the most promising contents. Anything from the meat family will usually be thick, gooey, and moisturizing enough to help get your rub on.

5 Shit in your pants.
For old time's sake.

If you liked this excerpt from *The Worst-Case Scenarios Survival Handbook: Masturbation*, be sure to order the book for hundreds of other ways to masturbate, including How to Masturbate:

- On Fire
- At a Parent-Teacher Conference
- On a Reality Television Show
- While Running from the Police
- While Employed as a Character at Disneyland
- During Bible Study and many, many more

GRAY'S ANATOMY OF LOVE

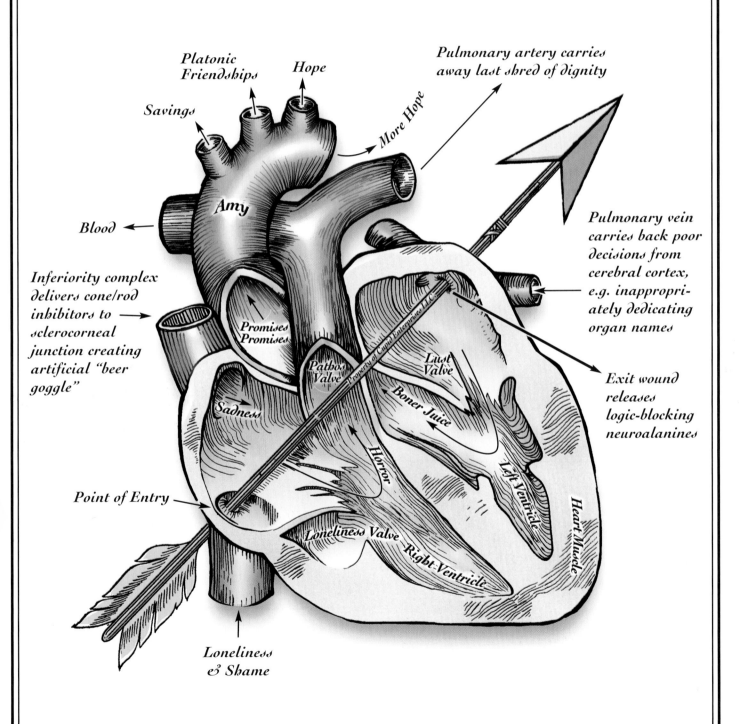

Platonic Friendships

Hope

Savings

Pulmonary artery carries away last shred of dignity

More Hope

Amy

Blood

Inferiority complex delivers cone/rod inhibitors to sclerocorneal junction creating artificial "beer goggle"

Promises Promises

Pathos Valve

Lust Valve

Boner Juice

Sadness

Horror

Left Ventricle

Heart Muscle

Pulmonary vein carries back poor decisions from cerebral cortex, e.g. inappropriately dedicating organ names

Exit wound releases logic-blocking neuroalanines

Point of Entry

Loneliness Valve

Right Ventricle

Loneliness & Shame

Researched by Sean Crespo

WHAT SORT OF MAN READS PL*YB*Y?

A young man in touch with himself and his own imagination. Self-reliant, and with an appreciation for his personal privacy, he keeps his hand close to his chest and an eye out for unexpected interruptions of his daily routines. With confidence in his ability to handle himself in tense situations, the PL*YB*Y reader wrings every last drop of satisfaction from his private pursuits. Helping him stand up to that challenge is his favorite magazine. Fact: PL*YB*Y is read by nearly half of all young men who eventually excell at tennis, handball, or arm wrestling, and spent at least $12 on fine spurting goods last year alone. To reach that young man, put yourself in PL*YB*Y. He does. (Source: 1973 TGIF.)

New York • Chicago • Detroit • Los Angeles • San Francisco • Midville • Atlanta • London • Tokyo

How to Write Love Letters

by P. J. O'Rourke

Preface

What nobler and more beauteous form can the arts of prose or poesy take than "les lettres amoureux"? For what finer inspiration is there than love? And what finer mode or manner of expression than love's letters? Private of intent are they, yet universal of intention. Couched in stately speech, yet bespeaking the more than speakable. Passionate, but as far removed from carnal gesture as is the slim papyrus reed from the throbbing funtunnel of that Tri-Delt in Art History, three rows down and two seats to the left, boasting a set of cupolas that make Santa Sophia look like Olga Korbut with a breadboard down her Danskin.

Chapter I
Historical Origins and Literary Background of the Modern Love Letter

Foolscap cheap and watery ink
Hold value dear for wit, I think.
Though cost they less than meat or drink,
They make the maidens fuck like mink.
    —Alfred, Lord Tennyson

Ever since some Neanderthal grunt-monger first smeared a "no-tar-pit-too-deep" pictograph on the cave wall with a handful of mammoth brains, love letters have figured big with the reading public—especially the squat-to-pee segment. The lit-biz big boys of every age have soaked up the slack between big sonnet contracts, or whatever, penning their way into the pants of local talent. Dante had his Beatrice. Abelard, his Eloise. Byron had his sister. And Aeschylus had a bunch of Greek boy scouts running around in French-cut fishnet togas playing hide-the-hemorrhoid with his Doric dangler. But, anyway, these guys could really swing a quill. They wrote letters that scaled the dizzying peaks of high-flown Parnassus. Letters that plumbed the sensuous depths of Styx-bound Elysium. Letters of brilliance, letters of beauty, letters that would make women do anything. Hum jobs, rim jobs, round the world, glass top coffee tables, Mazola parties, Alsatians in panty hose—that was nothing to these guys. One skim through a Cervantes mash note at a convent in Barcelona and there was a three-day run on the Spanish cucumber market. No kidding, Shakespeare used to have this girl who'd get down on her knees under the table at the Pig and Whistle with a mouth full of live caterpillars and make with full choke on the business end of his meat throttle. To coin a phrase.

Not only that, but today we owe about half the Modern Library and two feet eight inches of the Harvard Classics Five Foot Shelf of Books to this unbridled pursuit of pervo poontang. "To a Maid Made Bigge by What She Made Large" by Andrew Marvell, for example:

Full glad am I that fates have smiled
To bless thee with the gift of child,
And complimented proudly too,
That to our love thee think this due.
Yes, lest vain hubris bring me grief,
Decline must I this laurel wreath;
And state, for truth, I doubt it I
Whose source is this nativity.
    For as Hellic cities seven
        Vie for claim of Homer's birth,
    So seven cities-full of men
        Might claim the honor for thy girth.
But Oh, not sayest I deny
That oft togther we did lie.
Still thee were to such passion moved,
By verse of mine, thee set to prove
Thy love of me in ways arcane.   •
So turned thee round thy nether cheek
And pleasured me in manner Greek,
And pressed with care the kiss of France
With lips which girt my codpiece'd lance.
    Spent I in every crannied nook
    Or hole of thy fair form save one.
    Thus canst lay claim to fatherhood
        —*Mayhaps it was John Donne!*

Swell stuff, huh? Well, you can do it too. Maybe not with all the fancy iambic and pentameters and ten-dollar synonyms for "grapefruit tits," but every bit as effective when it comes to spray-painting the dead end of her honey hole instead of your ceiling light fixture.

Why? Because women *love* to get mail. And it doesn't take a three-year subscription to *Psychology Today* to figure out what "letter stuffed in a girl's mailbox" is a symbol for. No, sir! The way they lick those stamps with their long, provocative tongues, the way they make out addresses with gentle flicks of a felt-tip marker—it's clear as beer piss what women are up to. They want to take your private parts down to the post office and bang on them with a cancelling machine, then rip open your dork with a souvenir Gurka dagger. Crazier than shithouse rats, every one of them. But the point is, *any* piece of mail sets a girl's Kayro flowing, and if enough have your name on them, then some of that gash-gush is bound to splash your way.

So if you have your heart set on some parcel-post pussy, don't wait to develop the narrative style of a William "Dean" Howells; just start mailing away at the object of your affection and she's a shot quail. Girls prefer businessmen as sexual partners

because they have longer envelopes, but anything will do—Hi-Brow cards about her appendix scar, Rio Rancho brochures, back numbers of *Commonweal*. Or a cinder block in brown wrapping paper with a two-cent stamp and no return address, which won't do much for your Saturday nights, but it'll give her a postage due bill the size of the Israeli defense budget and it's good for a laugh. If you're as psycho-sexually troubled as I am, I mean.

Pretty soon she's thinking the Postmaster General has his whole junk mail fleet depth-charging her letter chute and then you're ready to hit her with the high-powered "billets doux[1]." But before you turn her doomed pudendum into a literary free fire zone, let's make sure you have your map coordinates straight, or you might call in an air strike on your own position and wind up with a set of fragged noncoms and a permanent assignment on the Ross Ice Shelf walking point for a herd of Musk elk, cooze-wise, if you know what I mean.[2]

Chapter II

Beginner's and Intermediate Love Letters

If to write the flowery prose,
You find yourself too lazy,
    Broads run for cover
    And soon you discover
Your love life's pushing up daisies.
    —William Burmashave Yeats

When you say "flowery language," the first thing that pops into a lot of guys' minds is "pansy." These are the ones who sprinkle their letters with words like "buckshot," "quarterback," "mackinaw," and "axle" to create a gruff and hairy masculine image in their girl friends' thoughts. This *works* alright except that most women's ideal sexual partner is sleek, graceful, and practically devoid of bodily hair—in other words, another woman. Which doesn't matter a bit since they all fuck with their eyes

---

[1] *That's French for "love letters," not to be confused with "love for French letters," which is what she'll have when you're rolling one down your ding-dong and getting ready to "dip sheep" instead of playing one-handed spit-in-the-carpet with Ms. Thumb and her four comely daughters every night the way you did before learning all the valuable lessons in this informative article.*

[2] *And, frankly, if you'd been willing to do your duty in Nam defending America from those hordes of smelly zipper-heads instead of flashing a crack full of peanut butter during your draft physical and then wrecking other people's expensive college campuses over some argle-bargle about colored people not having enough TVs, you would* know *what I mean.*

Handy Helps for the Novice

LE ORIENT EXPRESS
PARIS · PRAGUE · BUDAPEST · ISTANBUL

LA POSTE DU CHEMIN DE FER
TRAIN MAIL
DIE EISENBAHNPOST

4.20 dm
16 Veb.
1975

GDZ 5¢

ADDRESS
ADRESSE

PASTE

COLLER

OPPENID
CENZOR
UN VIDENT
3.3

HIER ANKLEBEN

An authentic envelope from the stationery desks in the first class compartments of Europe's legendary Orient Express. Cut out carefully, fold flaps in, and glue together. Guaranteed to immortalize the dreariest homesick prattle or Y-Teen Youth Tour itinerary.

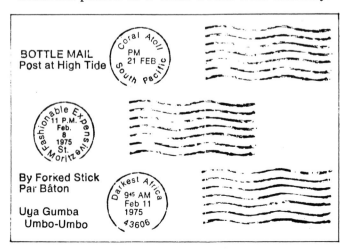

BOTTLE MAIL
Post at High Tide

Coral Atoll
PM
21 FEB
South Pacific

Fashionable Expensive
11 P.M.
Feb.
8
1975
St.
Moritz

By Forked Stick
Par Bâton

Darkest Africa
9⁴⁵ AM
Feb 11
1975
43606

Uya Gumba
Umbo-Umbo

FREE DERRY

12p

20

11 CENTAVOS
POPULARES

TIERRA OCUPADO POR LOS
REBELDES COMUNISTAS DE LOS
ANOES BOLIVIANOS

Exotic Stamps
For additional accuracy, make perforations around borders with pushpin or thumbtack before clipping.

The Postmarks of Adventure. Peel press-type film off backing, select postmark, place over uncancelled stamps on your love letter, and rub gently with blunt stylus or soft lead pencil.

Handy Helps Continued

MI-5

In Her Majesty's Secret Service since 1601.

No. 83 Whitehall
London SW 1
01-373-3032
Cable: SECSERVE

Hotel le Beaucoup Cher Très Plus Grand

Pour les Riches

RUE D'EXPENSE

PARIS, FRANCE

WING LOW HOY TRADING COMPANY

Street of the Monkeys, Macao   Phone: 14-2626

WEAPONS
NARCOTICS
WHITE SLAVERY

Impressive and unusual letterheads to add a certain cachet to your otherwise mundane correspondence. Cut along borders, match solid lines to the edges of a plain white sheet of 8½x11 typing paper, and deliver to a local Quick-Print. You'll have a lifetime supply of intriguing stationery—ideal for use with the Orient Express envelope. But that means you'll have to buy two copies of the magazine (we're not in business for our health).

Special Bonus Tip

To make authentic-looking teardrops, mix one tablespoon of salt and a dash of laundry blueing in a pint of warm water. Fill eye-dropper and allow drop(s) to fall from a height of fourteen inches.

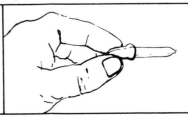

closed and practically the only place they ever put their hands is on your back where you don't *have* any hair unless you're Jewish and in which case you probably don't have any excessive masculinity problems anyway. But it's a bad idea, just the same, to try and seduce a girl by getting her to think of things that'll make her actually nauseous.

Elaborate, flowery language is important because women love big words. Though why women love big words is a mystery, unless it's because they're all secret Negros. Which might be the case since women love to sing and dance and wear stupid clothes and usually don't have much in the way of useful job skills. (Try slipping "bodacious," "abilitude," or "Ah sho' do be amplified ob makin' yo' acquaintancehood," into the next note to your sweetie and see what happens.[3] Also, when used with expertise, polysyllabic words, poetic inversions, and rococo phraseology can make wanting to plunge your pud up her giggle duct sound like a white-tie invite to the *Palais Stodet* for a twelve-course feed with the Belgian Queen Mother-in-Law. In fact, the importance of flowery language cannot be overestimated:

With proper use of "flowery language"

Oh beautiful for spacious skies,
For amber waves of grain,
For purpled mountain's majesty
Above the fruited plain.
America, America, God shed his grace
*   on thee*
And crown thy good with brotherhood
From sea to shining sea.

Without proper use of "flowery language"

You're good-looking because you have a big sky and your wheat is yellow. Also, your red and blue mountains are higher than your valuable farmland. United States, God should drop blessings all over you and put togetherness on top of your head which is filled with other praiseworthy virtues coast to coast.

Now, very few people emerge from an American public school education with words like "purpled" or "fruited" in their vocabularies—let alone the ability to use them with a straight face. So you're going to have to make up in writing style what you lack in learning and mushy sentiments about the landscape:

Dear_____,

The dorm is quiet. The air is heavy with my roommate from Cleveland. Outside, across the boulevard, the moon sets behind the Pick-and-Pay and my thoughts turn to you. Oh, Rose of Dayton, love binds you to me as epoxy resin does the self-stick tile in the rec room of your father's manse. Here are we—counties apart—yet love between us spreads in a band more wide and enduring than U.S. 127's asphalt expanse.

[3]*But don't come limping back here with an armload of bloody doctor bills if she carves a Harlem sunset in your face with a pearl-handled straight razor.*

Our love is like the Astroturf, unheeding storms which mar mere mortal weekends. No icy blast is proof against the clinging salt of our love.
So, to me fly straight,
Swift as an arrow,
Soon as you can borrow
Your mother's Camaro.

xxxxxooooo, etc.

Really, you've got to put yourself in the mood. A quick flip through the thesaurus, two jelly glasses full of George Dickle, and a vivid recollection of Elaine Guttenburg's blousefront the day she gave back all your Jay and the Americans singles and the three-foot Snoopy ought to do the trick. Or rent a print of *Elvira Madigan* (nix on the barfola, though). Or think about the lavender sachet in your mother's underwear drawer.

But if you still don't feel you're ready to pitch shit with the varsity, then warm up with some "bull-pen"[4] practice on everyday notes and messages like:

Meter Maiden or brave Officer of Law,
Far be it from my desire to bring down danger upon the heads of our fair cities' teeming myriads by lief of this, my motored carriage, in block of passage to yon hydra-yclept font of waters which need serve to sooth consumption by ere-threatened flame. But denizens of foul opiate's ways have lain hands upon my near-new Delco. And spirited it away.
Or:
Oh, Man of Milk, neglect not the protein dear to this young body's corporal health! Leave thee then not one but two fine quartfull ampules of thy nectar, pure and void of tint as is the broad expanse of arctic Thule and nearly, yes. as cold. But leave thee never now or yet ᵃgain the "half-with-half" congealed by Apollo's bright chariot, the sun, into warmish lumps which stank.

Until your confidence is in the kind of shape where it's hanging moons out minibus windows at the Kent State National Guard, be patient; with practice, you'll spout more euphemisms than a Boston Carmelite in a public health clinic with the clap-yo-hands. Then every sheet of stationery you put to Bic becomes a license to pound pussy, and every word you scrawl will stiffen nipples from Nantucket to San Jose—as long as you don't mean it.

And I *mean* it. They know that if you're writing a love letter and you're *sincere*, then you're writing a love letter because you're *in love*. And if you're writing a love letter because you're *in love*, that means you haven't got anyplace else to park your peter while you're wherever you are that you're writing from. And once women get the idea that their Sisters have walked out on your act, you're screwed—figuratively. Dropped like a used Pursette. It happened to the midi and it can happen to you.

[4]*Did you "get" it? And quit moving your lips.*

This brings us to two additional techniques of romantic correspondence, humor and rhyme. Humor is the more consequential of the two, particularly if you try to use it. A "laughing" woman, like a "laughing" hyena, is strictly a figure of speech. No zoologist ever meant to imply that if you told a hyena the one about "Two popes walk into a bar, . . ." it would rupture a lung, spit out its drink, or try to book you on Carson. The same goes double for women. And what a hyena *would do* if you got close enough to tell it a joke is by no means any prettier than what women do to comically inclined young men every day of the week.

Girls don't have a sense of humor. When all your plumbing is set up to do is manufacture babies and the main function of your outward features is to start fights and inspire suicide, life is no laughing matter. Tell your girl a joke, a perfectly hilarious joke, an absolutely smash-up-the-smoking-car-make - 'em - vomit - in - the - ice - bucket joke . . .

Old Rabbi is walking down the street and he sees a little kid sitting on the curb, playing with a pile of horse shit.
"Oi vey!" says the Rabbi. "What are you doink playing vit horse shit?!"
"I'm makin' a Irishman," says the kid.
"Ho ho ho ho ho," laughs the Rabbi, "but vhy are you makink a Irishman?"
"I ain't got enough shit to make a Rabbi."

. . . and all she'll say is something like "goodbye."

Women who like to laugh are even rarer than women who like body hair. If you find a girl who adores your puns and loves to run her fingers through your curly shoulders, she's probably a drag queen. The next time you're direct dialing her woozle you'd better check down there and make sure she's not holding her balls out of the way, especially if your knuckles come up smelling like the Chicago Ship and Sanitary Canal instead of Puget Sound.

Rhyme, on the other hand, flips them over on their backs so fast you'd think they had hinges. You get those words all rhyming up together and tintinabulating around on the page and it's music to a girl's ears. Which is exactly the effect you want—the minute they start hearing music in their ears, they think they're in a movie. And you know what goes on in movies these days. Boy, did you see *Wet Rainbow*? Ooo-ee! God *damn*. Anyway, you can polish up the old versification skills the same way you brushed up on the mush prose. It's a lot easier than it looks. You'd be surprised at how many words rhyme with each other. Mikado, avocado, and amontillado, for instance, all rhyme great.

Additional Study

By now, if you've been attentive, you should be well on your way to distinction as a home-town Casanova, considering what probably passes for distinction in your home town. Such learning is in itself meritorious, but for the student who wishes to delve deeper, a short glossary of the Female language has been attached:

A Short Glossary of the Female Language

English	Female
cock	*thing*
tits	*things*
cunt	*there*
no	*please*
yes	*do you love me?*
fuck	*dinner and a movie*
shit	*freshen up*

Chapter III

Advanced Composition

"Others only see your beauty; I see up under your skirt."
—Ralph Waldo Emerson
In a letter to Emily Dickens

There is little doubt that the love letter in its highest form is primarily the product of big, bloody, gory wars with heathen nations full of cruel, foreign-looking, bellicose desperados who get slaughtered by the millions and everyone is glad. Not that I subscribe for a moment to the theory that such carnage stimulates women sexually. Personally, I think it's a disgrace the way practically every prominent psychiatrist believes that just because women spend about one-fourth of their lives dripping blood all over the place, they therefore have an overpowering desire to see me do a lot of bleeding, too.

Just because every woman in America physically *threw* herself at anything with brass buttons on during the last big war and, when the men came home covered in the gore of untold hundred millions of hacked and shredded nips and krauts, jumped on cocks at such a rate that there resulted a "baby boom" of proportions unknown in the history of the world, is no reason to think that women are sexually stimulated by killing.

Nevertheless, those messy international altercations sure do fill the woods with cunt, and if you have any feeling for the fellow members of your sex, you'll do anything you can to start another one. Like using lots of gasoline and ribbing the crap out of any sheenies you happen to know about how the Arabs got the jump on them last time around—really rub

their noses in it; with the way *their* noses grow it shouldn't take too long to get something going. Everybody's got to do his part. Not like the last time when we had a perfectly good thing going and you college kids queered it getting killed and wounded right here stateside where it doesn't do anybody any good.

But when you finally cash in on all that paramilitary muff, "accidents" can still happen. If you're worried that your number may come up pregnant, try sending this famous telegram:

Dear <u>Miss Lucinda Vermicelli,</u>

The Joint Chiefs of Staff of the Armed Forces of the United States of America regret to inform you that <u>Pfc. Lawrence Hallihan</u> is missing you in action stop

If your love-light is a careful reader, she'll gain new respect for your importance with the Pentagon brass. But if her reading comprehension should be somehow impaired (say, for instance, by the emotional stress of six or eight months fishing spotless Modess out of her afro-clam), then maybe she'll throw herself in front of an uptown A Train, and what might have been a lifetime of child support payments will coat the rails with a thin scum from Columbus Circle to 125th Street and Lenox. Either way, you can't lose.

However, short of another swell world war, there's always a trump card we can pull on women which is, basically, that they're pretty easy to fool. In fact, they're practically famous for being tricked into the old in-and-out by "traveling Pap testers" or "county health inspectors" taking "deep throat cultures" to "check the spread of typhoid" ("Now, close your eyes and let me paint your tonsils!") or you-name-it.

Steal some business stationery and send out invoices:

Re: Your order of one 6" penis

We are pleased to inform you that a new shipment has arrived and your order can now be filled. Please pick up load at our warehouse apartment, 28½ College Ave, or phone for forwarding to your dorm.

No girl in her right mind will want to outright refuse delivery and risk getting involved in a lengthy court case over some obscure point of contractual law.

Or try a bargain. No woman can resist a bargain. Think what a bargain marriage is, for example, and *they* know that's what's kept them from starving all these years.

Or make your love-light a contest winner. That's another thing they love, getting something for nothing. Filling the old void, as it were. Something from nothing; that's where babies come from, after all. And without babies, what excuse would they *have*? But I digress:

Dear Occupant:
You may have already won an all-expense paid night at the luxurious new Hiway-Vu Motel. If you're a short blonde with large perky tits and answer to the name Suzy May Lasky . . .

And so forth. And if *that* doesn't work, why don't you just get 'em clipped off. I mean it. What the fuck? Sign up for that clinic in Casablanca, snip-snip and you're a dame. Who cares anyway? I hear they do a good job of it nowadays. Hardly anyone can tell unless they get up close. And they even turn the skin of your cock inside-out up inside you so you can feel it and everything. Then you wouldn't have to write any of this crap. Christ, you wouldn't even have to *read* it. You wouldn't have to do a goddamned fucking thing. Just sit around on your ass all day, eat bonbons, and read movie magazines, and the hell with the man who works. □

QUEST OF LOVE

Nineteen New Ways to Be Offensive
at a Wedding
by Ed Bluestone

1

Show up with a baby and claim he belongs to the newlyweds.

2

Cover yourself with glue to improve your chances of catching the bouquet.

3

Offer to show people pictures of the bride fucking a dog.

4

Tell people that you knew the bride before the sex-change operation.

5

Tell the bride that the only reason you can look at her is that you used to be a proctologist.

6

Instead of a standard gift, give the newlyweds a gift certificate to a drug rehabilitation clinic.

7

As you move down the receiving line, spit on each person.

8

Ask the bride's mother to give you a handjob.

9

Give the bride some Binaca, and tell her it kills the taste of sperm.

10

Propose a toast to the bride's nose job.

11

Steal the cards from the wedding gifts so that no one can tell who they came from.

12

Walk up to various guests and demand to see their invitations.

13

After the bride throws her garter start people chanting, "Throw your bra . . . . Throw your bra . . . . "

14

Tell people that the groom had to be given Quaaludes to keep him from backing out.

15

Tell the rabbi there's no money to pay him, and ask if he'll settle for shtupping the bride.

16

Assure the bride's mother that the groom is "hung like a horse."

17

Return a bra which the bride left in your car.

18

If there's a hunchback at the Jewish wedding, tell him that he has to wear one yarmulke on his head and another on his hump.

19

When the bride is coming down the aisle, push the organist out of the way and start playing "The Lady Is a Tramp."

A Purity Press Publication 75¢

What Every Teen-Ager Should Know

Nancy Reagan's Guide to Dating Dos and Don'ts

"A sane, sound book for modern young people embarking on the sometimes murky sea of premarital dating."—Rev. Billy Graham

"Teen-age questions answered with a frankness and honesty refreshing in these sniggering times."—Ann Landers

"A guiding beacon for today's turned-on, anything-for-kicks generation."
—Pat Boone

Introduction

Hi. If you are "twixt twelve and twenty" and a would-be dater, this book is for you. In it, I am going to deal honestly, and sometimes quite frankly, with the joys and pitfalls of teen-age dating in the hope that it may prevent your first corsage from shriveling up into a bouquet of nettles.

A dating manual for this day and age? one of your "sophisticated" chums may scoff. *Why, all that jazz about moral decency and lofty ideals is a lot of bunk and hooey!* Is it? Well, take a good look, fellows and girls, at the dangers that surround you in today's "anything goes" world. Everywhere a teen turns, he is assaulted by an avalanche of filth that lurks in many forms—pornographic movies, obscene novels, indecent plays, lurid magazines, prurient snapshots, seductive television commercials, suggestive song lyrics, immodest dances, salacious paintings, lewd advertisements, coarse poems, smutty radio shows, depraved newspapers, indelicate lithographs, perverse sculptures, shady stories, gross cookbooks, tawdry cocktail napkins, ribald postcards, libertine bumper stickers, provocative buttons, meretricious gestures, licentious operas, pandering food labels, and shameless zoos.

It's enough to make me sick to my stomach. Actually, after a drive through L.A., I often *get* sick to my stomach and have to spend a whole afternoon in the little girls' room. As a matter of fact, I think I'm already a little woozy, and I haven't even gotten to the first chapter yet.

Where does this nauseating tidal wave of smut and garbage come from? Well, you won't find out from the "Sex O'Clock News," but it is no secret that certain foreign powers would like nothing better than to see our country paralyzed and prostrated by a degenerate Supreme Court that sanctions petting sprees and free love as "freedom of choice" and "harmless kicks." While America rots from within, all the Russkies would have to do is rumble through Washington in tanks with those long, nasty things on top and pick up the pieces. Her youth "brainwashed" by so-called "liberated" codes of behavior, a mightly nation would be vanquished, laid low by deep kissing and petting parties.

But young people all love dates, and there is no finer preparation for marriage than a wholesome, well-rounded social life. I have received thousands of letters from concerned teens all over the country, begging for advice on this important (and fun!) part of adulthood, and I hope this book will serve as a useful and informative answer.

Hi.

Nancy Reagan

Chapter I

So You're Growing Up?

Dating is like dynamite. Used wisely, it can move mountains and change the course of mighty rivers. Used foolishly, it can blow your legs off. Scientists have calculated, for example, that if a man could harness even a fraction of the kinetic energy wasted in a single session of Post Office or Spin the Bottle, he could light up the entire city of Wilmington, Delaware, and have enough left over to discover and mass produce a cheap, effective cure for cancer of the larynx. Thus, it is so important to understand and harness the explosive power of the forces developing in your body.

Have you noticed that your body is playing little tricks on you lately? If you are a boy, you may have noticed your legs, face, arms, and chest are becoming covered with thick, black pubic hairs and your voice may be beginning to sound like a phonograph needle ruining your favorite stack of platters. If you are a girl, you may have noticed a painful swelling up here and some more funny business going on down there.

These dramatic changes can mean only one thing: cholera. If you are not among the lucky ones, then it simply means you are becoming a young man or a young woman, depending on how much flouride they dumped in your parents' drinking water. I know that such changes can often be difficult for growing teens, but try to weather the storm and "grin and bear it." There is always impotence and menopause.

During these trying teen-age years, a girl begins to "menstruate" (*men* stroo ate), and a boy begins to have "erections" (ee *wreck* shuns), normally only when called to the blackboard by his teacher. There is absolutely nothing abnormal about this, and, aside from voluntary sterilization, no known cure.

Not only is the miracle of growing up taking place inside your body, but it may be going on outside it as well. There are many names for this remarkable stage of development— "acne," "pimples," "blackheads," "whiteheads," "redcaps," "boils," "blemishes," "cankers," "zits," "pustules," "efflorescence," "breaking out," "pockmarks," "carbuncles," "suppurations," "polyps," "goobies," and "St. Anthony's Fire," to mention just a few. Perhaps one of your clever friends will notice this badge of young adulthood and jokingly dub you with an appropriate descriptive nickname, like "Crater Face," "Swiss Cheese," or "Vomithead." But perk up! Such bothersome side effects are all in Mother Nature's master plan, and they may very possibly disappear in time, leaving a healthy, glowing complexion on those portions of your face and neck not permanently disfigured by layers of horny scar tissue. You *can* treat your "boo-boos" right away, however, with frequent applications of hot, soapy water, mild astringent, or, in unusually severe cases, a woodburning kit.

Chapter II

Calling All Girls

It is time to clear up one myth about menstruation or "the curse" as many, including myself, prefer to call it. Many girls worry because their "periods" don't come as regular as clockwork, on the first or fifteenth of the month with the rest of the bills. This is nothing more than a silly wives' tale. The "cramps" you may feel, often no more noticeable than a rhythmic sledgehammer blow to the abdomen, only mean that the two little almond-flavored organs deep in your tummy are finally getting around to preparing a little home in case a baby wants to move in. This continuing cycle varies widely in different girls and may range anywhere from fifty-three to three days, depending on whether the little almonds want their owner to bloat up like a derigible or simply bleed to death.

This interesting process, often called "nature's egg-timer," was originally based on the lunar month of twenty-eight days. But with so many changes in our modern calendar to make way for silly things like Labor Day and Martin Luther King's birthday, the cycle is often keyed to other natural rhythms, like sunspots, quirky reversals of the earth's magnetic poles, or fluctuations in the stock market. (During these special days, it is wise to avoid anything that might interfere with this delicate phenomenon, such as swimming, ham radio transmitters, and remote-controlled streetlights.) My *own* cycle is based on the appearance of Haley's Comet, so although I am under the weather only infrequently, I am stocking up on you-know-whats now, because when my next one comes in 1985, it's bound to be a *whopper*!

One more word about your period. When it finally comes, you may find it a good idea to use a "sanitary napkin" to help stanch the massive loss of precious, irreplaceable

fluids from your vitals. If so, beware of fast-talking sales pitches claiming the Tampax-type tampon is preferable to the Kotex-type external napkin. The former may be somewhat more convenient, but it can lead both to unwanted feelings and risking your stock in the marriage market. As for the slight icky odor that occasionally results from the safer, saner napkin, a *schpritz* of feminine deodorant, Glade, or liquid benzene should make your strolls upwind of kennels and dog shows free from any possible danger of embarrassment.

Chapter III

Fellows Take Note

As for you boys, don't feel left out. If you glance down between your legs, where your vagina should be, you will see an odd-looking pink sac containing two little ugly things. Go ahead, take a look right now, but *keep your hands on the book* (more about *that* later). Quite a surprise, wasn't it? Well, the funny pink sac is called your "scrotum"

continued

(*skro* tum), and the two little ugly things are called "testes" (*teh* stees) and are why you can never know the ultimate, inexpressible joy of motherhood.

Believe it or not, your scrotum will respond to sudden changes in temperature, quickly raising or lowering your testes to maintain them at a constant heat level, something seen nowhere else in nature except by those few who have mastered the proper techniques of marshmallow-toasting. If you don't believe me, try rubbing an ice cube against your scrotum and see what happens. Now, quickly try a lighted match. Now another ice cube. Another match. Faster. Cube. Match. Cube. Ma—*aha!* Didn't your mother ever tell you not to play with matches? All joking aside, this is simply another example of the wonders you can find in and around your own body, stuff that has often led to many important scientific discoveries. For example, when my husband, Ronald, was in the Boy Scouts, he used this same natural principle for a homemade thermometer and won a merit badge in meteorology.

Chapter IV

The Nightmare of Wet Dreams

Nocturnal emissions, or "wet dreams" as they are often called, were once dreaded and traumatic experiences for young boys of the Victorian era. But today there can be little doubt that these perfectly normal, disgusting catastrophes are merely your body's way of "priming the pump" for the coming responsibilities of manhood and marriage, and a signal to your mother or laundry that you are ready for dating.

Should you have a nocturnal emission, do not worry. A few easy preparations for this can be made in advance. Each night, before your mom tucks you in, make sure she supplies you with two bath towels, an automobile sponge, a mop, a pail of hospital-strength disinfectant, a five-gallon can of industrial cleanser, a hammer, a chisel, and a two-handed paint scraper.

Chapter V

Playing with Yourself Is Playing with Fire!

Clint and Babs were returning from their church youth meeting. At her door, Babs turned and shook Clint's hand good-night. It had been a lovely date, and, thinking over the evening as he undressed back home, Clint noticed a strange feeling suddenly coming over him. In bed, Clint was still restless, puzzled by this new, overpowering sensa-tion. Suddenly, as Clint thought of Babs's unusually warm farewell, memories of an impure picture he had once found hidden in a Gideon Bible popped up unexpectedly. As did something else. Drowsily allowing his right hand to stray under the covers, Clint sleepily took the situation in hand and, before he realized what he had done, committed an act of self-pollution. The next morning, while driving to school to be sworn in as Student Council President, Clint was struck and killed by a speeding bus.

Such stories are common in the daily papers. Every day thousands of young men and women pay tragically for a single, thoughtless surrender to temptation. But even more victims of the "solitary sin" go unrecognized, their fates mistakenly diagnosed as "poor study habits," "tennis elbow," or a "slight case of the sniffles." The list is endless. But the untold misery brought by willful masturbation cannot be reckoned by mere statistics. One has only to look at our prisons, mental hospitals, and riot-torn campuses for the real cost.

Chilling, isn't it?

I'm no chump, you are probably saying as you read this, *but how can I, as an up-to-date teen, learn to guard against this treacherous and degrading habit?* First, a sound diet including eight glasses of pure water a day. Second, good health habits, such as brushing your teeth and having a thorough bowel movement after each meal. Third, avoid sweets and between-meal snacks. Regular exercise will also help sap excess energy in a helpful, constructive manner. Some popular sports you may enjoy are bicycling, swimming, skating, curling, basketball, golfing, polo, sledding, badminton, jai alai, quoits, table tennis, and snooker. Hint: if trouble still persists, it may be wise to make it a rule to slip on a pair of baseball gloves, heavy wool socks, or oven mittens before retiring. If these precautions fail, your dad will be happy to help handcuff your hands behind your back before you turn in.

As for you gals, don't get smug. Many young women regularly harm themselves with acts of self-pollution *even while sound asleep*, often dreaming of bizarre degradations involving beatniks, Negros, or worse. Because of this, it is advisable not to tempt the devil. Have your mother "keep on ice" such objects as pencils, candles, bananas, frankfurters, hairbrushes, and softball bats.

Now that I have the scoop on self-abuse, you say, *I'm going to practice these easy safeguards and pass the low-down on to my pals.*

And I can think of three people who will back you up on that: Clint's mother, father, and Babs.

"Playing with Yourself Is Playing with Fire!"

Chapter VI

Your First Date: Calling Her Up

Calling up a girl for a date for the first time can often mean a bout with those "telephone jitters." How to avoid them? It's easier than you think! Like anything you do, there's a *right* way and a *wrong* way. I'll pause a moment while you let that sink in. The most important thing to remember is *don't beat around the bush*. The forthright, direct approach is the best way to ask for a date, as any girl will tell you. Let's start with the wrong way first: Carl has two tickets to a popular movie approved by his local church group, and he wants to take Norma as his guest. Let's see what happens. . . .

Norma: Hello?
Carl: Hello.
Norma: Hello? Hello? Is somebody there?
Carl: Hello?
Norma: Look, who *is* this? If this is some kind of a joke, my father—
Carl: Uh, Norma, this is Carl from your Civics class, and I was wondering if—
Norma: Carl? I don't think I know any "Carl."
Carl: Well, I'm the one with the thick glasses who sits way back by the windows? Today when I spoke to you in the hall—
Norma: Listen, maybe you have the wrong Bancroft. There's a *Carla* Bancroft in our class. The homely one with those things all over her face?
Carl: Well, actually, that's *me, Carl* Bancroft. Anyway, you were with Moose Pojanski from the football team at the time? I mean, you were talking to him, mostly, but—
Norma: Oh, sure, sure, I remember. Okay, shoot.
Carl: Well, I was wondering, if you weren't doing anything Saturday night, perhaps you'd consider—
Norma: Saturday? Oh, gee, that's tough. That's the night I always wash my hair.
Carl: Uh, well, maybe Sunday? I could exchange—
Norma: And I always dry it on Sunday nights.
Carl: Uh, then how about Mon—
Norma: Then I have to set it. It's a real job, y'know?
Carl: Well, I suppose I could get tickets for Tues—
Norma: *Click.*
Carl: Hello? Norma? Gee, the line went dead.

Needless to say, Carl did not get to date Norma that Saturday. Now let's eavesdrop on a boy who knows how to use those telephone courtesies that spell "date bait," as he invites a girl for a horseback ride. . . .

Norma: Hello?
Moose: 'Lo, Norma? 'S Moose.
Norma: Oh, Christ, for a minute I thought it was Carl again.
Moose: Huh? Whoozat?

Norma: Some flit says he's in one of my classes.
Moose: Oh. How 'bout Saturday? Wanna?
Norma: Sure, but one thing.
Moose: Wha?
Norma: Don't forget the you-know-whats.
Moose: Huh? Oh, yah. Heh heh. Yah.
Norma: Listen, it isn't funny. I thought I missed it last month and I nearly freaked. If you want to go bareback, you can call up Carl.
Moose: Huh?
Norma: Some flit says he's in one of my classes.

See how easy it was? Moose knew that old saying about catching more dates with honey than you can with vinegar, and Norma knew the one about an ounce of prevention being worth a trip to Puerto Rico!

Chapter VII

What to Wear

Dating is like electricity. Used wisely, it can operate your dad's power tools, fry eggs, and run trolley cars. Used foolishly, it can electrocute every member of your family including your goldfish. Being a teen with taste means, then, that you don't try to "short circuit" your future happiness with provocative clothes that will "overload" your date with the temptation to tamper with your "fuse box."

If you are a girl, steer clear of clinging sweaters, layers of heavy makeup, sheath skirts with revealing kick pleats, and Capri pants so tight that the boys can read the date of a dime in your back pocket. Gals in the know favor the casual good looks of cardigan sweaters, simple pleated calf-length skirts bolstered by layers and layers of crisp and crinkly crinoline. And please, ladies, *sensible* shoes! There are now on the market several brands of attractive pumps made of sturdy materials that spell fashion flair both on the dance floor and along those invigorating woodland trails. Since you are still growing, try to have a little pity on Dad's wallet and buy them at least two and a half sizes bigger to give your poor toes plenty of wiggle room! But avoid patent leather. Nothing is a surer invitation to disaster than shiny shoe-tops are to a sharp-eyed, peeping Tom with a rudimentary knowledge of light refraction.

Proper foundation garments will help give your dating wardrobe that added "plus." Ruggedly made brassieres (preferably with a time lock), garter belts, hosiery, and dress shields give a girl added confidence on a date and help correct poor posture. Hint: if you are going on an unchaperoned date, an additional girdle or two can be a welcome "something extra" when the full moon rises and that "all-American" suddenly becomes "all hands"!

Boys, too, know that a neat and clean appearance goes a long way toward winning the respect and admiration of his date. Tight chinos, pointed shoes, and elaborate pompadours (perhaps hiding the "point" underneath!) impress no one. You can't tell a book by its cover, but if a candy wrapper says "nuts" on the outside, you can be sure there's one on the inside. Boys are also cautioned to especially avoid tight dungarees that can cut circulation to vital parts of the body. Last year alone, a respected clothing physician reports over fifteen thousand men suffered the loss of their genital organs, either by chronic shriveling or simple "drop-off." Don't let this happen to you.

Crew cuts, "butches," and flattops with well-trimmed sideburns are the rage with gals everywhere, boys, and few ladies can resist the buckle and swash that a pair of Hush Puppies or saddle shoes can bring to a fellow's feet. For more formal occasions, Dad may let you borrow a pair of his he-man and hefty brogues with those cunning little perforations topping off the toes in decorative patterns and swirls. And while we're at it, let's not overlook your underthings. Loose, comfortable boxer shorts are the best bet, but if your date will include some strenuous exercise, ask your mother to take you to the shopping center or sporting-goods store in your neighborhood the next time she goes and fit you out with a reliable brand of athletic supporter. Unless you're Frank Sinatra, it doesn't pay to be a "swinger!"

Chapter VIII

Meeting Your Folks

Dating a boy is like being taken out on a trial spin. If he's a careful driver, the trip can be a fine jaunt. If he's a careless motorist, you may find yourself back at your door with four flats and a shot suspension. This is why your parents take an interest in who you date. Your mom and dad have made a considerable investment in you and may have spent $10,000–$15,000 on you for food, clothing, partial rent, medical bills, education, and insurance alone, not to mention mad money and court fees. You owe it to your parents to let them take an interest in who may be handling their investment in their absence, and introducing your dates to them is a good way to begin. It is a delicate undertaking, for it is time for that giggle on the telephone to become a flesh-and-blood person, but simple politeness is the only "must." It is simply a matter of "getting to know you," as this example shows. . . .

The doorbell rings. Sue answers the door and greets Ben, her date for the evening.

Ben: Good evening, Sue.

Sue: Good evening, Ben. Won't you come in and let me introduce you to my mother and father?

Ben: Of course, Sue.

Sue: Mother, I'd like you to meet Ben. Ben, this is my mother.

Ben: How do you do, Mrs. Waspwell. It is a pleasure to meet you.

Mother: How do you do, Ben. It's a pleasure to meet you.

Sue: Ben, this is my father. Father, I'd like you to meet Ben.

Ben: How do you do Mr. Waspwell. It is a pleasure to meet you.

Father: How do you do, Ben. It is a pleasure to meet you. By the way, Ben, isn't your father the president of the country club?

Ben: Oh no, sir. My father is Jewish.

Father: Good night, Ben.

Ben: Good night, Mr. Waspwell.

Mother: Good night, Ben.

Ben: Good night, Mrs. Waspwell.

Sue: Good night, Ben.

Ben: Good night, Sue.

See how easy that was?

Chapter IX

Have Morals, Will Date

Now that your parents have met your date, it's time to go! But where? To an all-night beach blast? An unchaperoned pajama party? Perhaps to a double-clutch twist contest, a form of "dancing" that the late Igor Stravinsky once described as "simply petting set to music"?

Of course not.

I am reminded of the story of a boy who was looking at a list of "don'ts" posted on the swimming-pool bulletin board.

Think they forgot anything? asked a sympathetic buddy. *Yeah,* answered the boy, *"don't breathe!"*

Things aren't as grim as all that. There are many healthful and wholesome activities in which young daters may participate *and* keep their moral decency intact. Most communities have young-people's centers, and many church groups organize frequent hayrides, craft fairs, and special exhibits. But if your community lacks these, there are still 1,001 things to do that can give any guy or gal that special "lift."

Looking for something to do on a date? Take a gander at these activities available to young "thrill-seekers": folk dancing, travelogues, displays, youth rallies, guided tours of local industry, collecting pop bottles for worthy charities, sight-seeing hardware stores, reading to blind children, learning how to use a road map, unusual fêtes, playing Sorry, discovering points of interest, laying linoleum, building and operating your own weather station, identifying wild flowers, rummage sales, pets, repairing appliances, learning new words, washing the family car, remembering things, telling jokes, having shoes stretched, and making fudge.

Sound inviting? Dive right in, the dating's fine!

Chapter X

Making Conversation

Making "small talk" on a date can be one of the biggest problems for inexperienced daters. Conversation, like ten-

"You Don't Have to Pet to Be Popular"

nis, is best when the ball keeps bouncing back and forth. The surest way to keep the ball in play is to find out what you and your date have in common. Perhaps both of you are interested in sports, or you have complementary hobbies, or your fathers both make the same amount of money.

Once you establish something to talk about, you'll be amazed at how the conversation can flow effortlessly from one topic to the next. Ted and Marlene show you how....

Ted: It's a grand night, isn't it?

Marlene: Wonderful, Ted. Did you ever see such a moon?

Ted: Isn't that what they call a "harvest moon"?

Marlene: A "hunter's moon"? Don't do that, Ted.

Ted: Do you hunt? I had an uncle who once was a fine hunter.

Marlene: My aunt once painted a wonderful hunting scene. Stop that, Ted.

Ted: I didn't know you were interested in painting. Do you paint?

Marlene: No, but I enjoy sketching and swimming. Get that hand out of there, Ted.

Ted: Why, I bet you're a terrific swimmer. I know you're tops in skeet shooting.

Marlene: I mean it, Ted! But I'm not as good with a gun as my father.

Ted: Oh, does he skeet shoot, too?

Marlene: No, Ted, he was a marine at Okinawa, and now he's a sergeant on the police force.

Ted: It's a grand night, isn't it?

Marlene: Wonderful, Ted. Did you ever see such a moon?

Chapter XI

You Don't Have to Pet to Be Popular

To pet or not to pet, that is the question! Many young girls, eager to be "in" with the crowd, think that they have to act free and easy with every lounge lizard and couch commando to show that they are grown up, that they are "cool." I'm reminded of a story that happened to the daughter of an old friend of mine....

Pam, a naïve young girl eager to be "in" with the crowd, accepted a date with Stan, a boy whose reputation as a heavy petter was the talk of the cafeteria. When Stan pulled up in front of her home, Pam noticed that instead of coming in to meet her parents, he just sat in the car tightening his chinos and combing his pompadour while he honked his horn for her to hurry. Against her parents' advice and her own misgivings, Pam raced to Stan's car and drove off, the auto's shot suspension practically ruining the driveway. The evening was pleasant enough at first, but when 9:30 rolled around and it was time to head for home, Stan began to act differently. He began feeding Pam a line, telling her that "everybody petted" and those who didn't were hypocrites, or "prudes." He told her that he was "madly in love with her" and that she was a "slick chick." He talked about famous scientists who recommended petting on the first date, like Freud, Darwin, and Rollo May. Wanting desperately to be in the swim, Pam finally agreed and willingly submitted to an act of heavy petting in the back seat of Stan's automobile. When Pam's parents saw that it was almost 10:30 and Pam had not yet returned, they immediately notified the State Police. An hour later the police found Stan and Pam, but it was too late. Apparently they had been so busy heavy petting that the doomed couple had failed to even notice a speeding bus.

Sound familiar? It should. Official government figures show that an act of heavy petting is committed in the back seat of an automobile somewhere in the United States every fifty seconds, and the Highway Department reports the *exact same incidence* for motor-vehicle fatalities. To pet or not to pet?

The choice is yours.

Chapter XII

How to Say "No"

A girl once told me that when she stepped out for an evening with her sweetheart, her parents always gave her her own bottle of mouthwash so she could "freshen up" after necking with her fiancé. These "parents" obviously had a geranium in the cranium! Any parent who permits a daughter the opportunity to pass out free samples is in danger of having the entire store looted. What such parents are actually saying to the boy is, *Dear necker, if you can't be good, be careful. I know you are here to crack the safe. It won't be necessary. Here's the combination. Take what you want, but please tidy up after.*

Some flirts claim that, to click with the gang, you have to keep in circulation. One has only to look at a book that's been in circulation to see the results: dog-eared around the edges, stained with fingerprints and jelly, a weakened spine and half the insides missing, nasty cracks written along the margins.

Get the message?

A wise girl knows that saying "no" to petting is as important to her reputation as refraining from vaulting fence-posts, riding Western saddle, or engaging in excessive shinnying. "Many are cold," goes the saying, "but few are frozen." A boy in the know quickly realizes that there's more to an iceberg than the one-fifth on the surface that meets the eye and says to himself, *Finding out about the four-fifths of this doll that's below the surface is worth more to me than a thousand French handshakes!*

Of course, it's not always easy separating the sheep from the wolves, and the mildest-mannered boy can turn out to be the most unscrupulous kiss-collector if you let him. Should he try any monkeyshines, there are several workable methods. The commonest is simply to look your date squarely in the eye and, with a sweet but hurt expression, whisper, "Dave, I'm very disappointed in you." If words do not convince, it may be a good idea to carry along a persuader of a more forceful character. Among the most popular are police whistles, tear-gas pens, and blank pistols. Finally, if none of these are available but you do happen to have a cold drink in your hand, turn back to Chapter III and study again the effect of quick temperature changes on those ugly pink things.

That's the whole story, daters, and I wish you a grand, evening. And don't worry about making mistakes if you studied this book carefully. I guarantee you won't "miss the boat."

But you will miss the bus. □

How to Talk Dirty in Esperanto

Kiel Parole Malpure en Esperanto
by Richard Bonker and Henry Beard

So you didn't think you could! Frankly, it's as easy as a *furpie* if you follow my simple rules. There are many sound reasons for spending the next few hours learning them. To name a few: With Esperanto you can write graffiti on the walls of the restrooms of the United Nations, the World Court at The Hague, or the European Parliament at Strasbourg without shame, and on more common surfaces without fear of contradiction. With Esperanto you can derive considerable pleasure from uttering even the vilest phrase in Esperanto; although your language is from the gutter, it is from the gutters of the Champs Elysées, the Kurfürstendamm, Jermyn Street, and the Via Sant Angelo. And if afterward you should feel remorse, you are entitled to wash your mouth out with beeswax or anise or some other exotic astringent instead of ordinary soap. With Esperanto you can trade imprecations as an equal with members of foreign-born minority groups whose native caterwauls—with their varmint-like barkings, pagan speech-rhythms, and moronic, singsong syllables—are so much more appropriate to scatological usage than the noble cadances of English. You can expound at great length on the chastity, racial characteristics, and sexual inventiveness of their mothers without risking the kind of comprehension that has them reaching for knives to supplement their disappointing vocabularies. And should you, by great good fortune, enter into an altercation with a fellow Esperan-

tist, the great commitment to international brotherhood and understanding that you share with your antagonist will quickly overcome the bitterest of enmities, and you will be able to adjourn speedily to a nearby trattoria, there to partake of a toast of beeswax and anise to Dr. L. Ludwig Zamenhof, the creator of Esperanto, and to us, of course, for correcting his puzzling oversight of not having included any dirty words in Esperanto in the first place.

FIRST: pronunciation! Master these rules and you will be able to speak Esperanto like a native!

Esperanto is phonetic; letters are always pronounced alike no matter where they appear! B, d, f, h, k, l, m, n, p, s, t, v, z, are prounounced exactly as in English, so don't worry about them.

a	....	Father made me do it.
ĉ	....	tits
c	....	Chew on these, big boy.
e	....	there
g	....	gobble
ĝ	....	Gee, you sure have a small cock, needle-dick daddy.
ĥ	....	German "Achtung!" (The closest English equivalent is suck.)
i	....	cherry
j	....	yoni
ĵ	....	pleasure pit
o	....	old dirt road
r	....	French "merde" (pronounced mer-r-r-de)
ŝ	....	shit
u	....	boobs
aj	....	Spanish fly
aŭ	....	go down on
ej	....	foreplay
eŭ	....	"eh" plus "oo"
oj	....	joint
uj	....	Oh, ick, it's all gooey!

Now that wasn't so hard, was it? Don't be ashamed to consult this list whenever you feel the need. And, one more thing, remember: In words with more than one syllable, the stress is always on the next to last syllable. In words of only two syllables, the first is stressed, since it is also the next to last.

SECOND: grammar! Esperanto has the easiest grammar in the world! Memorize these rules and you will have no trouble with the language. All Esperanto words consist of a root[1] and an ending. The root gives the meaning of the word and the ending tells what part of speech it has. Nothing could be simpler and there are no exceptions in Esperanto.

Now watch as we make our first whole sentence:

Liroj mangas viadon.
LEE-roy MAHN-jass vee-AHN-doan.
Leroy eats meat.

Isn't that easy! What we really wanted to say was "Leroy eats shit," but our Esperanto dictionary unaccountably refused to list it. Nevertheless, we push on with:

Sandra lekas pilkojn.
SAN-drah LEH-kass PEEL-coin.
Sandra licks balls.

all of which are in the book. Notice

1 As soon as you've had your little laugh, we'll go on.

how useful the affixes are:

Sandra lekadas pilkegojn.

SAN-drah leh-KAH-dass peel-KEH-goyn.

Sandra frequently-licks large-balls.

In Esperanto, the verb *veni* means "to come." Using the suffix *-uj*, which means "container," we get *venujo*, scumbag; whence:

Li venas en la venujon.

LEE-VEHN-ass EHN LA veh-NOO-yon.

He comes into the scumbag.

Other useful appurtenances of *veni* are *venajo* 'come-substance' or 'jism,' *venegulo* 'a real comer,' *venestro* 'come-leader'(useful at orgies), etc. With these preliminaries out of the way, we are all set to go to town (or around the world) with this larger passage:

Saluton! / Kiel vi fartas?[2] / Gage bone! / Ĉu vi havas la plumon? / Jes, mi havas la granda forta plumon, sed la inko estas malpura. / Malbene! / Kia idioto mi estis, ne uzi la venejon.

Hello there! / How are you faring? / Jolly good! / Have you a pen? / Yes, I have the large strong pen, but the ink is rotten. / That is awful! / What a fool I was not to use the scumbag.

We've gone as far as we can without some bona-fide dirty words. We won't let the spoilsport editors who compiled the dictionary have the last word; Esperanto is nothing if not adaptable. Dirty words are as easy to come by as a well-engineered teat—provided my patented system is followed.

THIRD: Vocabulary!

Example: **Asshole.** This could be rendered accurately as "anus open-ing," but this somehow lacks vividness: *anoaperturo.* A much better rendering would be "windhole." Thus, add *vento* to *truo* to get *ventruo.* Another more colorful rendering would be to borrow the Chinese expression "fart-eye." Thus: *fartokulo.*

Example: **Furburger.** This rather eloquent euphemism for the vulva is simply rendered by noting that the Esperanto for "Hamburg" (the alleged city of origin for the meat pattie) is *Amburgo.* Add to this the word for "fur" to get *felburgo.*

Example: **Twat.** This one's harder. "Twat" is from an old English expression for "hole in the hedge." The Esperantan rendition for this is impossibly long—"growing-thing-fence-hole," i.e., *kreskaĵbariltruo.* However, the essence of "twat" is "bushy," which is best rendered (inasmuch as the Esperantan for "bush" is "little tree"—too long a word) as *broso* 'brush'.

Example: **Prick.** This is directly translated as *pikilo,* but to get a shorter word, we truncate it to *piko.* Another possibility might be to make use of the suffix *-il* which means "tool" or "instrument of." Thus, if *fuki* is the verb "to fuck," then *la fukilo* means "the tool to fuck with" or, in other words, cock or prick.

Example: **Shit.** There are a number of baroque possibilities here, such as *noktomalpuro* 'nightsoil', which seems excessively prudish, and *brunaserpento* 'brown snake', which is evocative but clumsy. The best bet is to use the common root found in other languages, as is the custom in Es-

Nouns:	-o	singular
	-oj	plural
	-on	singular noun used as direct object
	-ojn	plural noun used as direct object
Verbs:	-as	present tense
	-is	past tense
	-os	future tense
	-us	conditional mood
	-u	imperative mood
	-ant	present participle
	-int	past participle
	-ont	future participle
Personal pronouns:	mi	I
	vi	you
	li	he
	ŝi	she
	ĝi	it
	ni	we
	ili	they
Adjectives:	-a	(-aj, -an, -ajn for plural, singular as direct object; and plural as direct object, respectively)
Adverbs:	-e	
Conjunctions, prepositions, and related words:	la	the
	kaj	and
	sur	on top of
	sub	under
	je	on (abstract) as in "*on* the rag"
	al	to
	de, da	of
	kun	with
	sed	but
	kiu	who
	ĉu	"do" as an auxilliary, as in "*Do* you give head?"
	jes	yes
	ne	no, not
	kio	what
Useful affixes: (suffixes and prefixes)	ek-	sudden action
	fi-	shameful, nasty
	mal-	the opposite of
	pra-	very old
	-aĉ	contemptible, disgusting
	-ad	frequent or continuous
	-ec	abstract quality of (-ship or -ness)
	-eg	great size
	-et	small-sized
	-in	feminine
	-uj	container

2 The word *farti*, contrary to your expectations, means "to fare" in Esperanto. Makes a jolly pun, though: "How do You do?" puns with "How are you farting?"

USEFUL SENTENCES

Esperanto	Pronunciation	Translation
1. *Leroj merdas.*	LEE-roy MEHR-dass.	Leroy shits.
2. *Leroj ekfimerdas.*	LEE-roy eck-fee-MEHR-dass.	Leroy nasty-shits-sudden.
3. *Leroj kaj Sandra merdadas montegojn da pramerdo.*	LEE-roy kai SAN-dra mehr-da-dass mon-TEH-goin da pra-MEHR-doe.	Leroy and Sandra frequently-shit great-sized-piles of antiquated-shit.
4. *Vi estas dek funtoj da merdo en kvinfunta sako.*	VEE EHS-tass dek FOON-toy da MEHR-doe ehn kveen-FOON-tah SOCK-oh.	You are ten pounds of shit in a five-pound bag.
5. *La grandioza kvalito da via merdo garantas aboleri la konkurson.*	La gran-dee-OH-zah kval-EE-toe da VEE-a MEHR-doe ga-RAHN-tass ah-bo-LEH-ree la kohn-KOOR-sohn.	The superb quality of your shit is guaranteed to wipe out the competition.
6. *Fuku vin!*	FOO-koo VEEN!	Fuck you!
7. *Peki estas homa, fuki estas divina.*	PEH-kee EHS-tass HO-ma, FOO-kee EHS-tass dee-VEE-nah.	To err is human, to fuck divine.
8. *Li fukas ŝian broson.*	Lee FOO-kass SHE-ahn BRO-sohn.	He fucks her twat.
9. *Vi ekfukas ŝian broseton kun via pikego.*	Vee eck-FOO-kass SHE-ahn bro-SEHT-tohn koon VEE-ah pee-KEH-go.	You quick-fuck her tiny-twat with your giant-cock.
10. *Mi pendegas.*	Mee pehn-DEH-gass.	I am well hung.
11. *Via pendeco estas malkredeba.*	VEE-ah pehn-DEH-tso EHS-tass mal-kreh-DEH-bah.	Your state of being hung is highly questionable.
12. *Li pendas kiel hamstro.*	Lee PEHN-dass KEE-el HAM-stro.	He is hung like a hamster.
13. *Viaj veniloj aperas muite kiel spinakaco.*	VEE-aye veh-NEE-loy ah-PEHR-ass MOOL-teh KEE-ehl spee-nah-KAH-cho.	Your genitals bear a remarkable resemblance to moldy spinach.
14. *Estes mia esprima deziro ke fulmo frapus frapus vian pinon.*	EHS-tass MEE-a ehs-PREE-ma deh-ZEE-roh keh FOOL-ma FRA-puss VEE-ahn PEE-non.	It is my express wish that your penis be struck by lightning.
15. *Estas mia konjekto ke via patrino estas ne strango al cirkauprenoj de hejmaj dorlotoj kaj fojnejokortaj bestoj.*	EHS-tass MEE-ah kohn-YEK-to keh VEE-a pa-TREE-no EST-ass neh STRAN-goh ahl tseer-cow-PREH-noy deh HEM-mai dor-LOT-toy kai foy-neh-yo-KOR-tai BES-toy.	It is my conjecture that your mother is no stranger to the embraces of domestic pets and barnyard animals.

peranto: "*merde*" to form *merdo*. It's an effortless step from the construction of dirty words in Esperanto to the compilation of short phrases. Remember, a little imagination goes a long way.

FOURTH: Practice! Translate these sentences into Esperanto.

1. The weather is nice. It is pleasant here. That is a pretty dress. Let's fuck.

   Vetero estas agrable. Estas placa ĉi tie. Tiu estas beleta kostumo. Ni fuku.

2. There seems to be some error. Your ass is occupying the position which rightfully belongs to your head.

   Apera esti ia eraro. Via posto okupas la pozicion ke laŭrajte apartenas al via kapo.

3. You are a booby. Would you be so kind as to bend over so that I may insert this kumquat into your rectum?

   Via estas naivegulo. Vi estus afabla ŝufice kliniĝi tiel ke mi esteblos enmeti ĉi tiu kumkvaton en via anuso?

4. Please correct me if I am mistaken, but are you not accustomed to eating shit?

   Mi petas korekto min se mi eraras, sed ĉu vi kutimas ne mangi merdon?

5. Shame! You should have your mouth washed out with beeswax and anise!

   Honto! Vi lavu vin buson kun abelvakso kaj anizo!

6. Can you direct me to the nearest medical facility? My penis has been struck by lightning.

   Ĉu vi povas direkti min al multoproksima medicina efiko? Mia piko estis frapont de fulmo.

As a final test of your newfound skill, translate the following passages at your leisure into English. And remember, practice makes perfect!

Passage No. 1

Mansignant la konstitucion kun minaĉo, ili devigas Ĝ. Ê. Uver leki la pilkojn de F. Ĝ. Ŝin dum Elen Keler masturbas kun kolumbo.

Passage No. 2

Ili fukas panjon sur litkovrilo de la amerika flago kun dileto de tagaĝa varmeghundo dum pisant sur la Biblio kaj frajon kaj reprodukto de "Amerika Gotika."

Conversation

Pardonu, fraŭlino, mi vidas ke vi portas verdan stelon. /Jes. Ĝi estas ĉar mi parolas lingve. /Kiel vi fartas hodiaŭ? /Mi fartas bone. Ejnstejn edzigis lia kuzinon en Skenektadi. /Ĉu vi observas ofte birdmigradojn? /Ne. Mia patro estas okulisto. /Mi esperas ke Ejnstejn estis plena de boneco. /Ĉu mi pruntus tason de teo? /Jes. Kiu estas la pli alta: hundido aŭ tekruĉo? /Mi ne konas. Mi ne fartas jam de multaj tagoj. /Je kioma horo vi aŭdas la veterprognozon? /Videmandas multajn demandojn. /Ĝi estas car mi demandas ilin. Demetu vion ŝtrumpojn. /Ni aŭdis unu horon da muzikaĵoj per gramofono. /Demetu nun vian brakteningon. /Estas ne vorto por "brakteningon." /Vi komprenis min sufiĉe. /Antaŭ tri tagon mi vidis teatraĵon de Leroj. /Ĉi tio estas koko. /Ho ĉu estas tio koko? /Ĉi tioj estas pilkoj. /Kial ekzistas tia multigeco da haroj? /Nun vi demandas la demandojn. /Mia patro estis okulisto. /Mia patro edzigis Ejnstejn. /Kiel mi faras pri tio? /Metu ĝin en vian buŝon. /La okulo estas granda! /La pli bono vin vidi! /Kial vi grutas? /Mia anguinalo jukas. /Mia patro jukas neniam. /Fuku vian patron! /Mi fukas ja. Tial mi ekzistas. □

Hi! I'm Anita Bryant. And I can cure homosexuality in just 10 days!

DO YOU FIND YOU DON'T FIT IN WITH THE REST OF THE GANG? DO TOUGH GUYS MAKE HIGH, FUNNY SOUNDS IN THE BACKS OF THEIR THROATS WHEN YOU WALK IN THE ROOM? HAS YOUR LOCKER BEEN "TRASHED" MORE THAN TEN TIMES IN THE LAST TEN DAYS? DOES SOMEONE KEEP PISSING IN YOUR LUNCH BUCKET?

IF YOU'VE ANSWERED YES TO ONE OR MORE OF THESE QUESTIONS, THEN CHANCES ARE YOU ARE A HOMOSEXUAL.

WHAT IS HOMOSEXUALITY? IT IS A DREADED SICKNESS THAT CAN BE CAUGHT FROM AN ATHLETIC COACH OR AN ENGLISH TEACHER. NOW, THANKS TO MONEY, HOMOSEXUALITY CAN BE CURED. HOW? HERE'S HOW. HEY.

SEVEN DEADLY SIGNS OF HOMOSEXUALITY

1 Carrying your books funny.
2 Short-sleeve shirts.
3 Spending too much time with girls.
4 Wearing wristwatch backwards.
5 Being careful with parents' car.
6 Yoga.
7 Being polite to policemen.

WHAT YOU GET

★ Playboy bunny decal
★ Something plaid and woolly
★ One pack of Chesterfields
★ Plain leather watchband
★ One pair of pliers
★ Reading selections from An American Dream, Deliverance, The Call of the Wild, and Field and Stream
★ Playboy key chain
★ Nice big cordovan brogues

SATISFIED CUSTOMERS SAY:

Anita,
You bet. I tried it. I ain't queer No-Mo. Fucked me a girl last night, right in front of her mom and dad. Hope to meet more girls in jail.
Big Wave Dave
Vancouver, Canada

Anita,
Your course is the best. Really, couldn't love it more. I repair my own car now. Isn't that wonderful? Don't you think, or don't you?
Derek Madrigal
Fire Island, N.Y.

Anita,
Hey, wow, like your course was really super heavy. I really dug it. I used to have a ten suck a day habit; now, none if any suffice me. Thanks, and a tip of the fine stocking cap.
"Four-eyes"
Cambridge, Mass.

ANITA BRYANT'S HOMO NO-MO MACHO-BUILDING COURSE

Hell, yes, I'd like to be normal like you. Here's my bucks. Please send me the complete course. I realize that if I am not completely cured in ten days, my money will be spent.
Send $5.00 to:
Anita Bryant's Homo No-Mo
635 Madison Avenue
New York, N.Y. 10022

Name_____

Address_____

City_____ State_____ Zip_____

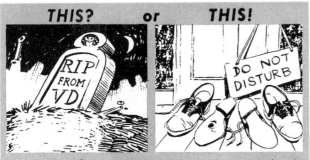

The Hughes Engagement Guide

by John Hughes

"Many a man has fallen in love with a girl in light so dim he would not have chosen a suit by it."

Maurice Chevalier

Everyone from William Shakespeare to Mickey and Sylvia has said that love is blind. Love does not see with the eye, they say, but with the heart, and if you've ever tried to make it through the stock quotations with your heart, you can begin to see the problem facing so many grooms today. These men, who suddenly find themselves writing poems and attaching them to single yellow roses, worrying about what they look like naked, and shaking baby powder into their underpants, are in no condition to objectively assess the pros and cons of the little gal who's got them in such a dither. Many a man wigged out on male hormones has stumbled up the aisle of love bellowing "I do!" only to wake up six months later with a sebaceous harlot where once there had been a fairy princess. It is a sad story, but for 90 percent of us, it is the story of our lives.

■ HER BODY

Basic rule: "Everything gets bigger, hairier, and closer to the ground."

Some women hold up better than others. Some age and wrinkle, gain weight and distort almost overnight, it seems, while others last for years. Examine the six primary female phyla illustrated below. Determine the one that most resembles your fiancée.

How She Will Hold Up

TODAY	TENTH WEDDING ANNIVERSARY
Cute as a Button	Fat as a Cow
Voluptuous Sex Kitten	 Mangy Old Cat
 Pixie	Hillbilly
Exotic	Bizarre
Sultry	 Swarthy

■ HER BREASTS

Breast Declivity as Effected by Age and Volume

Type	Large	Medium	Small
Age	18-20	18-20	18-20
	22-25	22-25	22-25
	30+	30+	30+
navel			

Note movement of the nipple downward.

■ THE FIRMNESS TEST

To fully evaluate the long-haul capability of the bosom to retain shape and character, you have to measure the firmness. In the case of full-busted girls, the breakdown of the fibrous tissue connecting the lobes may already be in progress and will accelerate at a disheartening rate after marriage. A small breast that would score well in a droop test and on a cup curve may not have sufficient firmness to retain shape and could become an unsavory "potholder"-variety bosom in a short time.

Her Breasts Are:
Small 3 points
Medium 2 points
Large 1 point

They are as Firm As:
Auto Seat 3 points
Kaiser Roll 2 points
Rosin Bag 1 point

Score_____

Results:
6 points.......Breasts alone are reason enough to marry her.
5 points.......Breasts and good cheekbones are enough.
4 points.......Breasts okay, but she better have a job.
3 points.......She needs a job, paid-up car, and videodisk machine.
2 points.......She better have two jobs, family money, and a great face.
1 point........An alien force has taken control of your mind; seek refuge in another country.

■ A BREAST CHECKLIST

1. Examine the bosoms under full-light conditions (does not include candles, moonlight, or colored light bulbs) and note the appearance of: hair on the areola or red welts indicating plucking of areola hair, moles or warts, networks of blue veins, stretch marks.
2. Moisten nipples, then blow on them to make sure they erect properly.
Do you like the way they look?
3. Do you honestly like the shape of her breasts? The color of her nipples?
4. Will she do strenuous exercises to keep her pectoral muscles in tone?
5. In the unlikely event that it would become necessary to save your marriage, would she consent to cosmetic breast surgery?

■ HER PERSONALITY

At the Party	No Personality	Too Much Personality
She wears a…	coat.	slit skirt, no panties.
She drinks…	Pepto-Bismol.	Heineken's with a Chivas chaser.
During cocktails she…	sits in the car.	asks the waiter if he's ever fucked a U. of Colorado grad.
At dinner she…	chokes on a piece of meat.	announces that the oysters look like a part of her body, and invites the host to take the first guess.
After dinner she…	sits in the kitchen with the help and tells them she feels ugly and won't blame them if they hate her, because she hates herself.	does a Grace Jones impression and tells the hostess the joke about the football player who spikes the baby.

■ HER GENITALS

As important as they are, oddly enough, they don't change that much, and it's very difficult to get a bad set. Since the criteria for judging the beauty of female genitals are so very low, you will have to find a deformity case or a hermaphrodite to marry an ugly set. Children will affect the muscle force and grip factor, but, overall, what you see now is what you'll see for many years. The downy covering of youth will give way to something hairy and coarse, but space-age cosmetic science has developed several safe and effective ways to keep genital hair at a reasonable level. The only real red flag is if your fiancée has a very low personal grooming standard or a feminine-organ malfunction.

■ TAKE A SECOND LOOK!

You've admired the paint job, you've kicked the tires, but have you looked under the hood? Take a good long look at her and make sure you haven't missed a colony of hairy moles in her armpit.

Example A   First glance.

Example B   A closer look.

■ BEWARE!

Beware of the girl who's holding it in! There are many fat women in the theme bars and office pools of our country who are passing as thin women only through extraordinary devotion to grueling exercise programs and dangerous diets. Once these women get married, they'll have to let go and become what they really are—huge, fat pie wagons who will feel no compunction about wearing black slacks and blouse to the beach. They never lose this weight and will add another twenty or thirty pounds with each child. These gals are very clever and often manage to snare nice-looking men. They go right into childbirth, home mortgage, and furniture investment, so that when the metamorphosis from slender to zeppelin is complete, the husband is too heavily invested, emotionally and financially, to get out. You can avoid getting hitched up to one of these latent behemoths through early detection.

The Five Signs of Future Fat

1. All of her clothing is too tight. She is struggling to keep in a size she outgrew long ago.
2. Short legs and waddling gait.
3. She insists on total darkness for sex.
4. Her hair looks fabulous. She is concentrating on the one part of her body that will not get fat.
5. She eats the lime in her Perrier water.

■ HER MIND

Phi Beta Kappas are swell, but they can't cook and they don't make the leap from quantum physics to the ironing board with much grace. All you should want from a girl is enough sense to manage the house, hold a decent job, and not embarrass you at a dinner party by asking the British ambassador if her dress makes her look fat. Here is a simple intelligence test for prospective brides.

Question:
"What is at the core of our current problems with Mexico?"

If she answers:
"I just love this song, turn it up! *Oooo*, I love the nightlife!"
She is a dumbass.

If she answers:
"You haven't phrased the question very well. Are you referring to the natural-gas pricing debacle or the general ill feeling toward the Yanqui?"
She is a smartass.

If she answers:
"We're not very nice to them; let's fuck, then I'll make you dinner and vacuum out your car."
Don't wait for the wedding. Elope and buy her anything she wants.

■ HER FAMILY

Unless you have the good fortune to marry an orphan, your bride will be but the tip of the iceberg when it comes to the total marriage package. In fact, she may represent as little as 20 percent of what you actually marry. After the honeymoon, you will have to face the fact that all those miserable swine in wild suits who made your wedding reception such a forgettable experience are now *your* family.

Evaluate Her Relatives

Step 1

Find out how many there are, where they live, what they do for a living, and how likely they are to need money or a place to stay.

Step 2

Check with police to see if any of her family have been involved in organized crime or have committed crimes. Try to determine if there are any unsavory characters in her family who could surface and embarrass you, should you get famous, rich, or elected to public office.

Step 3

Ask yourself, "Are her brothers and sisters the type of people I want my children to call aunt and uncle? If both she and I were killed, would I want my children raised by her parents?"

■ SPECIAL CONSIDERATION: THE ONLY CHILD

Be aware that if you marry an only child, you will be solely responsible for the care and keeping of her parents when they reach their senior years. In conventional families an unmarried sister or brother takes the parents, and the other family members contribute to the upkeep bill, or they all kick in enough to send the parents to a trailer park in Sarasota. But with the only child, there is no one to share the burden, so you must bear it alone. At worst, it could mean adding an apartment to your present dwelling and having a pair of sour old people peeking in on you for the rest of their lives (be reminded that living with a real family is a wonderful elixir for the elderly, and they often hang on for years longer than anybody would have thought). At best, it will mean writing checks, and visiting an old-folks home on holidays, and lying to your wife about how happy her parents seemed. Don't be fooled by prenuptial assurances that her parents have pensions and savings and that their future is taken care of. Whatever they have put away, it isn't enough: In twenty years, thirty thousand of their dusty old dollars may not be enough to buy a six-pack of Maalox.

■ HER OFFSPRING

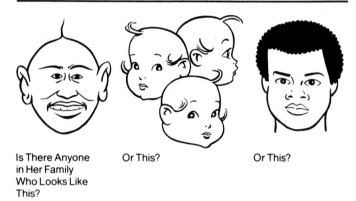

Is There Anyone in Her Family Who Looks Like This?

Or This?

Or This?

■ HER HEALTH

It seldom occurs to the man in love that his fiancée could be struck down by a cruel disease he thought only existed in made-for-TV movies. Nor does he think that she could be a miserable whiner who catches bugs like a frog. It's a wise groom who does his homework and peeks into her medical history. A simple way to get a bead on what sort of health her family enjoys is to bring up the subject in a casual dinner conversation with the family.

Sample Dialogue

You: The pork roast is superb, Mrs. Franklin! Oh, that reminds me. What did Kathi's grandparents die of?

Mrs. Franklin: Bumpsy died of stomach cancer, and, let's see...Poppy Charles died of tuberculosis.

Mr. Franklin: There is a load of cancer on my mother's side. Dad had Parkinson's. Now, Kathi's Grandma and Grandpa Twilley both had congenital heart trouble *and* Hodgkins, which is a real coincidence, to find people from two separate families with that combination!

Kathi: Well, who had Lou Gehrig's disease, then?

Mrs. Franklin: Auntie Carol and Uncle Raymond and, I think...

You: Can you excuse me? I have to go make a long phone call. I'll see you all in a week or so.

It's also good policy to encourage your fiancée to have all nonemergency medical problems remedied *before* the wedding. Many fathers of attractive daughters hold off on such things as dental work, glasses, cosmetic surgery, etc., in hopes that the new husband will have it done at *his* expense. Fool him and hold out.

Also, you should find out how your girl stands up under pain. Girls have an extraordinary talent for blowing up common ailments like colds and blisters into major illnesses. You can usually judge if your fiancée is a weepy whiner by the way she handles menstruation. Does she stay home from work when she has her period? Does she require special treatment and favors, like help getting in and out of automobiles? Does her period last more than a week? More than a month?

■ QUICKIE PELVIC EXAM

At some point before the wedding, include in one of your romantic interludes a pelvic exam. Although you will be doing things her gynecologist does, the context in which you do them will confuse her. However, be certain that you are tender and gentle and that you kiss her occasionally and refrain from referring to her clitoris as her ''glans clitoridis.''

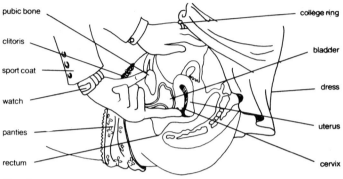

Step 1
Inspect the external genitals for discoloration, bumps and swellings, unusual hair distribution, or lice. Give her a hug and tell her you love her.

Step 2
Insert middle finger into her vagina. Lovingly ask her to cough, and test her stress incontinence (involuntary flow of urine during laughter, sneezing, or coughing). Check for Bartholin cysts, and measure the strength of her pelvic-floor muscles (AKA Hong Kong fuck muscles). Nibble her ear and caress her breasts in a circular motion from the nipple outward to include the entire breast, and note any lumps or growths.

Step 3
When she is sufficiently aroused, insert your index finger as well. Note the size, shape, and position of her ovaries, uterus, and tubes. Be on the alert for any growths or inflammations. Palpate her uterus and see if it causes her discomfort.

Step 4
Concentrate on her clitoris until her hips begin to move in an automatic fashion and her back arches and she begins to breathe heavily through her nose and mouth accompanied by head thrashing and guttural groaning. Promise her a house and a baby, then withdraw the index finger from her vagina and rapidly insert it into her rectum. As quickly as possible, determine the tone and alignment of her pelvic organs and adnexal region. Note any lesions. As she struggles, gauge the tone of her rectal sphincter muscle.

Step 5
Discuss any negative findings with a gynecologist, or consult a women's-organization hot line.

■ SEX

Basic rule: ''She will learn to cook but not to fuck.''

The real issue of premarital sex is how she does it and how often she does it. The food gets better but not the sex; so if you don't like it now, you'll hate it later. If she's good, keep in mind that it might just be her drive for the diamond that's motivating her and once she's settled down and comfy she may lock up the cookie jar forever.

Reading the Sex Fake
The sex fake is a romantic ploy designed to confuse men. It makes women seem sexier than they really are. It's a marvelous tool for maximizing impact without increasing output. It is a deep, probing kiss that curls your toes. It's a spontaneous handjob with cocoa butter that makes you forget that you were going to ask for a blowjob. It is a moist hand that you think is a mouth. It is thirty seconds of foreplay that feels like an hour.

Question:
''If she uses the sex fake on me and I'm satisfied, what difference does it make?''

Answer:
''Theoretically, it makes no difference, except that the sex fake is too demanding and time-consuming to pull off for a lifetime. Generally speaking, it ceases on the Monday following the conclusion of the honeymoon. That's when you'll find out what you really married, and, of course, by then it'll be too late to turn around.''

■ THE MANIPULATIVE SKILLS OF THE SEX FAKE—A Sample Dialogue

Jim: Remember what you said last night? That we could fuck tonight?

Jill: I don't remember that.

Jim: Sure, you said…

Jill: Kiss me. [*Pause.*]

Jim: Let's do it, okay?

Jill: Just lay beside me and…Why do you have to grab at me all the time? Can't you just appreciate me for myself?

Jim: I'm sorry, but I want to fuck, is there anything wrong with that?

Jill: No. Of course not. You're so selfish. Oh, forget it! Take out your thing and I'll hold it. Come on!

Jim: This isn't the way I wanted it, but… [*Pause.*]

Jim: Ah! That feels so good. [*Pause.*]

Jim: Could you move your hand up and down, sort of?

Jill: Why don't you tell me how to do everything?

Jim: I'm sorry.

Jill: You take all the fun out of it. [*Pause.*]

Jill: Are you going to take a long time? My arm's tired from tennis.

Jim: I'll go like a bunny. [*Pause.*]

Jim: Want me to hold yours?

Jill: Jim! You said you were going to hurry! You're taking forever! Are you thinking about another girl? You are!

Jim: No, I'm not!

Jill: Yes, you are! Take me home!

Jim: No, please! No! There's no one else!

Jill: Yes there is! You can put that disgusting thing back in your pants and drive me home! I don't want to see it as long as I live!

Jim: Please, you have to listen to me! There's no one else!

Jill: Okay, maybe I believe you. Why don't we go get something to eat, and we can talk and straighten this out.

Jim: You mean it? Thanks. I'm sorry.

Jill: You should be. I'm more than a sex machine, you know. All I do is fuck, fuck, fuck! I have a brain, you know!

Jim: I know you do. I'm so sorry. I'm just an asshole, I guess.

Jill: Yes, you are, but I love you and I can't wait to get married. It'll be lots and lots of fun. Boy, am I hungry!

■ GIVEAWAY LINES

"I want to do it, but I have my period. Damn! I'm so horny!"

"Would it be okay if we didn't do it just this one time?"

"After we're married, I'll be more comfortable. Right now I'm real uptight. And it isn't exactly romantic in a car, you know. Can you understand that? I love you."

Is It a Real Orgasm?

The honest female orgasm is three to fifteen rhythmic contractions of the outer third of the vagina at .8-second intervals (the contractions follow the beat of the song "Surfin' USA"). Unless these contractions occur, you can regard her groaning, moaning, clawing, kicking, begging for mercy, and shouting filthy religious epithets as bargain-basement histrionics.

■ A WORD ABOUT NUNS AND WHORES

There are two groups of women who do not bother with the sex fake. They are nuns and whores. You don't want to marry either. You'll know if you have a nun on the line by her absolute insistence on maintaining the virginity of her wazoo, her mouth, her breasts, her hands, her eyes, and her handkerchiefs. You'll love her wit and intelligence; she'll be as sweet as peaches, kind as all get-out, and a pal and a half. But she will drive you berserk. You'll never convince her to have reasonable sex on a regular basis, and the only way you'll get her pregnant is to whack off in her bathwater.

A whore is easily identified by the number of compliments you get on her from friends, family, and total strangers. She'll think up things to do that *you* will think are sick. She'll put out and put out and put out. Even if you're not around, she'll put out and put out and put out. If you so much as stumble on the career path, she'll be gone like spit on a skillet. And you'll never know how much of your paycheck is going for gifts to tennis studs and UPS delivery men. She cannot and will not cook, clean, or give a fly's patoot about anything north of your dork or south of your wallet.

■ HER MAINTENANCE HABITS

The Strip Test

Women are amazingly adept at concealing flaws. The more skilled a woman is at making up her face, the better her wardrobe, the keener her accessory sense, the greater the probability that she is hiding something. What you must do at the outset of a serious relationship is get an accurate picture of what she has and what she doesn't have. This is best accomplished during an overnight stay. As she sleeps, you will have an excellent opportunity to study each facial region at length. You'll be able to lift up bangs and see what's underneath, check to see if her eyelashes are real, and smell her as she really smells. In the morning, position yourself outside the shower, so that when she emerges washed clean of foundations and blush-on, you'll get a good look at the naked truth. If she lives at home with her parents and an overnight stay is impossible, try to get her to take a nap. Make sure you schedule a very early Sunday morning, unannounced, breakfast drop-in and get her to a swim party or hose her down for a clean look.

With Eyebrow Plucking | Without Eyebrow Plucking

With Facial, Sloughing, Toner, Moisturizing, Pore Shrinking, Sealer, Base, Highlighter, Lip Gloss, Lip Liner, Eyeliner, Eye Shadow, Mascara, Eyelashes, and Blush-on.

Without Facial, Sloughing, Toner, Moisturizing, Pore Shrinking, Sealer, Base, Highlighter, Lip Gloss, Lip Liner, Eyeliner, Eye Shadow, Mascara, Eyelashes, and Blush-on.

With Hydrogen Peroxide | Without Hydrogen Peroxide

■ AFTER YOU RENT YOUR TUXEDO…

Make sure you make emergency arrangements with an out-of-town friend for accommodations in the event you get to the church and decide, for whatever reason, that this marriage isn't for you, because there will be a lot of people looking for you, among them: a raging bride with seventy-five friends laughing behind her back; a spleenful mother of the bride; a gaggle of relatives who have driven hundreds of miles with fry pans and lettuce spinners; your mom, who told you she was a slut in the first place ; her brothers, who think you've damaged the goods and now don't want to pay for them; grandmas and grandpas who have sent ten thousand letters to friends the world over announcing the news : a foaming father of the bride, who has invested his motorboat money in the wedding and can only recover 40 percent, and *that* only if he stiffs a few suppliers; the Al Duchin Trio, who will be among the suppliers stiffed; the department-store salesclerks the country over who have to write up refund slips for all the presents you won't get; your dad, who bought you a brand-new car because you were finally starting to act like a man; your friends whose cocaine wedding present you've already snorted up your nose at the bachelor party; your office manager, who juggled all the vacation schedules so that you could take your honeymoon; all the bitchy old broads who got their vacation schedules rearranged; and United Airlines, which will be making the Chicago-to-Honolulu run with two economy-class seats empty on September 5, 1980.

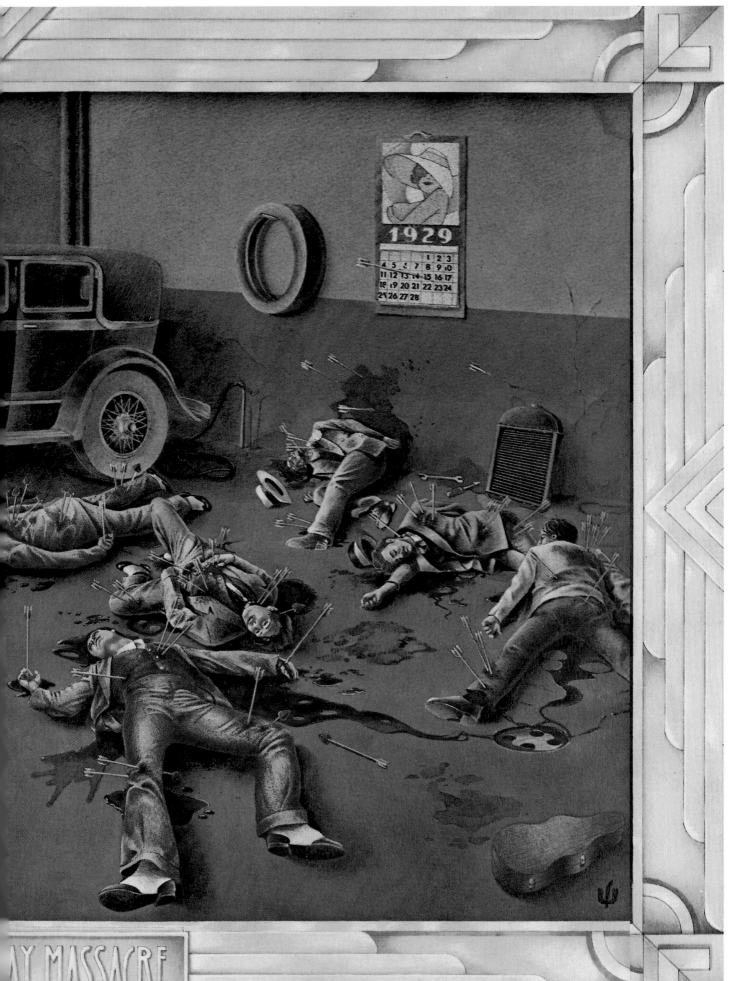

FOTO FUNNIES

The Amazing Adventures of
TIME BASTARD

FRANCE, MAY 30, 1431

CAPTURED BY THE ENGLISH, THEN FURTHER ENSNARED BY THE TREACHERY OF BISHOP CAUCHON, JOAN OF ARC, THE HEROINE OF ORLEANS, COMMITS HERSELF TO GOD AND AWAITS THE PUNISHMENT OF FIRE. SURELY, NO ONE CAN SAVE HER NOW, NOT EVEN THE DIVINE VOICES WHICH HAVE GUIDED HER SO LONG.

...ET NE NOS INDUCAS IN TEMPTATIONEM, SED LIBERA NOS A MALO.

AMEN

OR CAN THEY?

MON DIEU!

PLEASE, LET'S KEEP IT IN ENGLISH, FRENCHY. TIME'S A TICKING

HAVE... YOU... COME TO SAVE ME?

IN MY OWN WAY.

WHATEVER YOU'RE GOING TO DO, PLEASE HURRY! THE GUARDS WILL BE HERE IN LESS THAN A HALF HOUR.

HALF AN HOUR? WELL, I'LL JUST HAVE TO THINK OF SOMETHING, WON'T I?

OH!
OH MY!
OH MY GOD!

ZZZZIP

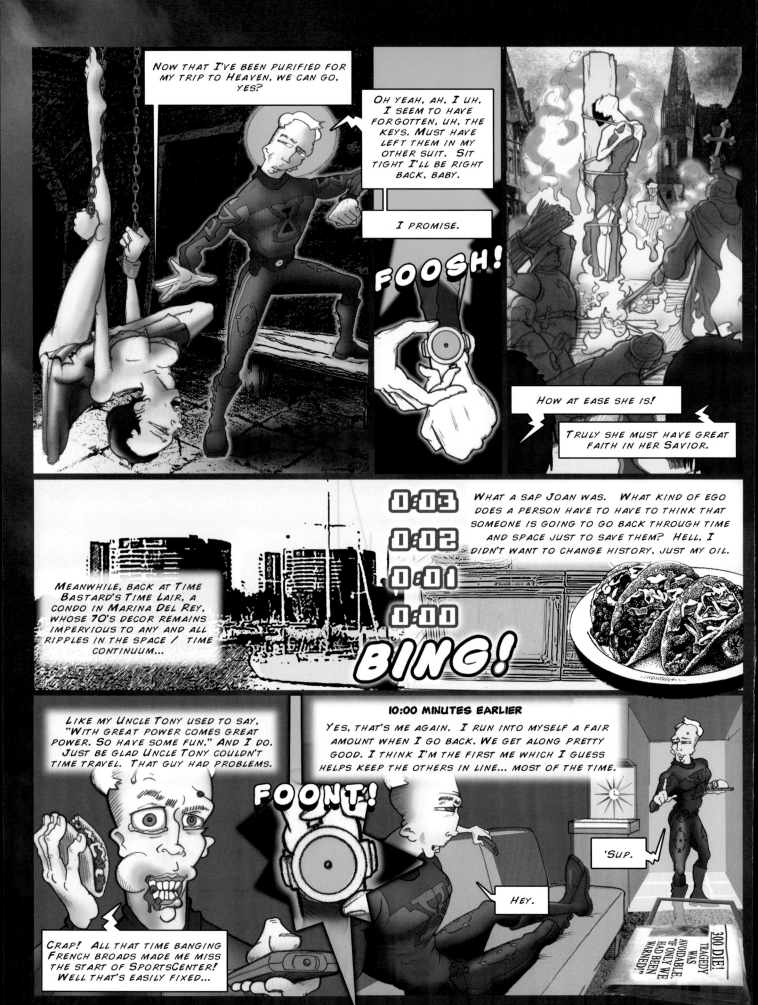

THIRD BASE

50 CENTS   **THE DATING NEWSPAPER**   **APRIL, 1956**

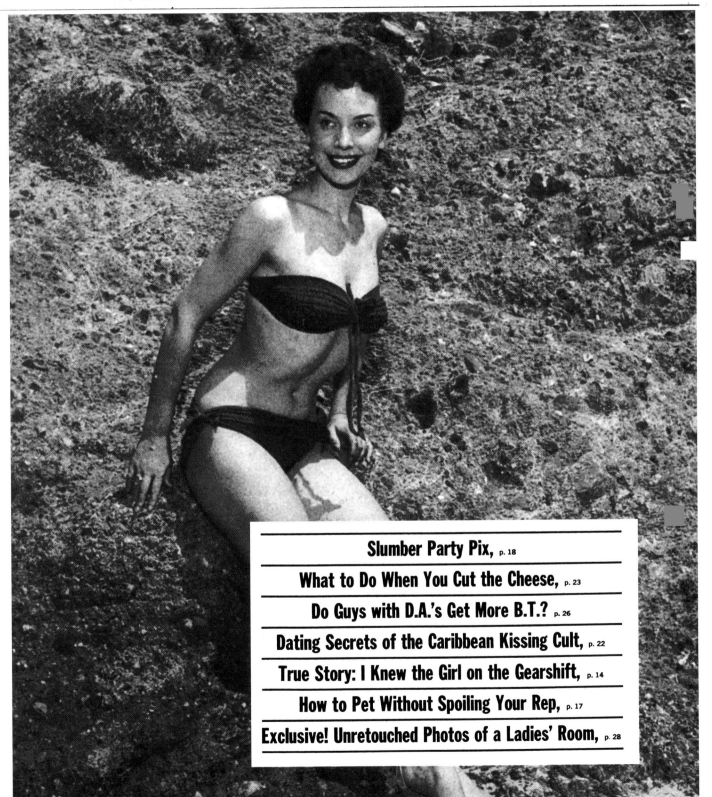

Slumber Party Pix, p. 18

What to Do When You Cut the Cheese, p. 23

Do Guys with D.A.'s Get More B.T.? p. 26

Dating Secrets of the Caribbean Kissing Cult, p. 22

True Story: I Knew the Girl on the Gearshift, p. 14

How to Pet Without Spoiling Your Rep, p. 17

Exclusive! Unretouched Photos of a Ladies' Room, p. 28

Sounding Off

STUPID RULES

We think it's about time for the hypocritical members of the parent-teacher click responsible for obsolete standards and regulations to wake up and die right!

Here we are in the middle of the twentieth century in the age of the Bell X-9, Compatible Color TV, push-button gearshifts, and so much wheat we don't know what to do with it all, and pretty soon we'll have cars that drive for a year on a lump of atomic stuff the size of a Fig Newton, and still you'd think we were living in the Dark Ages when everyone was dumb, and they burned you at the stake if they caught you with a chemistry set, and you had to be home by nine on weeknights and ten on weekends so the barbarians wouldn't sack you.

We at *Third Base* think it's stupid to have the same rules now. For one thing, kids today are smarter and don't think the world is flat or worship cats, and because we count with numbers instead of letters and don't have to sit down and conjugate everything before we write it, it takes a lot less time to do homework.

We categorically ask permission for everyone over the age of fifteen to be allowed to stay out until ten on weekdays and eleven on weekends. What's one more hour? That's less time than it would take for the Russians to wipe us all out in a sneak attack!

SCHOOL FOOD

Here is the menu for lunches in the Philadelphia area high-school system for one week last month:

MONDAY
Cut Ziti Macaroni w/ Meat & Cheese Sauce
Baby Lima Beans
Mashed Potatoes
Italian Bread & Butter
Rice Pudding
Milk

TUESDAY
Hamburg & Gravy
Mashed Potatoes
Spinach
Dinner Roll & Butter
Prune Cup
Milk

WEDNESDAY
Tomato Soup w/Rice
Choice of Peanut Butter & Jam or Chicken Salad Sandwich
Mashed Potatoes
Fruited Jell-O w/Topping

THURSDAY
Spanish Rice
Shredded Cabbage Salad
Applesauce
Bread & Butter
Mashed Potatoes
Milk

FRIDAY
Fish Stix w/ Tartar Sauce
Mashed Potatoes w/ Onions
Sliced Pickles
Hard Roll & Butter
Sugar Cookie & Dixie Cup
Milk

We think it's time to let the dietician know we're wise to what's going on!

ROYAL SHAFT

Here is another typical example of the royal shaft we at *Third Base* are always getting. Of course, none of this is ever reported in *Junior Scholastic*.

After last month's issue came out, my desk was searched and a copy of *Catcher in the Rye* and a pack of Luckies, planted by stooge room monitors, were confiscated, and also some other personal items, which were planted, too; a letter was sent to my parents causing me to be grounded and to lose a week's allowance; I was sent to the end of the line at milk lunch; and I had to clap erasers for a week.

How much longer are we going to put up with these storm-trooper tactics?

THIRD BASE, The Dating Newspaper

Editor in Chief	Top Assistant Editor	Advisor
John Boni	Hank Beard	Mr. Neely

Helpers
Terry Catchpole, Lynn Goldsmith, Chris Miller, Marc Rubin, Walt Smith

Spelling	Cutting and Gluing	Cokes
Idie Emery	Ellen Taurins	Sheila Goldfarb

Staff
Red Ruffansoar, Stu Pendusdork, Zeke Steenyne, Bea Dmitri, Ivan Kutchakokoff, Charles U. Farley, Seymour Butts, Wilma Fingerdu, Peter Gozinya, Harry Wazoo, Dewar Balzac, Harriet Beecher Meete, Lotta Crabbe, Buster Hymen, Ida Hardon, Helen Bedd, Shirley Jism, Phil Adio, Connie Lingus, Hugh G. Rekshun, Kenny Dewitt, Wanda Feelmi, Leon Twotsky, Clyde Orris, Helen Howzyanakis, Harry P. Ness, Lope DeMule, Claude Balls, Stella Virgin, Hugo Jerkov.

Third Base, The Dating Newspaper, Locker 341, Warren G. Harding High School, Phila., Penna. Copying the compositions in this paper into a blue book, theme book, notebook, or anything else without a permission slip from *Third Base* isn't allowed. Compositions sent to us that we didn't ask for won't be read if we can't read your writing or the pages are all stuck together.

DATE-LINE

Sure, I know that a lot of the kids in school say I'm bad and slutty, but all I know is I'm having a real blast and I don't have pimples, or rashes on my hands, or go home all nervous-jervis from holding back with a date. If I like a fella and he showed me a nice time, I'll pet with him. I don't care *who* knows it, and that includes my parents,
Mr. & Mrs. _____ of _____,
_____, U.S.A.

My dumb girl friends are always saying don't do any heavy petting unless it's with your steady. Well, first of all I don't have a steady because I like playing the field. Anyway, my drippy girl friends only say that because none of them have a finished basement or a fallout shelter to fool around in, or boyfriends with cars to park someplace with.

Don't anybody get the impression that I'm easy, or boy-crazy. I just like to pet. It's faroutsville and a hundred times neater than ordinary smooching or necking. Once you been petting with a smooth operator, you can't go back to necking. And as long as a guy keeps his hands to himself and doesn't try for the "danger zone," what's the harm in sending him home happy? And besides, I like petting.

Anyway, I'm a doll that's always been curious about things, like wondering how many different ways you can pet and stuff like that. And I never thought I'd go even beyond my craziest dreams the night I was sitting in The Hop Shoppe with some of my nerdy girl friends. We were drinking some Cokes after the Friday-night school dance, a real drag, and our championship football team first string broke through the door on their way home from a night practice. I thought they were acting real sharp, doing cool things on the way to the fountain like punching each other out on the shoulders, banging into tables, and saying, "Excuse me," and making rebel yells even though we live in the North. Real sharp stuff. Natch, my square girl friends said they were creeps. "Ugh, raunch time," they kept moaning, especially when the team did something neat. So there I was, sitting with three dullsville spastics, watching the team having a cool time. I wished I was with them instead, and that goes double for the dreamboat who played halfback. He was the snazziest-looking, the only one wearing shoulder pads over his school sweater, and he had his comb inside the front loops of his chinos, so it looked like a long black belt-buckle. It really was neat and I could feel myself get interested. He noticed it, too, so imagine how I practically creamed in my jeans when he actually came up to our booth and pushed a malted in front of me. But leave it to my blow-lunch girl friend to spoil things.

"Don't drink it, it's probably poisoned," she said, a real sarc remark if I ever heard one, but Dreamboat had a come-back reply. "Hardeeharhar," he said, and that shut her up. I took a couple of sips and one of the guys on the team yelled over from the fountain so everybody could hear, "Hey, that's the malt with the booze in it." What a great slash! Everybody laughed. Except my cubey girl friends. "Gross-out, gross-out," they kept saying. I told them if they weren't having a ball they could go. I was staying. Janie said that since we all came to the dance together we should all go home together or it would look "bad." I didn't care, so they just splitsville and left me in the booth with Dreamboat.

Right away I wanted to let him know I was interested, so I asked him to loan me his comb. He said that if he did, his pants would fall down because the ends were connected to his belt. "Smooth," I said, and he pushed a quarter into the booth juke for six big plays, one fast and five slow. We got up and danced the Slop and the latest "Bandstand" stuff while the rest of the team hung around and bird-dogged me with their eyes. They must have known me from before because I could hear some of them whispering, "It's Make-Out Mary," and "For a heavy pet, she's the doll to get." Well, like I said, I'm not ashamed for liking what I like. Everybody found that out when I got the idea for double and triple dating, two or three guys and me, myself, and I out for a good time. Then I got the idea for a group date, and five or more guys would meet me a block from my house and we'd go out. Boy, when you've had five or six fellas all slipping their straws into your malted at once, it's really dragsville when you have to go back to two or three.

Anyway, the team kept bird-dogging me, and I recognized one or two of them as being one-fifth of a date I had once. Don't ask me why, but I was getting all hepped up by them looking at me, even though I was dancing with One and Only. I really wanted to pet with him and feel his frantic kisses up, down, and all around my mouth and even maybe—for him I'd do it—my neck. I couldn't wait. Besides, I hadn't gotten petted in about a week and I was ready-Freddy.

After the six dances were up, we all squeezed into a raked Hudson and began layin' rubber through town. I was on Dreamboat's lap, and since we were all crowded I was getting excited by all the touching and rubbing. My ankles began to sweat and it turned my slave chain green. I could hardly think straight, I was so excited. Then I got pressed and squeezed even more when the cat driving made a bunch of sharp turns so everybody could land on top of me from the swerves. I usually get mad from a dumb trick like that, but I liked it this time. These guys sure knew how to get a girl going. We ran a few red lights, and then one of the tackles in the front seat pulled out his comb and fixed his D.A. That made me even more hot and bothered. I just couldn't stand it anymore and leaned back, stuck out my lips, and closed my eyes to look as dreamy-looking as I could. I stayed like that for a couple of minutes and I guess they must have noticed something about the way I looked because the car stopped.

"Hey, she's dead!" the wingback said, and they all laughed. Sarc, sarc, sarc, I thought, and breathed harder. Then everybody got so quiet all of a sudden and you could hear an ignition key drop. Jeepers, I thought, I heard about girls who did things with a whole football team, and now I was going to be one of them. I never dreamed it would happen to me, or even that I'd like it when it did, but I was wrong. I was even

continued on page 8

3

Interview

Make-Out Man Tony Redunzo

**"I was never on a date
I didn't make out on!"**

THIRD BASE cut class one day and went to Nathan Hale High School for this special interview with a make-out artist. We asked around the halls and in the caf during fifth lunch, "Who's the biggest make-out man in school?" Everybody, but everybody, said the same thing: TONY Redunzo, "Fast Tony," "The Mover," "Operator Plus," a junior transfer from Waldon Vocational, the school that burned down last month.

THIRD BASE: Tony, how do you become a make-out artist?
TONY: Practice makin' out a lot.
THIRD BASE: How do you do *that*?
TONY: With a chick.
THIRD BASE: What if you can't get one to practice with?
TONY: Tough.
THIRD BASE: Uh . . . everybody says you can make out with anybody.
TONY: Yeah. I just got a way with chicks. Ever since I was a kid.
THIRD BASE: How do you do it?
TONY: Well, now it's easy. If a chick goes out with me, I know she's a make-out on account of my rep. She must want what Tony's after, see, or she wouldn't date me. But if you're a guy just startin' out, you gotta use the techniques.
THIRD BASE: That's what we want to know, Tony, the techniques.
TONY: Like I said, it comes natural to me. But no matter what, you always gotta be sincere with a chick. Even if you gotta phony it up. Always dress sharp and be snazzy lookin', keep your suedes brushed, keep your cool, an' know the words to all the latest tunes. That's the basics. Then you go shoppin' for a chick to click with.
THIRD BASE: What's the first thing you do when you spot a doll?
TONY: Get 'er lookin' at me. Usually, I walk over near where she's standin' an' crash into her accidental.
THIRD BASE: Accidental on purpose.
TONY: You got the idea. Now I look 'er over. Give 'er the Redunzo up-an'-down. Sometimes a stuck-up chick'll make a face or stick her tongue out at you, but that's okay 'cause that means she's lookin'. That's when I turn it on and just stand there real cool an' undress 'er with my eyes.
THIRD BASE: Wow! Undress her?
TONY: Just down to the brassiere. You don't wanna scare her off. Now she's all set for me to make the big move.
THIRD BASE: You ask her for a date?
TONY: I start combin' my hair. Right in front of her. With this.
THIRD BASE: Hey, that's a neat comb.
TONY: Yeh. It's a custom job. I made it in shop. Now she knows I mean business, so I don't waste any time. I wanna see right away if she's a make-out or not. So I ask her the big question, point blank.
THIRD BASE: No kidding!

The *big* question?
TONY: Yeh. How late can you stay out? See, if they're allowed out after nine o'clock without permission on a school night, you know her folks have given up on tryin' to control her. A doll like that does what she wants an' she's prob'ly a hot ticket. It ain't failed yet. I even know some chicks can stay out late as ten, ten-fifteen without special permission.
THIRD BASE: What're *they* like?
TONY: *You* figure it out.
THIRD BASE: Wow!
TONY: You said it. Ready, willing, and able. Best of all, though, are the dolls who don't have to be in until eleven.
THIRD BASE: What about *them*?
TONY: I dunno. I gotta be home by ten-thirty myself, but it figures they gotta be something wild.
THIRD BASE: What about a doll that has to be home *before* nine?
TONY: You talkin' weekends or durin' school?
THIRD BASE: School.
TONY: Total loss. Just go pull your pud instead of wasting time on a drip like that.
THIRD BASE: How else can you tell if a chick'll make out?
TONY: Sometimes I use the straw technique.
THIRD BASE: What's that?
TONY: Let's say you're at the soda fountain after a date an' it's your treat. In a case like that, I usually go all out an' order a cherry Coke. There's something about a cherry Coke makes a doll think she's bein' treated special. When it comes, only put one straw in it. Get the picture? Now you take a swig and push the glass over to her. If she drinks from the straw, chances are she's a make-out, 'cause she don't mind getting her mouth where your mouth was.
THIRD BASE: I didn't know that.
TONY: Live an' learn. But, it don't count if she wipes the top of the straw with her fingers first.
THIRD BASE: If I tried that, my chick would probably

say, "Hey, where's *my* straw?"
TONY: Could be she's worried about germs. A lotta chicks are takin' Hygiene class. Hi, Gene.
THIRD BASE: Lookin' keen.
TONY: What's the scene?
THIRD BASE: In between.
TONY: What?
THIRD BASE: Between your legs.
THIRD BASE: After you start making out, how far can you go?
TONY: Depends on if they're hot-natured an' how much. Some chicks are heavy make-outs. Just touch 'em an' they're all over you. But most chicks, you gotta help 'em along. Blowin' in their ear gets most of 'em excited. Then when they start getting passionate, start coppin' a few feels. A lotta times they're so excited they don't realize what's happening. But you always have a comeback reply in case they say, "Keep your hands to yourself," "Private property. No fishing allowed," or something like that. Just act surprised an' say, "Gee, I didn't even realize what I was doin'," or "It just happened." Just say it sincere.
THIRD BASE: What if she don't say anything about feelin' her up?
TONY: Then you know you can get some more. Go for a grab *under* the sweater. Sneak your hand under an' work up, slow. Then let a finger slip inside the brassiere. When it's in there, go for the nipple. It's the little point at the end of the tit. That really gets 'em boiling.
THIRD BASE: Do you get a lot of bare tit?
TONY: Shit, yeah! Almost always. I got a special routine for it.
THIRD BASE: What?
TONY: Trade secret.
THIRD BASE: Come on.
TONY: Okay, okay. You're wheelin' a chick home after a date an' you go park someplace dark. First thing she'll say is "How come we're stopped?"
THIRD BASE: Boy, sounds like you know *my* chick.
TONY: What's 'er name?
THIRD BASE: Mar—uh, you wouldn't know her. So what do you do then?
TONY: Just say something

like, "Don't worry! I ain't gonna try nothin'. Everybody knows you're a "good girl," so I wasn't even thinkin' about makin' out." Now, if there's something a doll don't want to be called, it's a "good girl," an' pretty soon she'll be tryin' to prove she ain't. I get most of my bare tit with that routine, but it always brings on a case of B.B.

THIRD BASE: Blue balls.

TONY: You said it. Only thing left is go slam the ham.

THIRD BASE: How far do you usually go with a chick?

TONY: Oh, I figure to get dry humps about half the time. You gotta have space, though, like a sofa or on the beach. You can't dry hump good in the car. Unless you're a midget. Usually a chick'll let me give her some dry fingering instead.

THIRD BASE: How's that feel?

TONY: Real!

THIRD BASE: Sex appeal.

TONY: Good deal. Sometimes though, you get chicks'll say, just for example, "Gee, Tony, I'd love to make out with you, but I'm afraid of what'll happen. You're so wonderful, I wouldn't trust myself once we got started."

THIRD BASE: You actually had girls say that to you?

TONY: I said just for example, didn't I? All you gotta do is put on an innocent face an' say, "Gee, don't worry about that. I can't mess around for real. I'm plannin' to go to college." Talkin' college relaxes 'em, lets 'em think you won't do nothin' dumb to ruin your life. Then, while you're talkin' about how you're gonna major in shop or mechanics, you start in on her. You're on your way.

THIRD BASE: Boy, you got every angle covered.

TONY: Wait, there's more. Another routine is the "Redunzo reverse." Tell the chick, "Don't worry, I won't touch you. I don't trust myself, so I'd better not even kiss you. You know about us hot-blooded Italians, so I'm not takin' any chances." Two bits says the chick'll tell you, "I know when to stop," or "I'll tell you when

For Your Wallet

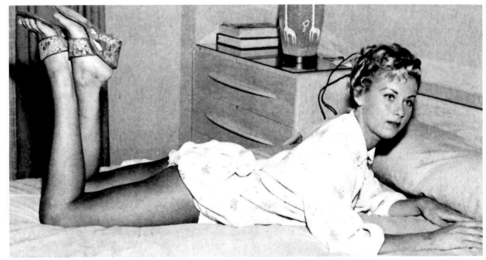

you're going too far." But they don't.

THIRD BASE: Where's the best place to make out?

TONY: Nothin' like a nice, soft sofa, but you gotta get inside the chick's house for that.

THIRD BASE: How do you do that?

TONY: When I take 'em to the door, I say something off the subject, like "Can I use your bathroom?"

THIRD BASE: Terrific.

TONY: Now, she won't just say no. She'll tell you that goin' upstairs might wake up her folks or something. Some guys lose their cool right there and they give up. Just start hoppin' up an' down a little and say you gotta go real bad. If you're outside, sort of look at her old lady's roses like they'd be okay inna pinch. If she still says no, ask can you come in for a glass of water on account of you're thirsty. You gotta have that comeback ready. Boom. You're inside.

THIRD BASE: What next?

TONY: Drink the water, but slow. Then, on the way out, you say with a surprise that you got a couch or a sofa at home just like hers. "Lemme see if it feels the same," you

can say, and then you go try it out. Once you get on that sofa, you're hard to move.

THIRD BASE: What if her old man shows up?

TONY: I got a special one for that. See, I can make myself throw up, just like that. So, if one of the fossils makes the scene, I just blow a little lunch, and everything's cool. You know, I felt a little sick, so she was gettin' me some aspirin. See, what you do is kind of half gargle, half cough, like this. Oh, sorry.

THIRD BASE: Yeah, I see what you mean.

TONY: Never fails.

continued

5

continued

THIRD BASE: That's neat.

TONY: Smelly feet.

THIRD BASE: What's a treat?

TONY: Beatin' your meat.

THIRD BASE: Tony, how do you start foolin' around? You know, what's the first thing you do to make out?

TONY: Inside the house or inna car?

THIRD BASE: Both.

TONY: Hunnerts o' ways. See, the idea is to get 'em thinkin' about it, get 'em on the subject, but do it real casual, like. Start in with one of your lines. I got a whole bunch of 'em. Like, I'll ask the chick if she got a girl friend named Kay. When she says yes, you say, "Oh. Then if you see Kay, tell her I want her." Get it? If you see Kay . . . F-U-C-Kay. Or you can say, "Do you know my friend, Buster Cherry?" Get it? Buster Cherry? And when she says, "No," you say, "Tits O.K." That puts you right onna subject.

THIRD BASE: Heyyyyy!

TONY: Right. An' if she laughs, you know she's wise an' you can start makin' out pretty quick. If she gets mad, usually she'll say something like "Watch your tongue." But that's okay, too. You still know she's wise, or why did she get mad? Either way you know the situation.

THIRD BASE: What if she doesn't have a girl friend named Kay?

TONY: Stay cool, go to another subject. Like if I was in my Merc, I'd say, "How's about drivin' down to the Cuban airport and watch the Spanish fly?"

THIRD BASE: That's sharp.

TONY: You bet. She's gotta laugh 'cause it's a joke. If she does, great. If she says, "Huh?" that's even better, 'cause now you can explain the joke. Either way you're on the subject. Then you say how you'd never use the stuff, even though you got a box of it at home, 'cause if a chick don't like you enough to make out with you, you won't force her. Sincere bullshit like that. Works alla time.

THIRD BASE: You actually got Spanish fly at home?

TONY: Nawwww! I just say that.

THIRD BASE: Oh.

TONY: Now, if I'm inna car, I got it made in the shade anyway, 'cause I've put all kinds of lumpy stuff, pieces of junk and nuts an' bolts an' my kid brother's old sled, in there under the upholstery, so if she don't wanna bust her bums, she's gotta sit in Tony-boy's lap. Of course, you gotta look out, 'cause sometimes they'll bring along a phone book or a big textbook or somethin' like that and kind of slip it in between, you know? Their mothers tell 'em to do that.

THIRD BASE: What do you do then?

TONY: Depends. If it's a phone book, I'll say, "Excuse me, I gotta look up a number," or if it's like a history book, maybe I'll go, "Hey, I been wondering, just when was the Louisiana Purchase?"

THIRD BASE: Sharp!

TONY: Another good starter is this *National Geographic* I stole from a dentist. There's a section about tribes without clothes in it, an' you can see the pictures. I keep it on the back seat or in the glove compartment. Sometimes I let it slip outta my book bag. That's always good.

THIRD BASE: Hey, can I see this?

TONY: Just don't take it outta the car.

THIRD BASE: I won't. What other ways is there?

TONY: Over here on the dash I painted "Class of '69" in nail polish.

THIRD BASE: Class of— Oh, yeah. I get it.

TONY: Right. She's bound to ask about it. If she don't, you bring it up casual. Say, "Hey, look at what my dumb buddy did for a joke and I can't get it off." Boom. You're on the subject. You got her thinkin' about it.

THIRD BASE: What page does it have about the tribes?

TONY: Inna middle someplace. Another way is just say something French like "we-we" or "Fi-fi" an' take it from there. Anything French is automatically talkin' about the subject.

THIRD BASE: Hey, look, you can see tits an' everything.

TONY: I told ya.

THIRD BASE: There's something gunky stuck on the page here.

TONY: If you're out after a prom or a hop or something, you got a great way to get on the subject just by talkin' about the wrist corsage you got her. Talk about the bees goin' in the flowers and what they do and stuff like that.

THIRD BASE: It won't come off.

TONY: A real neat starter is tellin' the chick right from the beginning that you're thinking about becoming a priest, but you wanna see if you're cut out for it. Tell her she's a test date so you can see if you can control yourself from makin' out, 'cause if you can control yourself with her, you can resist anything.

THIRD BASE: Look, what is this stuff anyway? Oh, gross!

TONY: The more you don't try anything with her, she gets more upset that she's resistible. Sooner or later she's all over you, tryin' to get you hot. I got a hand-job that way once.

THIRD BASE: That's genius.

TONY: Bet your ass.

THIRD BASE: Lotta class.

TONY: Inna grass.

THIRD BASE: Tony, what's the biggest problem in making out?

TONY: There's two. One is gettin' from the front seat of the car to the back seat without a chick suspectin' anything. Pretend you dropped something important back there like your comb and you gotta go look for it. She'll usually help you out and there you are.

THIRD BASE: What's the other problem?

TONY: A chick wearin' a one-piece dress up to the neck. I'm talkin' if you wanna try for some grabs. It's almost impossible, so you gotta get in there through the sleeves. It's rough, but if you can get past the dress shields, you're hittin' on all eight cylinders.

THIRD BASE: Who makes out the best?

TONY: Blondes an' nurses. My best make-outs was blondes. Nurses really know the score, too.

THIRD BASE: You made out with a nurse?

TONY: Naw, most of 'em are older 'n me. But I heard. They know all about protecting themselves, so they do it more.

THIRD BASE: How can you tell if a doll'll go all the way?

TONY: Lotsa ways. If a chick sits with her legs apart, or chews gum and wears make-up, you just *know*. If they got big tits, they'll do it, too. Your best bet, though, is a chick with skin trouble. They're always doin' it 'cause that's the only way they can get guys. Same goes for real uglies, too. You can get anything from an ugly chick. Only thing is, people see you with her and they know you're after one thing. Then you got your ordinary pig or beast. Really foul, but they'll fuck a duck.

THIRD BASE: Lots of luck. Did you ever go all the way?

TONY: Are you kiddin'?

THIRD BASE: Gee.

TONY: One time I was makin' deliveries onna after-school job and this married chick——

THIRD BASE: Married?

TONY: You heard me. She was married an' her husband was out of town someplace. Well, she gave me a tip and while she was doin' that, she gave me a French handshake. Right then I knew.

THIRD BASE: What's a French handshake?

TONY: Come on. You know.

THIRD BASE: No.

TONY: You're shakin' hands, right? And one of you tickles the palm with the middle finger. It's a signal the Frenchies use when they got the hots. They go around givin' French handshakes till somebody says yes. You do it like this.

THIRD BASE: Ohhhhh. We call it "Tickle your Fancy."

TONY: Well, it's a French handshake.

THIRD BASE: What about the married chick?

TONY: Turns out she's a real sex fiend, see. One of those lymphomaniacs. They gotta make out almost every day. Something's wrong with their nerves makes 'em that way. She was somethin', boy. Really somethin'.

THIRD BASE: Did you go all the way?

TONY: She had her clothes off an' everything. I could

see her hair.

THIRD BASE: Down there.

TONY: You said it. She had grown-up tits an' all.

THIRD BASE: What happened?

TONY: I must of been there for three hours. Fantastic.

THIRD BASE: Did you do it? What happened?

TONY: Ahhhh, she was havin' her period.

THIRD BASE: Oh.

TONY: But we was gonna. It's just that it was the twenty-eighth of the month.

THIRD BASE: Tough.

TONY: Yeh. Should of known. All chicks get it on the twenty-eighth every month like clockwork. I might as well of stayed home and pounded the peter.

THIRD BASE: Nothin' neater.

TONY: Nothin' sweeter. □

HEARTY HAR-HARS

John Wayne and Marilyn Monroe got married. That night they were taking off their clothes in the motel room. John Wayne removed his shirt.

"Why, what's that?" said Marilyn Monroe, pointing to the hair on his chest.

"Oh, that's my grass," replied the actor. He then watched as Marilyn Monroe took off her blouse and her brassiere. "What are those?" he asked.

"Those are my babies," she replied. Then John Wayne took off his pants and his underpants.

"What is *that*?" cried Marilyn Monroe.

"That's my car," said John Wayne, who then watched as Marilyn took off her girdle and her panties. "What's that?" he asked, when she was finished.

"That's my garage," she explained.

"Well, I'll make you a deal," said John Wayne. "I'll let your babies play in my grass if I can park my car in your garage!"

Spell "pig" backwards and then say the word "slow."

The angle of the dangle and the square of the hair divided by the heat of the meat equals the cube of the tube!

A **THIRD BASE** BONE-US!

Cut out this score sheet and save!

NAME_____PHONE_____BUILD_____
HAS TO BE HOME BY_____AGE_____PERIOD_____MAKE-OUT: Yes___No___
NUMBER OF DATES: Alone_____Double_____Other_____HOME ROOM_____

SCORE

BASE: 1st___,_____2nd_____3rd_____Home Plate_____
Caught ih rundown between____and____:___ Thrown out at____:____Picked off at____
KISSES: Regular_____French_____Other_____
PETS: Rubs_____Grabs_____Nudges_____Fondles_____Slaps received_____
SKIN FEELS: Between bottom of sweater/blouse and top of skirt_____
Bare back inside sweater/blouse_____Bra strap: Back_____Shoulder_____
DANGER ZONE: Down there_____Near there_____Around there_____
BRA: Unhook_____Slide down_____Falsies: Yes_____No_____
TOTAL FEELS: Over clothes_____Over bra_____Under clothes/bra_____
FINGERS: Dry_____Wet_____Broken_____JOBS: Hand_____Other_____
LOVER'S BALLS: Yes_____No_____

"Sorry, Debby, but the car just won't start!"

When you go parking, take it into extra innings with our miniature battery-operated 45 rpm record player. Comes with recordings of car breakdown noises, howling wolves, rattlesnakes preparing to strike, rats fighting, and Russian bombers. Fits easily under hood; can be hooked up so first turn of ignition starts it going. A bargain at $24.98. Datemate, Inc., 2330 Western Blvd., Bayonne, N.J.

IN TROUBLE?

If she is, so are you! Don't be a yo-yo! Send for complete, easy-to-use Pregaway Set. Kit comes with four professional suction nozzles (including universal adapter for all makes of vacuum cleaners), one dozen horizontal main girders from deluxe Erector Set, rubber dart pistol with six darts and twenty feet of dental floss, five-ounce can of Drano, fly-casting rod with tiny rattles, and other proven fetus lures, and complete set of bus schedules to all major cities in U.S. (specify hometown). Only $39.98. Pregaway Products, Postale #34, Nogales, Mexico.

SALTPETER METER

❦ Stands for how much S.P. you can eat and still get it up by reading book listed.

❦❦❦❦ Red hot
❦❦❦ Not bad!
❦❦ O.K.
❦ Read your sister's diary instead!

❦❦❦ *God's Little Acre*
❦❦❦ *Peyton Place*
❦❦❦❦ *Lady Chatterly's Lover*
❦❦❦❦ *Tropic of Cancer*
❦❦❦❦ *Kinsey Report*
❦❦❦ *Blackboard Jungle*
❦❦ *By Love Possessed*
❦❦ *Catcher in the Rye*
❦❦❦ *Battle Cry*
❦❦❦❦ *Amboy Dukes*
❦❦❦ *National Geographic,* May, 1955

AMAZING DEVICE!

Are you embarrassed because you are powerless to contain or disguise the clouds of smelly gasses that you emit in cars, at dances, or on a date? Then what you need is the Super Safety Fart Emulsifier. Streamlined case clips to belt, looks like an ordinary pen holster, but actually contains a tiny tank of propane, jet nozzle, and sparking wheel. A single push of power plunger lights flame in nozzle and sends pulse of blazing gas into odor zone! Fart is safely, odorlessly detonated. Can also be used to melt frozen car-locks.

Send $9.98 to Wangies, 430 Washington St., Fall River, Mass.

FALSIE RADAR

They won't fool you anymore when you're wearing this U.S. Army surplus Radar Bogus Bosom Detector. Originally used by the FBI to detect Russian spies posing as women, it gives off a telltale warning buzz when it spots a pair of phony knockers. Find out before the tenth date! Send $49.95 to Wreltne Products, 5001 Valdalia Blvd., Las Cruces, Calif.

BOSS NEW SLASHES

Up my moon with a gravy spoon!

Kiss my foot, three joints up!

Stick your thumbs in your rear and walk on your elbows!

What I eat today, you eat tomorrow!

Roses are red, violets are blue, something in the toilet looks like you!

Your mother drives a pickle truck!

Is that your face or did your pants fall down?

Eat it raw through a flavor straw!

Make like a hockey player and get the puck out of here!

WANT TO PUCKER?

Turn ordinary kissing sessions into osculation orgies with these lip aids, every one made by over-sexed Italian hula-dancers in Tijuana, France!

Male Add-a-Lip. Your mouth can be bigger than nature made it with this special strap-on device. Giant lips made of lifelike rubberoid fit snugly over your own tiny lips. $3.98.

The Embouchure. She's sure to get hepped up when you put on a pair of these famous musicians' lips with the "tickler" on top! This is the special lip it takes years for horn players to develop. Specify B-flat trumpet, alto sax, B-flat clarinet, oboe, or French horn. $4.98.

Puffo. Thin lips can be enlarged without artificial devices with Puffo. When Puffo, shaped like a human fist, is applied to your mouth by you or a friend, your lips quickly become larger, softer, more sensitive. $2.98.

Immigrant Lips. The same kind that made America great. Each lip a genuine replica of a foreign mouth as recorded on lip prints at Ellis Island. She'll be happy to let you go "round the world" when you're wearing these "lips of many nations." Italian, Greek, Spanish, Arabian, Scandinavian, Slavic, Irish, $4.98 per pair. Polish, $3.98 per pair.

The Lipschitz. Are Jewish lips really differentville, like you hear in the locker room? We have a limited number of these special "uncircumcised" lips in stock. Find out for yourself! $5.98. (Sorry, Arabian and Jewish lips cannot be mailed in the same order.)

The Boston Blackie. If only half of what you hear about the coloreds is true, then you should give these babies a try! And there's a bonus: they make your teeth look whiter! $4.98.

Ubangi. The biggest there is. Really wild! For professional make-out artists only! As advertised in *National Geographic.* $7.98.

Prolongo. You won't want to come up for air when you use this miracle substance on your lips. Secret ingredients make your kisses last longer, and a safe, powerful adhesive makes it harder for her to break away. Comes in handy easy-to-apply stick. $1.29.

To order, send amount for items desired, plus 25 cents to cover postage and handling, to Pucker Products, Box 1159, Penn Station, N.Y. NOTE: All items sold for the prevention of cold sores and chapping only.

7

Personals

LEARN KISSING, French-style, from experienced petter—how to work the tongue, where, and why. Send 25 cents for booklet that tells you other things to do with your tongue besides talking! Box 45.

THREE SHARP CHICKS from Rosensweig Junior High, real cute, interested in meeting some cool cats for purposes of P & N, G & R. Write Cherry Bumps, Box 22. No drips or brains, please.

Look sharper, increase your combing pleasure with these grooming aids! These items from Mr. D. A. have saved many steadies from breaking up! All items scientifically tested for safety and hygiene.

THE MIGHTY JACK—Just about the finest grooming aid on the market today. This special ten-inch rattail has extra-thick prongs for total stimulation and will maintain its rigidity for deep penetration. Special back piece Splitter for straight, true D.A.'s every time. When you whip out The Mighty Jack, they know you're not fooling around! $2.50.

THE DINGER—Our most popular combing device. It bends to any shape, lets you comb from any position; no need to stop combing just because you're in a tight spot. Flexible, rugged; fits anywhere at all! $2.25.

THE BLACK BOMBER—A comb for you cats with problems. Do you have a tendency to comb too fast, so it's all over just when you're getting started? How about you husky guys who can't reach all of your head? The Black Bomber gets into all those hard-to-reach places with fifteen inches of rubberized plastic and over fifty titillating teeth. $3.

THE VIBRO COMB—A real breakthrough of modern science. Special, battery-powered motor stimulates your hair right down to the roots, excites your follicles, and leaves your scalp tingling. If you can't have her fingers in your hair, use ours! $5.

PROLONGO—Keeps your hair erect for hours. Don't be embarrassed by a limp, floppy head of hair halfway through a heavy make—look cool all the time. Prolongo actually maintains, lengthens, and stiffens your hair, without smelly glues or messy cements. $3.50.

KOMBA SUTRA CARDS—Unique playing cards show comb positions used all over the world, including techniques never before seen in this country. Completely illustrated, nothing omitted or hair-brushed out. Learn the French two-hand technique, the Italian quickie, the Greek reverse. Many more. $4.98.

Rush me the safe, hygienic grooming devices I have checked below. I certify that I am at least twelve years of age.

___Mighty Jack ___Dinger ___Black Bomber ___Vibro Comb
___Prolongo ___Komba Sutra

Name_____

Address_____

City_____State_____Zone_____

PLAIN JANES! Do you spend Saturday night at home playing checkers with your creepy kid brother while the gang is out having a swell time just because you're a little on the homely side? Let Mixmaster, the scientific dating service, find you Mr. Right. Just send your name, telephone number, and $1 to Mixmaster, Box 208, Stuyvesant Station, Phila., Pa. We'll do the rest!

PIGS! PIGS! PIGS! PIGS! We've got 'em all at Pig City! All kinds! All sizes, All shapes! All ugly! All willing! You name it, they'll do it! Kissing & Feeling, Petting & Necking, Grabbing & Rubbing, Kissing (French-style), Second Base, Third Base, Fingering (dry), Humping (dry), Squeezing & Nuzzling, Groping, many more. Great for parking, parties, or just messing around. $1 per pig. Write Pig City, Box 208, Stuyvesant Station, Phila., Pa. We'll do the rest!

BUNCH OF REAL CUT-UPS want to meet chicks who like hanging around, making the scene, and doing stuff. Some S & N. No pigs. Box 30.

C. G. is a C. T. and I have the B. B. to prove it. H. V.

BUDDY HOLLY is alive! Play "Peggy Sue" backwards at 16⅔. Got any other clues? Send to Danny, Box 43.

Daisy chain, every Friday. Box 14.

CHARLEEN: Why did you drop out of school on Wednesday? Sue said you had asthma and Roger says you told him your aunt in Arizona died. I know you've been seeing other guys, but you're still the one and only for me. What gives? Love, Don.

It's in the chipped beef.

LEFT REAR SEAT open in my '53 Merc for next three Sats. Mooning and snickering, some downshifting. Dennis, Box 38.

GIRL, 16, looking for other girls to stand around with outside drugstores and walk up and down street from seven to ten on Saturday nights. Must know latest slashes. Waving and smoking O.K. Betty, Box 14.

I'm sitting in math class and my creepy boyfriend thinks I'm writing him a love letter, but I'm really writing this ad. I'll do anything you can do with four feet on the floor. Write Janet, Box 17. No fumps or funkydabs.

DIRTY WORDS to all the top songs: "Lipstick on My Collar," many more. Write Rob, Box 50.

DATE-LINE *continued*

hoping it *would* happen. Then, all of a sudden, Dreamboat's hot, frantic lips were pushing against mine, and before I knew it, it happened. One guy after the other. I was being gang-kissed. Wildsville. I was dizzy with excitement, and I could hear voices in the background saying, "Me next," "Me next." I knew it wouldn't be right to let one have it and not the others. They kept kissing me, and every so often somebody's tongue would squeeze through my lips and push up against my teeth. There's always some nerd has to spoil things, but I kept my teeth together. As far as my own mouth and tongue goes, I'm saving it for Mr. Right.

After it was all over, they all said I was a good sport about it and that they still respected me. Dreamboat, specially. He said I was the kind of girl he wanted to see more of. The rest of the team said the same thing while they started driving back. I knew they meant it because they even didn't want it to look bad for me to come home with a whole bunch of guys like that, so they dropped me off about three miles from my house. I got home all dreamy-eyed and thinking that now that I was gang-kissed, ordinary petting would be dragsville. I started wondering about what new things to do. Well, whatever they are, I know they'll come to me sooner or later . . . alligator. □

HOW TO BE
LOATHSOMELY
REPELLENT
TO WOMEN

**by John Doe as told to
Sean Crespo and James Pinkerton**

Are you being forced to engage in excessive amounts of exhaustive love making, many times against your will? Lord knows I've had this problem. Often I simply collapse, spent and aggravated, on veritable piles of recently sexed models. I can only assume you must battle similar annoyances, and my heart goes out to you and your over-thrusted loins.

Whatever your reasons, you took the time to seek out my book, *How to Be Loathsomely Repellent to Women*, and I applaud your savvy.

Sadly, however, there isn't any *one* trick to repulsing women; as with anything worth doing, making yourself completely and utterly undesirable involves a number of approaches, which I call the **6 B's**. (The B, you'll note, is the second letter of the alphabet; remember this, as it will come in handy for remembering the six B's.)

Let's begin.

TIP #1: Be Ugly

Some lucky people are genetically predisposed to having challenging, even radically unsettling features. For the rest of us, be it a shovel to the face or dangerous hobbies involving leaps from great heights, ugly features take effort—and a willingness to do irreversible structural harm to our bodies, emphasis on the face! So, if you've been cursed with high cheekbones, evenly spaced eyes, and at least most of your teeth (as opposed to one giant tooth or teeth with 3 feet roots facing outward), you've got some work cut out for you.

But don't despair—a quick trip to your neighborhood plastic surgeon might be all you need to get on the path to looking truly, violently loathsome. The budget-conscious among you, however, may simply wish to purchase the largest portion of vodka from the nearest bulk store, then seek out the steepest flight of steps in your area.

Let Nature take its course.

Now for those of you genetically gifted with an unsightly, vomit-inducing appearance, don't get *too* cocky. You still have to worry about the neck down. To ensure that your sexual appeal is completely non existent, be careful with your life choices, or what I like to call the **LC** (or Life Choices). Yes, that job down at the construction site might pay well—but isn't a sedentary desk job a more effective method for achieving that pale, doughy physique guaranteed to repel women? Remember: office settings combine the best of the worst in a man, with a gradual deadening of body *and* spirit. There's nothing more attractive than spiritual wholeness and toned muscles; avoid these at all costs. A simple cubicle and a chair to pour your daily widening ass into could be your best friends.

Think you're not at risk? Studies show even one brisk open-air walk on a lunch break can heighten your self-esteem and force you to lose the weight you'll need to be repulsive. The next time you get the urge to take a stroll, ask yourself: "Where is my mouth, and what can I be putting into it right now?"

TIP #2: Be Alone

"What could possibly repel a woman more than a man with no functioning social skills?" you ask. The answer, of course, is fat people. And yet many first-timers assume that showing off their poor social skills and awkward conversational gambits is their best bet for repulsing the opposite sex.

This is a common mistake. In reality, most women are so emotionally a shambles from past relationships that acts of rudeness, attempts to discuss comic books, or loud, beefy farts are actually more likely to turn them on. Back when I used to go to bars (before the endless requests for sexual encounters drove me away), I once punched a girl in the jaw. Two weeks after the arraignment we were married.

You will find that the best policy for becoming a below-average Joe is simple avoidance. Latch yourself onto science fiction or sports instead. Let their immersive worlds, endless statistics and respectively tarty costumes be your shield.

"But how do I avoid making contact with an entire gender, especially one that comprises over 60% of the world's population?" Good question. The answer lies in the **three N's**, although to be fair two of the three N's are spelled without N's: a **N**octurnal lifestyle, **G**od-like speed, and the **A**bility to use the shadows themselves as a medium for travel. If the three N's prove too difficult to master, consider dressing as a Tolkien character. It achieves a similar effect and involves taller hats.

Speaking of Tolkien fans, what better way to avoid the ladies than by making it official and becoming a hermit? That's right. It's as easy as never going outside ever again! Plus, after a good long stretch of hermitude, if you do happen to come upon a female by mistake (though how you could mess up *staying inside* is beyond me), the visible shivering due to her presence and your startled reactions each time she speaks will more than ensure she won't be bothering you again.

If you're *still* not sure how to be alone, here's an example of how a conversation between you and a woman should go:

WOMAN: **So, what did you do this weekend, anything fun?**

YOU: **(unable to answer because you are not there)**

WOMAN: **Who the hell was I even talking to?**

Now get out there and stay inside!

TIP #3: Be Poor

If a life of complete solitude or physical deformity isn't your cup of tea, the route of financial paucity should compensate you nicely. There's actually nothing to it but *nothing*, so it's remarkably easy to memorize the steps with the **three D's. D**on't work. **D**on't borrow. Above all, **D**on't trade anything to anyone (books, CDs, beaver pelts) in case you mistakenly wind up with an item of slightly higher value. I once traded some valuable family heirlooms for a single comic book. Unfortunately, that comic book turned out to be Issue #1 of *Superman*. I don't need to tell you who ended up on the profitable side of that transaction. (It was me.)

Nothing turns a girl on like success, so avoid it at all costs. Look for low-end jobs in administration and photocopier maintenance, and be sure to mention your lack of money during the rare times you do see women (see Tip #2). Always carry OXO cubes about your person if proof is required; I find pulling out two, then excusing myself to go to the bathroom so I can "mix up some supper" tends to work wonders for getting the right impression across.

If you do happen to be wealthy, try to get rid of it in one lump, instead of letting it drip away through a series of idiotic swampland-condo investments or other doomed ventures—because who knows, a Sound of the Quakers record label sounds bad, but this is America. People might get behind it.

Donations are a particularly efficient tool for the wealthy, and the more horrible the destination of your money, the more horrible you will appear to women. Contribute vast amounts to *American Association of Racial Purity* campaigns, or sculptors building mile high *Monument to Rape* statues. Stick to being poor and you should be fine. Unless you punch her, in which case you might wind up with a Tudor and a joint account.

TIP #4: Be Bruce Villanch

TIP #5: Be Wrong

There is no better way to become loathsome and repellent to the female gender than to be, in all manner and method, in all you say and do, utterly and completely wrong. If you are still having trouble getting women to hate you, well, brother, you're going about things all wrong— but not the *right kind of wrong*. The *wrong* wrong. Which is right and therefore wrong. Right? Wrong. Moving on.

The following are suggestions and examples of previous, successful wrongnesses on my part:

- **Gut haddock on her back/stomach during coitus.**
- **Smile broadly in the mornings, and when she asks why you're so happy, tell her, "I had that dream where you fall into a bottomless pit with broken glass floating around in it, and the further you got, the happier I got."**
- **Suggest intercourse in inappropriate places, like your mother's bedroom, the bathroom, or "up the ol' shitbox."**
- **Buy intensely uncute pets, like cobras and ferrets. Train them to go right for the fucking eyes at the slightest provocation.**

- **Learn the ends of all movies; pretend you only guessed the ending.**
- **Gamble her younger relatives away.**
- **Wear multiple necklaces of gold letters that spell out other women's names.**
- **While she sleeps, give her heated BIC pen tattoos of other women's names.**
- **Your genitals should be referred to as "the old filthy cock" at all times when mentioning them at dinner parties and social events, which should be often.**
- **Build up a resistance to certain mild poisons. Cover your skin in them.**
- **Always "slip" when going for a handshake with her female friends.**
- **Rally actively against women's suffrage.**
- **Surprise her by wearing blackface to important mixers.**
- **Adopt a child without telling her. Name the child "ashtray," then pull out seven cartons of cigarettes.**

TIP #6: Be Dead

You've tried everything. Being ugly, being alone, being poor, being Bruce Villanch, and being wrong in every conceivable way…yet still women plague your life.

Like an overweight marathon runner or equiphobic jockey, the sad truth is that you are simply not cut out for the task you have chosen. You are just **too damn appealing** to the graceful gender. I can sympathize, as I myself am awesome. But let me assure you, you will never achieve the necessary state of loathsomeness to remain untroubled by women the rest of your days.

We have now arrived at your last chance for freedom, and as Sartre pointed out, the only real choice you ever get to make: Should you kill yourself or not?

The answer is an overwhelming yes. With that settled, the only question remains how. As you don't want to give any women the chance to sneak into your bedroom and have sex with you before you get the chance to off yourself, I would advise doing it as quickly as possible.

Guns, knives, toasters and tubs, all of these things will do the job and do it pretty efficiently. Avoid drug overdosing, building jumps, and drownings. They all provide a small but statistically very real chance of being saved. A surprisingly resilient body or exceptionally favorable currents can be your worst enemy. You never know what might stop you from killing you.

And to ensure that women don't try to engage in post-mortem relations with your body, it's best to set a series of booby traps near your corpse. Sharpened sticks at the bottom of a camouflaged pit, maybe a bucket of venomous snakes left teetering on top of a door —heck, mummies. And if any of those you-hungry ladies should get past those traps, they're sure to get a mouthful of surprise when they realize too late you've covered your genitals with arsenic paste and SARS.

Well, that's about all. I hope this guide has been as informative as it was informative. Good luck and don't give up becoming loathsomely repellent to women. I didn't, and look at me now!

Posthumously Yours,
John Doe

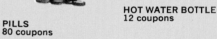

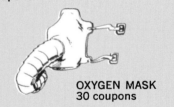

EXCUSE ME, AREN'T YOU THE LADY I JUST MET BEFORE?

YES!

YES!

YES!

YES!

YES!

WELL, WILL THE LADY WHO CAN WALK THE FURTHEST LIKE TO GO OUT WITH ME SATURDAY NIGHT?

ON SECOND THOUGHT...

WHAT WAS MY FIRST THOUGHT?

CHALK!

PEANUT OIL!

BIG HENS! SMALL HENS!

SO I WAITED FOR THAT FATEFUL EVENING. IT SEEMED SO STRANGE... WISHING, FOR ONCE, THAT THE HOURS WOULD HURRY BY...

I THINK IT'S THE MEN WHO WEAR TIES.

I THINK I'M THE MAN...

DID I THINK SOMETHING?

AS I WHEELED TO HER DOOR, I COULD ACTUALLY FEEL MYSELF BREATHING.

M-MUSTN'T B...BE NERVOM? NERVOSH? NERVOO? *NERVOUS?*

ROO 200

TAP TAP TAP

THEN, SUDDENLY, SHE WAS BEFORE ME, HER SKIN SO SOFT IT SEEMED TO DRIP LIKE A FULL COURSE I-V BOTTLE.

WHO'S HERE? IS SOMEONE HERE?

AS SHE ROLLED TOWARDS ME, MY VERY SOUL SEEMED TO GET CAUGHT UP IN THE WHIRLING MAELSTROM OF THOSE GLEAMING SPOKES.

FORGET THE MOTOROLA, BABY! YOU AND I ARE GOING TO DO THIS PLACE FROM TOP TO BOTTOM...

2

IT SEEMED SO NATURAL TO HAVE HER BESIDE ME IN THE ELEVATOR AND, AS COUPLES FALLING IN LOVE DO, WE PASSED THE TRIP IN SMALL TALK.

PRESS THE BUTTON.

WHAT?

COALS!

TRY FOUR.

STARCH!

TRY SIX.

LEMONS!

TRY... DID I SAY SOMETHING?

WHEN WE GOT THERE, WE DISCOVERED THAT A YELLOW MOON HAD BEEN PASTED ON THE CEILING BY OUR LOCAL CHAPTER OF THE "SENIOR SCOUTS." BENEATH IT, HER AGE SPOTS SEEMED TO GLOW LIKE SEQUINS.

WHY DON'T WE START OFF WITH A COUPLE OF QUICK OXYGENS?

WHAT?

I GUESS WHEN YOU REALIZE YOU'RE IN LOVE, THE FIRST THING YOU WANT TO DO IS SHOUT SWEET NOTHINGS INTO EACH OTHER'S AMPLIFIERS. THEN YOU SUDDENLY RUSH TOWARDS EACH OTHER.

AAH... YOUR HANDREST FEELS SO GOOD IN MY ARMS.

SNAKES.

DANCE AT YOUR OWN RISK!

CLINK

IF YOU LOVE ME AS MUCH AS I LOVE YOU, SAY "WHAT."

WHAT?

YOU... YOU'VE MADE ME THE LEAST UNHAPPY MAN IN THE HOME!

FROM THAT MOMENT ON, WE WERE INSEPARABLE! EVEN NOW, THE MEMORY OF THE DAYS THAT FOLLOWED IS VIVIDLY ETCHED IN MY MIND LIKE THE FOOTPRINTS OF A HOUSE-FLY ON STEEL.

WHAT?

WHAT?

I LOVE YOU.

DID I SAY SOMETHING?

WHAT?

WHAT?

X-RAY

WE UNDERATE TOGETHER, WE TOOK THE WRONG MEDICINE TO-GETHER, EVEN DROPPED IN FOR A MATCHING SET OF HIS-AND-HER X-RAYS!

3

AND ALTHOUGH I KNEW SHE HAD BEEN A WELL-BRED AND RESPECTABLE WOMAN, I WAS STILL A MAN... A MAN DRIVEN BY A RAGING DRIZZLE OF DESIRE.

MARGARET, I WAS WONDERING... TONIGHT, DO YOU SUPPOSE MAYBE WE COULD...

REALLY, OSCAR.

YOU RASCAL, YOU! YOU WANT TO THINK ABOUT KISSING AGAIN.

NO, MARYBELLE, I WAS HOPING WE MIGHT THINK ABOUT SOME-THING FURTHER!

NO, FRANK, I CAN'T LET MYSELF... AT LEAST, NOT UNTIL AFTER WE'RE... ASHTRAYS!

THAT NIGHT I COULDN'T FALL ASLEEP. I WAS UP TILL NINE-THIRTY, PRAYING THAT THE NEXT DAY I MIGHT WORK UP THE COURAGE TO POP THE FATEFUL QUESTION.

QUESTION... QUESTION... I'M GOING TO ASK THE QUESTION... I KNEW IT A SECOND AGO...

AND AFTER THE SUN HAD RISEN AND DRAPED ITS GOLD CURTAIN BEHIND THE SECURITY BARS ON THE WINDOW...

AUDREY... I... I LOVE YOU! WILL YOU... WILL YOU... WILL YOU... MARRY ME?

ALL RIGHT, I'LL TAKE THAT CHICKEN!

OH, MY DARLING! I'LL HAVE THEM CALL THE CHAPLAIN AND WE'LL BE MARRIED TOMORROW!

ONCE AGAIN, I COULDN'T FALL ASLEEP. MY MIND KEPT TRY-ING TO CONCENTRATE ON THE NEXT DAY WHEN MY HAPPINESS WOULD AT LAST BE ASSURED! I TRIED COUNTING SHEEP.

AND THE NEXT DAY, AFTER I SWALLOWED SOFT, I FINALLY WORKED UP THE COURAGE TO ASK HER TO MARRY ME!

PLEASE, DARLING.

ALL RIGHT, I'LL...

WE'LL BE MARRIED IN THE CHAPEL TOMORROW.

THAT NIGHT I WAS TOO EXCITED TO SLEEP MORE THAN FOURTEEN HOURS. THEN I ROLLED RIGHT OVER TO HER ROOM AND BLURTED OUT THE QUESTION.

...TRAINS, FISH... WILL YOU BE MY WIFE?

ALL RIGHT I'LL...

I'LL ASK THE NURSE TO CALL THE CHAPLAIN TO COME TOMORROW...

EAGERLY I WAITED FOR THE NEXT DAY! THEN FINALLY... WHEN I MET HER IN THE DINING ROOM...

W....WILL... WILL YOU...

OOPS! I DROPPED MY TEETH IN THE SOUP!

THE END

Pornog-raphy
for the
Dumb

by Norman Rubington

Someone you know, someone near and dear to you, may be a mute. You may be a mute yourself.

But what the hay. We're all equal under the belt. There's nothing wrong with the average dummy when it comes to the old in-out.

Here, translated into sign language from the obscene works of the notorious Akbar del Piombo, is a sample of salaciousness for the speechless. What is the sound of one hand reading?

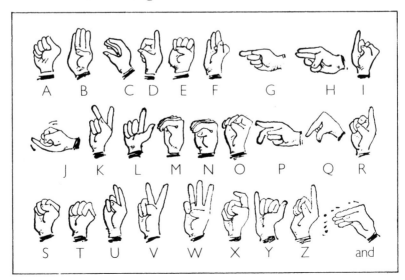

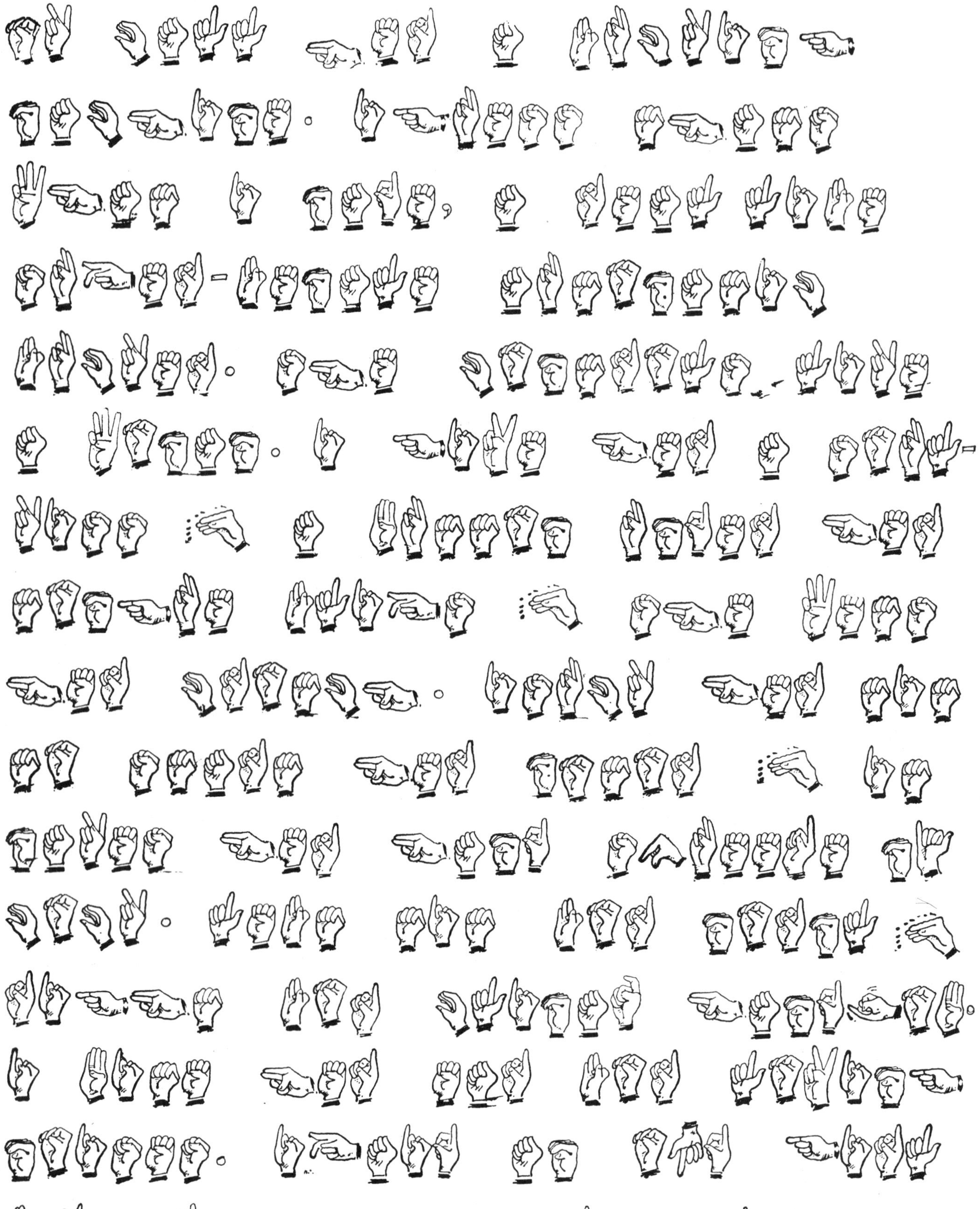

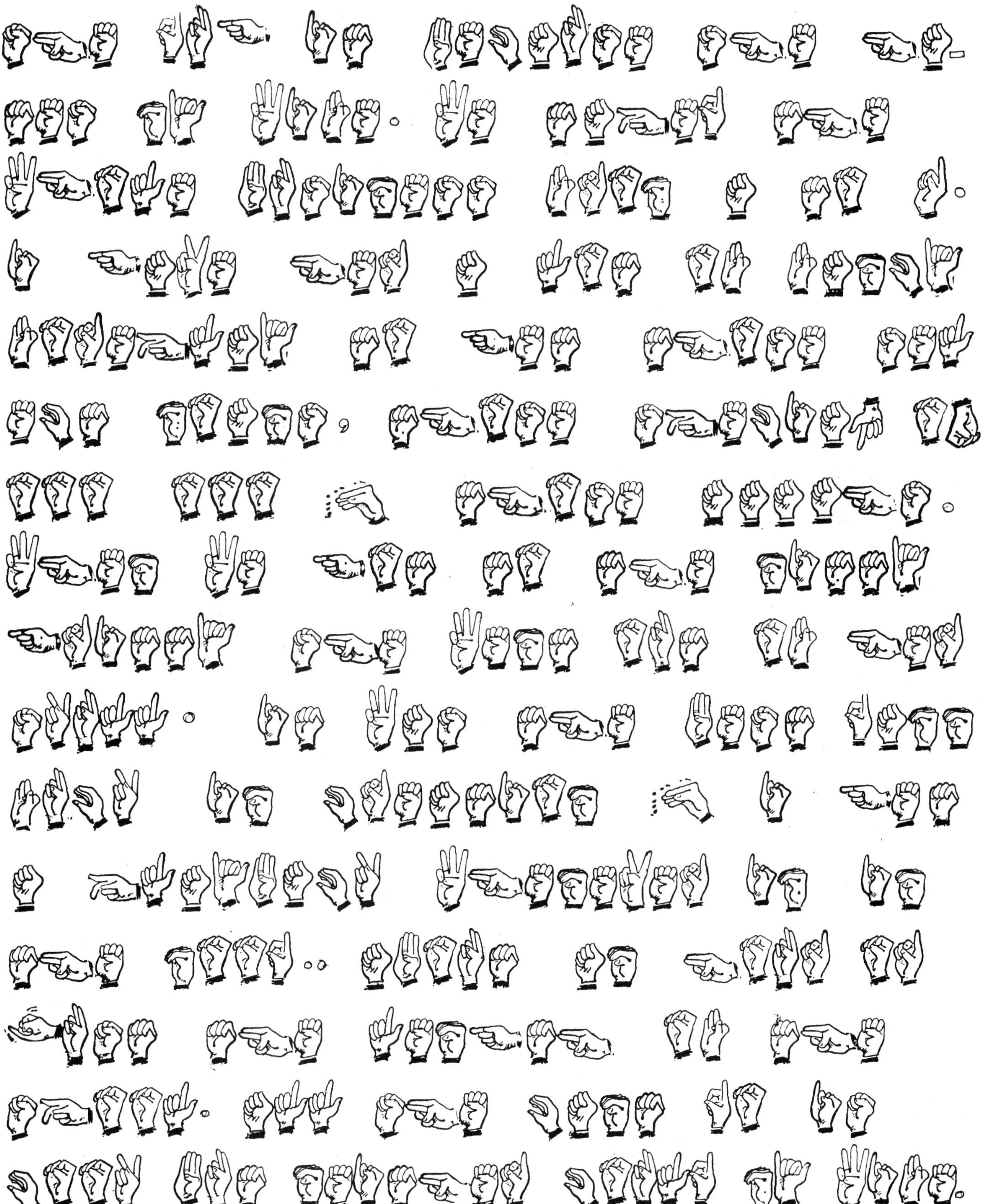

© RUBINGTON 1975

Mother's Little Helper

a self-abuse pamphlet
by Anne Beatts

In the absence of a popular feminist literature of stroke books for women, it is hoped that the following will help to fill the gap. . . .

Coitus Interruptus

When I first came to dour, gloomy Ravenscroft/Fisherman's Cove/St. Michael's Hospital, I never suspected that the dark, twisted younger son of the Earl/cod fisherman/but brilliant brain surgeon would come to exercise such a strange fascination over me.

Even after that morning in the deserted cupola/cove/surgical dispensary, where I had gone on the pretext of looking for my embroidery/some seashells/a bedpan, when he found me in tears and put his arms around me to comfort me, I thought his interest merely feigned, a polite gesture that was part of his natural aristocracy/New England courtesy/bedside manner.

How could he, who could have any noble lady/local girl/nurse he wanted, take an interest in a mousey governess/tourist/junior probationer?

But now, as he reached out for me, I began to realize that his cold, proud exterior concealed a warm, beating heart. Yes, I reflected as he crushed me against his ruffled shirtfront/oilskins/starched white tunic, even years of shutting himself away from everything except his hawks and hounds/codfish/patients hadn't closed his heart to me. The warning Old Melissa/Mrs. Abernathy/Matron had given me was wrong. He could feel, he could love. And it was I whom he loved.

"Cathy, Cathy," he repeated, his voice choked with emotion, his hands

wandering over my body, his face pressed against my hair. "Will you, my darling, will you?"

Just then the door of the cupola/fisherman's shack/surgical dispensary flew open. A voice thundered/drawled/barked, "Leave Ravenscroft forever!"/"Isn't it time for summer people to be goin'?"/"Report to Matron at once!"

Hot tears of shame sprang to my eyes. But as I tore myself away from his arms, I could not keep from saying his name: "Dirk, oh, Dirk!"

—after all lady novelists with three names

Sodomy

Now we come (catch the clever double entendre?) to something really naughty and, some people think, just a teensy bit wicked. Yes, girls, you know what I mean. The "back door." Now, before you wrinkle up your pretty little noses, just give it a chance to sink in. Lots of really famous people are all in favor of this one . . . Jean Gênet **and** Norman Mailer, for instance. And we all know how **significant** they are.

After all, fainting and pretending to be such a delicate plant was for your **grandmother**, not for a big girl like you. Shame on you for being so squeamish! We're not actually that sensitive in that area, if the truth be told. You probably won't find it at all unpleasant (provided you remember to wash thoroughly before and afterward with a strong carbolic soap—Caswell-Massey makes a divine one). Make sure **he** washes too, because disease can be a no-no! And don't let him touch you anywhere else while It's going on.

Then, you can just lie there and **enjoy** it! UHMMMMMMM!

—after Joan Garrity
(*The Sensuous Woman*)

Autoeroticism

CHILDREN UNDER SIX NOT ALLOWED ON TEETER-TOTTER UNLESS AN ADULT IS PRESENT

Rape

He advanced toward her, the fluorescent light glinting off his open switchblade.

"Whatsa matter, dontcha wanna be nice to me, Teach?"

As his body came closer, she could hear her own heartbeats. She drew in her breath to scream but could only whisper, "No, no . . ."

—after Bel (*"Up the Down Staircase"*) Kaufmann

He advanced toward her, the sunlight glinting off the barrel of his pistol.

"Wal, a purty lady like you ain't ascairt of a Union sojer, is you, ma'am?"

As his body came closer, she could hear her own heartbeats. She drew in her breath to scream but could only whisper, "No, no . . ."

—after Margaret Mitchell

He advanced toward her, the firelight glinting off the blade of his rapier.

"'Sblood! Is't that milady wilt spurn her noble suitor?"

As his body came closer, she could hear her own heartbeats. She drew in her breath to scream but could only whisper, "No, no . . ."

—after the Baroness d'Orczy

He advanced toward her, the moonlight glinting off his neck plugs.

"Va na ga va va gagagaga?"

As his body came closer, she could hear her own heartbeats. She drew in her breath to scream but could only whisper, "No, no . . ."

—after Mary Shelley

Bestiality

Ellen shifted position slightly and looked down at his sleeping form. His beloved head, with its rough luxuriant mane, was pillowed on her lap. The dark eyes were closed now, but she could feel the warmth of his breath. Even in the half-light, she could see his strong, beautiful body, capable of carrying her whole weight with ease. As he slept, his powerful shoulder muscles rippled under the skin, which was dewy with a faint film of sweat.

Suddenly, she felt him stirring. He raised his head, nuzzled her cheek, and whinnied.

"Oh, Gramps, it's all right! Blaze is going to be all right," Ellen said.

—after Anna Sewell
(*Black Beauty*)

Sublimation

Bonwit Teller
Dear Bonwit Credit Account Customer:

Thank you for paying your account so promptly. We have extended your credit to ~~UNLIMITED CREDIT~~

We hope you enjoy shopping at Bonwit's.

Sadism

Inasmuch as it would become necessary and, indeed, imperative to rid ourselves of the restrictive authority of the male, the goal of revolution would be to halt the functional obsolescence of masculine dogma by the reversal of its subjective tenets, formerly perceived by both sexes as moral obligations, or "commandments." Take as a case in point the injunction to refrain from the elimination by violent means of others of our species: It is at best of dubious authorship, and even if we give credence to the supposition that it was handed down from a higher authority, it is readily apparent that Moses himself, motivated by what even Freud had to admit was totemic fear of the all-powerful Father, was in

Marxist terminology enslaved by an economically exploitative relationship (easily threatened by the withdrawal of manna) and thus merely a self-appointed lackey of the supreme male chauvinist, Jehovah. Therefore, in order to achieve the actualization of a valid expression of that nature, which is felt to be feminine, it is evident that the first stage in the ongoing process of liberation in fact requires a corresponding invalidation and negation of all concepts and ethical systems that have been formulated by the repressive strictures of a male-dominated universe. Under this heading we may include logic, justice, truth, beauty, and the Pythagorean Theorem. And besides, women could pee standing up if they wanted to!!!

—after Kate Millett

Heterosexuality

The silken curtains surrounding the bed fell away at a touch, and she was revealed to his gaze, her pink and white bosom heaving slightly as she slept. Her feet were like tiny white doves in her little pink slippers. Her golden hair curled over her white shoulders. She looked so fresh and beautiful, it seemed as though she had just that moment closed her eyes. He bent to kiss her rose-leaf lips. On the instant, every bird in the palace garden began singing, and everyone in the palace woke up and went on with their tasks, exactly as if they had not been sleeping for the past hundred years.

—after *The Red Fairy Book*

Masochism

12:30	2	**THE SHINING HOUR** Brad comes out of his coma to find that Dot has left him.
	4	**TOMORROW IS ANOTHER DAY** Dot has a brain hemorrhage when she hears about Cindy and Brad.
	7	**ALL MY SORROWS** After finding out that Cindy has left him, Ronald has a serious accident on the way to meet Dot.
	9	**REACH FOR THE MOON** The only person with Ronald's blood type is his illegitimate son, who is also Brad's doctor.
	11	**TEMPEST IN A TEAPOT** Cindy tries to shield Ronald from finding out that his illegitimate son is a drug addict.
	47	**MADRE DE DIO** Nunca diga "Canadian" se non dice "Club."

—after all major networks

Group Sex

As she cruised down Park Avenue in the hazy winter twilight, Bitsy fell into a reverie about her past lovers. She had to admit . . . she'd been out with some real doozies.

There was Waldo, the pudgy do-it-yourselfer who wanted to build her a whole new box.

And Roberto, the sensitive South American amateur bullfighter who preferred her ears to her tail.

She thought with a special fondness of Binky, the crazy dentist from Hackensack who'd brought her home to eat his mother.

Yes, she'd done them all. You name it, she'd tried it. In spades. Chinks too. Christ, at least she hoped she wasn't prejudiced.

But none of them had given her what she was looking for. None of them had pressed that magic little button. Where was it, anyway? She knew it wasn't her navel. Filling that with cream cheese had done absolutely nothing for her.

Bitsy surreptitiously adjusted the Pursette that she wore instead of panties. But no, there was never a flicker . . . except for that time with the two albino hairdressers from the Hotel Great Northern and the trained slug. Maybe if she had thought to remove her Pursette . . .

But who knew? Who could say? Where would it all lead? When would she ever find the One . . . or Two?

She realized that if she didn't hurry she'd be late for her rendezvous with the zoo keeper and his twin brother. She crossed to the other side of the Avenue and began walking uptown.

—after Joyce Eberts
(*The Crazy Ladies*)

Incest
Lovely Lady, dressed in blue,
Teach me to be just like you.
If it's true that God is Three-in-One,
You bore your Father's only Son.

Lesbianism
yesterday was a bitter day and because outside was so cold and inappropriate I went over to freda's for some coffee and she didn't have any coffee so we had goat's milk ironic really because that time in westbeth with the trouble over the elevator and then together we both went to joan's where the doorbell isn't working just like old times I said thinking of mexico and brave joan who had been to the dentist's too and recalled the time the barman was so rude to her played with her white cat and I wondered was the cat male or female and she said neuter so I thought the day was too and with a sudden swoop of clairvoyance speak of the devil alice called disguised as a marine so we all met alice at the restaurant without any cigarettes because of the doorbell and the cat stayed at home feeling bitter no doubt but the cigaretteless restaurant had fat-cat cushions warm and friendly-feeling and joan said something really sweet so that made the day sweet too if you get what I mean so maybe it was bittersweet after all like the chocolate that alice gave me in the taxi and I went home with alice to have two very good orgasms, one bitter and one sweet.

—after Jill Johnston

Exhibitionism
Q. I am a tall Australian girl with all her own teeth and a weakness for British rock musicians. In my book I used several dirty words. Since then I find I am driven by an irresistible desire to appear on television and talk about sex. I have achieved international exposure and was featured in two sleazy sex-papers and on the cover of a major American news magazine. Recently I stated in a women's-magazine article that I prefer not to wear any panties. Is there any hope for me?

A. I see no reason why you, like any other woman, shouldn't find happiness and fulfillment through marriage —as long as you remember that you catch more flies with honey than with vinegar. (See the heading "Honey vs. Vinegar" in the chapter on a richer sex life through the use of food in my forthcoming book, *Every Woman Could If She Wanted To, But Why Bother When Mah-Jongg Is More Fun?*)
Next Month: "VD, the Disease You Get from Toilet Seats"
—after Dr. Rose N. Franzblau

Voyeurism
(*Consciousness I*)
Meanwhile, Steve's lovely wife, pert, lovely actress Jayne Meadows, sat dangling her toes over the edge of their kidney-shaped swimming pool, taking time out from romping with Randy, their full-grown English sheep dog, and tutoring the disadvantaged child of their Mexican gardener, to go over a part and whip up Steve's favorite dessert while we chatted.

Her sunny exterior betrayed no sign of the inner turmoil that must have raged within. Phrasing the question as delicately as I could, I asked her, "Jayne, there's been some nasty rumors going around this burg, and I'd like you to clear them up for our readers. For instance, why is it that you and Steve are forced to sleep in separate bedrooms?"

Jane laughed her full-throated throaty laugh. "Don't give it another thought, Rona," she said. "Steve and I are forced to sleep in separate bedrooms because I like the window open and Steve likes it closed."

COMING NEXT MONTH
The Lennon Sisters: "If Only We Were Black!" Sandy Duncan: "How My Operation Changed the Way I Look at Sex!" Liz to Jackie: "You Can't Have My Dick!"

Voyeurism
(*Consciousness II*)

Tooth Makers Help Convict Three-Time Sex Offender
PERTH, Australia (UPI)—The Honorable Justice Blackmer set an unusual precedent in allowing dental molds as admissible evidence in the case of George Osborne, accused of the brutal rape-murder of a 14-year-old girl.

Osborne, 31, a Melbourne resident, was picked up by police here on vagrancy charges. While undergoing some emergency dental repairs in custody, the prison doctor noted the similarity between Osborne's upper bite and the photographic record of toothmarks left on the dead girl's body by her assailant.

Osborne today was convicted of slaying Lucy Brigham, 14, of Perth, and was sentenced to life imprisonment. He is awaiting trial for two other similar sex crimes that have occurred in the Perth area during the past six months. It is not known whether tooth molds will be used by the Crown in the prosecution of the other two cases.

Voyeurism
(*Consciousness III*)
I had been sitting in the same chair in the Apple office on Wigmore Street for three days and nights. When he walked in I could hardly believe it. Was this thick, cloddish, unshaven boor in the dirty mohair sweater the guy that millions of teenage girls were creaming for? I guessed so.

I followed him out to his car and lay under it.

He came around the block again before I had finished brushing off the tire tracks. This time he stopped the car, opened the door, and grunted. I hopped in.

I tried to tell myself that I wasn't in love with him, that his grunts were too pretentious, but it was hopeless.

The bedroom of his elegant townhouse was covered in priceless Oriental rugs. The Oriental rugs were covered in dogshit from the puppy he brought home. I was supposed to clean up the shit, wash the kitchen floor, make the beds, pick up his clothes, fetch the paper, sit, beg, and roll over.

The pathetic lot of groupies who were always hanging about outside would stare at me enviously as I washed down the front steps on my hands and knees.

We went to visit a friend in the country. The lady of the house took me aside. "Be grateful for every second you spend with him," she said. I knew what she meant.

"I'm here to give you whatever will make you happy," I told him.

He only grunted.

He was drinking a lot by then. But there were the good times. We had our own special world, with special games and rituals, things only the two of us shared. For instance, every night when he came home from the recording studio, he always had the same pet greeting for me: "What's for supper?"

In bed he was perfectly adequate, as long as you didn't expect too much of him . . . as long as you didn't expect anything at all, in fact. But it didn't really matter that he was such a lousy lay. Being with him meant so much more to me than sexula gratification. It meant fame, prestige, and a big fat advance from Straight Arrow Books.

—after Francie Schwartz
(*Body Count*)

Fetishism

Pour 1 cup chilled heavy cream into chilled bowl and beat slowly with the whip until cream begins to foam. Gradually increase beating speed and continue until a) beater leaves light traces on surface of cream and b) a bit lifted and dropped will softly retain its shape. (In hot weather, it is best to beat over cracked ice.) Gently fold in 2 Tbs. sifted confectioner's sugar and 2 Tbs. kirsch. Turn into cheesecloth before refrigerating to ensure that the cream stays beaten. A fitting accompaniment for a *mousse au chocolat.* May also be served with Sacher-Masoch Torte.

—after Julia Child

Oral Sex

The tips of her persimmons had already begun to harden, and as she caught a glimpse of his round turnips and firm, fleshy scallion, she felt her honeydew go mushy. The next thing she knew, he was inserting a finger into her artichoke and forcing her to bury her nose in his cabbages. She nibbled daintily on his brussels sprouts and ran her fingers up and down his asparagus while he gobbled her tangerine. The intensity of his passion was turning her avocado to guacamole. Abandoning his lychees, she bit down hard on his rutabaga, causing him to emit a strangled cry of pleasure and upset the entire fruit and vegetable stand.

—after the *National Lampoon* □

Love
The Gathering™

Trading Card Game Starter Set

A World of Socializing without Leaving Home

written by Mason Brown, Sean Crespo
art by Keith R. Newton and Richard Carbajal

INTRODUCTION

You've just become part of *Love: The Gathering*, a universe of fantastic genders, powerful differences, and enormous loneliness…the world of *Love*. Start playing to see *if you can get some.*

OBJECT OF THE GAME

Love: The Gathering is won when either the **Male** or the **Female** player loses all of his or her **Dignity Points**. Players begin with 20 Dignity Points, but attacks from various Creatures and Relics will inflict **Humiliation** throughout the game. Be the last Male (or Female) standing.

KINDS OF CARDS

There are two decks — a Male and a Female deck. Each deck contains Vibe cards, Creature Cards, and Relic Cards.

VIBE CARDS

Your deck contains 7 Vibe Loci from which creatures draw their strength. These locations provide the "Vibes" which strengthen or weaken the attacks of different characters. For instance, to attack with a **Eurotrash Playboy**, the Male player would need to use 1 **Night Life** Vibe card, as well as 2 of any other kind. The 7 Vibe cards are: Work, Home, Recreation, Night Life, Vacation, The Internet, and Dark Alleys.

CREATURE CARDS (Male, Female)

All creature cards use the same basic layout:
A Male is a character with a penis who wants to sleep with Females.
A Female is a character without a penis who wants to acquire one.

RELIC CARDS

There are 3 kinds of Relic Cards — Possessions, Events and Artifacts.

A **Possession** is an object such as **Candy**, **Roses**, or **Lingerie** used to enhance your character's abilities or to block an opponent's attacks.

For example, the Male player may attack with a Jewelry Card. This card can inflict 2 Humiliation points, which can either reduce the Female player's Dignity Point total or completely vanquish a lesser creature, such as an **Hispanic Maid**.

An **Event** is a card representing an important occurrence. For example, the Female player may render a Jewelry Card worthless by countering with an **Appraisal**. However, sometimes Event cards themselves may be countered. For instance, Pregnancy is often a crushing blow to the Male player, that is unless he is able to counter it with a **Bumpy Ride in a Car with No Shocks Card**, a **Fall Down a Long Winding Staircase Card**, or an **Inconclusive DNA-Match Card**, at which point the Pregnancy is discarded and the Female is declared **Barren** for five turns and has to live with her sister.

An **Artifact** is a card representing special, powerful objects such as **Viagra**, **House Keys**, and copies of **Dianetics** that enhance a character defense or attack for one hand before going to the Graveyard pile. These cards are particularly rare, and only the less powerful ones, such as **Jell-O Shots** or **Tongue Stud**, will appear in starter decks.

PLAYING THE GAME

1. Scoping Phase
2. First Contact Phase
3. Conversation Phase
4. Skirmish Phase
5. Mating Phase
6. Escape Phase (Marriage phase if Escape Points are **Overwhelmed**)
7. Gossip Phase

ADVANCED RULES

Further *Love: The Gathering* game play rules can be found upon purchase of the Deluxe Set, available for $49.99. The Compleat rules can be purchased at Love Academy Stores, available for $149.99 at 5 convenient Nashua, NH locations. The Deluxe Compleat Advanced edition with automatic shuffler and faux-marble Graveyard is available only from Jim.

FAT CHICK

Creature

Offense: 1   Defense: 4
Vibe: 1 Nightlife

D, Blocks **all** food-based attacks.

"For a fat girl, you sure don't sweat much"
— anonymous admirer

1/4

EAGER HIGH SCHOOLER

Creature

Offense: 1   Defense: 1
Vibe: 1 Recreation

Sacrifice Eager High Schooler: Target
Creature gets -2/-0 until end of turn.

*"Women reach their sexual peak at 35. Men
reach it at 18. Yet they rarely peak together."*
— Cool Uncle

1/1

ICE PRINCESS

Creature

Offense: 3   Defense: 6
Vibe: 2 nightlife + 4 of any other kind

Impervious to all seduction. Can only be
defeated by the Rape card.

"That isn't Chateau Petrus!"

3/6

MOVIE PRODUCER

Creature

Offense: 6   Defense: 5
Vibe: 3 work and 3 other

First Strike. **Prenuptial Armor** allows
only 1/2 damage from Marriage Attack. If
attacked by **Underage Girl,** card must
move to France pile.

"What say we make a private movie?"

6/5

ANOREXIC GIRL

Creature

Offense: 2   Defense: 1
Vibe: 1 Recreation

Weightlessness grants Flying Ability.
Alcohol attacks are doubled.

*"The stomach is an enemy. The mouth a
traitor. The only thing you can trust is your
hunger."*

2/1

MID-LIFE ZOMBIE

Creature

Offense: 1   Defense: 1
Vibe: 1 Home

Powers double when paired with a
Regional Convention Card.

*"Do you have any Irish in you... Would
you like to? Okay, I'll be going now."*

1/1

SMALL-MARKET WEATHERMAN

Creature

Offense: 2   Defense: 1
Vibe: 1 Work

Provoke (Tapped Female cards retain **slap** ability).

*"Looks like I've got you hot and wet inside
with a 90% chance of insemination!"*
— Tornado Jones, meteorologist at KKAN,
the Winnetka Falls CBS affiliate

2/1

PHANTOM FAMILY

Creature

Offense: 0   Defense: 0
Vibe: 1 Home

Phantom Family comes into play with two
+1/+1 counters on it. When all counters
are gone, Phantom Family is considered
met and its power to beguile is removed.

*"I thought we were having Christmas at
your house this year."*

0/0

TRADING CARD GAMER

Creature

Offense: 0   Defense: .5
Vibe: 1 Internet T1 connection

*"So... I was wondering if, you know, maybe
you'd like to, I mean if you're not busy, uh,
me and some friends like this game, it's real
fun, uh, and I mean, if you'd like, maybe
you'd like to come by... sometime and, you
know, um, ...Did you see 'The Matrix'?"*

0/5

PASSABLE TRANNY

Creature

Offense: 7   Defense: 1
Vibe: 3 Dark Alleys

Can only be played in conjunction with a **judgment enchantment** such as **Favorable Lighting,** or **Beer Goggles.**

"OOOOOOOOH! GOD, NO! NO GOD, NO GOD, NO!!!"

™ & © 2003 National Lampoon

7/1

AOL TROLL

Creature

Offense: 2   Defense: 1
Vibe: 1 Internet

If played with 2 (Vacation Vibe Graphic), AOL Troll acquires Frequent Flier ability and will appear at your house. Add +3/+0.

"Dance like no one is watching. Sing like no one is listening. Eat like no one is paying."

™ & © 2003 National Lampoon

2/1

MONTHLY VISITOR

Event

Vibe: 2 Home + 2 other

Destroy any Male, Relic Card with impunity.

*"She's angry, red and heavy.
She's nature's blood floodgate.
She's the worst thing that could happen.
Just pray she isn't late."*

— *Irish Children's Rhyme*

™ & © 2003 National Lampoon

EMOTIONAL BAGGAGE

Possession

Vibe: 1 home + 2 others

Deals 2 damage against every creature in play.

"My feelings don't come with rollers!"
— *The Book of Harlequin*

™ & © 2003 National Lampoon

PERSONAL TRAINER

Possession

Vibe: 2 recreation + 2 others

+2/+1 to all creature cards. Remains in play until destroyed by a "Comfort Food" enchantment.

"Six-pack your bags! We're going to Ab-ville!"

™ & © 2003 National Lampoon

TROPICAL DRINK

Possession

Vibe: 1 Nightlife + 1 other

Subtract 1 from target creature's defenses. Used with **Lampshade Card,** charm increases, Double attack.

1 part pineapple juice, 1 part mango juice, 1 part rum equals 2 legs parted.

™ & © 2003 National Lampoon

COPIES MADE

Event

Vibe: 1 home + X others

Inflict X Humiliation upon release of home sex video.

"This isn't 'A Bug's Life'!!!"
— *Blockbuster customer*

™ & © 2003 National Lampoon

HOME

Vibe

™ & © 2003 National Lampoon

DARK ALLEY

Vibe

™ & © 2003 National Lampoon

AOL JOE'S GUIDE
to understanding online profiles
by Joe Oesterle and Mason Brown

Hey. AOL Joe here. Ever since the dawn of unlimited hours, I've been online searching for dates. And after comparing my real-life encounters with women to their online profiles, I've learned quite a few things about how to translate their descriptions of themselves. Here's a few tips:

- ➤ When a woman is "waiting for her Prince Charming," she's actually a monstrous connubial vampire hoping to suck out 2 month's salary from the next man she meets.
- ➤ A woman who will only admit to enjoying "long walks on the beach" in a completely anonymous profile has a zest for life rivaled only by Karen Ann Quinlan.
- ➤ The only person who really dances like no one is watching is Denise Pellegrini of Butler, N.J. and she has a good excuse—she works in a home for the blind.

Thinking about going online yourself? Use my guide to profiles to avoid common beginner mistakes. Or don't blame me if you find yourself at a "munch" in the Valley, talking to a woman with an Adam's apple so big you can bake a pie out of it. **Good luck!**

	> WHAT THE PROFILE SAYS	> AOL JOE'S TRANSLATION
MEMBER NAME	DaddysLilAnjul	Special Agent Hank Turnbull
LOCATION	Live with my parents, Duh!	Quantico, VA.
SEX	Female	Male
MARITAL STATUS	I'm still in high school. Duh!	Married to the same goddamned woman for the past 17 years.
OCCUPATION	I don't have an occupation. I'm only 14, du-uh!	Special Agent, Federal Bureau of Investigation
HOBBIES AND INTERESTS	Soccer, Cheerleading, Dressing up like Sailor Moon.	Softball, bowling, dressing up like Sailor Moon.
FAVORITE GADGETS	This 'puter my Daddy bought me.	Glock .40
PERSONAL QUOTE	"I'm your genie in a bottle;	"You have the right to remain silent…"

	> WHAT THE PROFILE SAYS	> AOL JOE'S TRANSLATION
MEMBER NAME	ZaftigGurl	Keep hands clear during feeding times
LOCATION	Could be close to you ;-)	Could be. I see a lot of fat girls everyday.
SEX	Female	Fat girl with cats
MARITAL STATUS	No one has been deemed worthy.	Are you the one? No one has ever been drunk enough to stay more than one evening.
OCCUPATION	Office Manager	Job title was secretary until she came in and bitched for a raise, which they didn't give her, hence the glorified title.
HOBBIES AND INTERESTS	Karaoke, quilting, cooking	Getting into sweats and eating comfort food while softly sighing about a cancer drama on Lifetime.
FAVORITE GADGETS	Are books considered gadgets? Tee-hee!	Knife and fork
PERSONAL QUOTE	"I can count my true friends on one hand."	"I am so terribly lonely."

	> WHAT THE PROFILE SAYS	> AOL JOE'S TRANSLATION
MEMBER NAME	CandleInMyAzz	This is a man who really loves candles up his ass.
LOCATION	Candlewood Arms Apartment complex	Okay. This guy really, really loves candles up his ass.
SEX	Male	Of course it's a guy. You ever try to stick a candle up a chick's ass. HINT: You don't try it twice.
MARITAL STATUS	Divorced	Ex-wife got sick of sticking candles in his ass.
OCCUPATION	[Left blank]	Editor-in-chief, National Lampoon
HOBBIES AND INTERESTS	Taking a candle and putting it in my ass.	Taking a candle and putting it in his ass.
FAVORITE GADGETS	A candle (in my ass)	A candle in his ass
PERSONAL QUOTE	"Boy do I love a candle in my ass."	He's not lying. This guy's a bonafide, ass-candle freak. God love him.

	> WHAT THE PROFILE SAYS	> AOL JOE'S TRANSLATION
MEMBER NAME	MyNaMeIsAmY. mY NicKnAmEs ArE: AmEs, AmYkiNs, PrInCeSs BuBbLeBuTt and AmEsTeR.	AnNoYiNgCuNt
LOCATION	CaLiForNiCaTiOn! WeSt SiDe, BaBy!	A hellish strip mall 2 hours from the coast.
SEX	FeMaLe @}-,---'-----	I hadn't guessed. Who else has that kind of time on their hands?
MARITAL STATUS	SoMeDaY, HoPeFuLlY	Please don't breed.
OCCUPATION	AzUsA CoMmUnIty CoLlEgE	4 credits short of working as a cashier.
HOBBIES AND INTERESTS	ChIlliN' LiKe A vIllAiN, KiCkIn' It, KeEpIn' It ReAl, BeIn' A StOnE cOlD fOx	Trying to steal other, more vibrant cultures.
FAVORITE GADGETS	My CeLlY	Just call it a phone, you bitch.
PERSONAL QUOTE	"SeX iS eViL. SeX iS sIn. SiNs ArE fOrGiVeN. So LeT's BeGiN!"	"I'm a virgin."

	> WHAT THE PROFILE SAYS	> AOL JOE'S TRANSLATION
MEMBER NAME	OneManWoman	She wants it. She wants it bad.
LOCATION	Home is where the heart is!	Have a seat... On my mouth!
SEX	Female	Yes, please! Grrrrrowr!
MARITAL STATUS	Please no IM's. I've already found my soul mate.	Apparently you've never met me. AOL Joe. ;)
OCCUPATION	Devoted wife to the greatest husband in the world and loving mother of two.	If it's discretion you want, don't worry, baby – AOL Joe can keep a secret.
HOBBIES AND INTERESTS	Doting on my husband. Watching him coach the kids' soccer.	Loving my family with all my heart. Blah, blah, blah.
FAVORITE GADGETS	I don't need gadgets. I have a family. <Contented sigh>	AOL Joe doesn't need gadgets either. Nothing beats flesh on flesh. <Extremely contented sigh>
PERSONAL QUOTE	"A healthy family is a sacred territory" No gross cyber-sex IM's please.	AOL Joe, this means you. Any more and I will report you to TOS. "Stop playing coy with me. I know where you live. I was at soccer practice. The little one looks just like you."

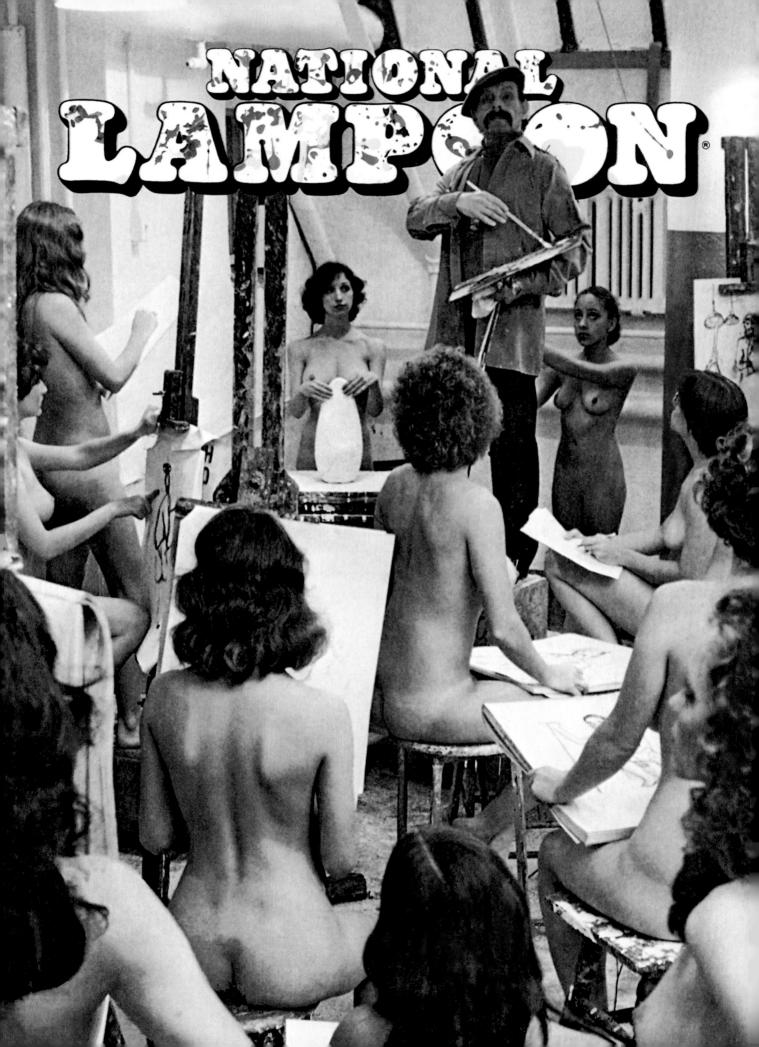

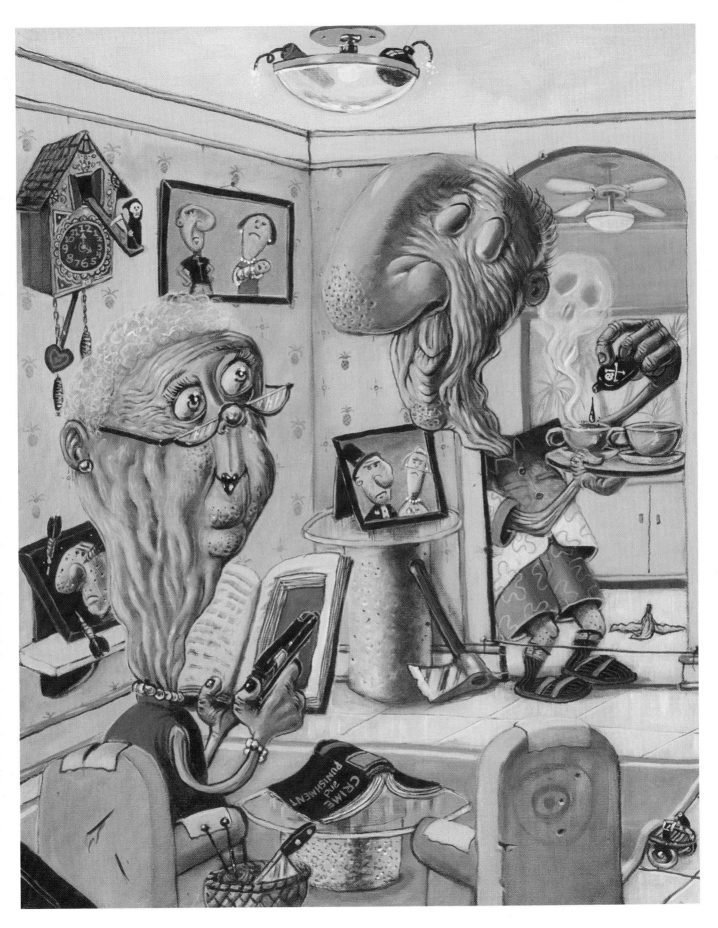

LOOK OF LOVE

This Magic Moment

Gary Dennis Stickles Cheryl Margaret Hendershot

"The Shutterbud" Wedding Photography by BUD WILCOX

This Magic Moment

"Sweeter than wine, Softer than a summer night."

Cheryl Margaret Hendershot

and

Gary Dennis Stickles

were solemnly joined in holy wedlock

on August 2nd 19 79

We Tell the World

And Send Forth Invitations

Cheryl Henderslott, Airman, to Walk Down Aisle

Mr. and Mrs. Willis T. Hendershot of 461 Landon Lane, Emporia, have joyfully disclosed the betrothment of their eldest daughter, Cheryl Margaret, to Airman Spec. 4 Gary Dennis Stickles of Mound City and the Chanute Air Force Installation, Chanute, Kansas.

The bride-to-be is a 1979 graduate of the Dwight D. Eisenhower High School, where she was Downtown Emporia Ad Captain for *The General*, which is the DDE yearbook. Her father is a deputy stamp officer with the Federal Bureau of Alcohol, Tobacco, and Firearms, Emporia Field Office, and her mother is a homemaker.

Airman Stickles was graduated in 1977 from the Fourth Consolidated School District High School of Mound City, following which he enlisted in the United States Air Force, rising rapidly to his current rank of Spec. 4 in Food Delivery Systems. Airman Stickles is the son of Mr. Horton Stickles, a weighmaster with the Kansas Department of Highways, the late Mrs. Alma Stickles, and his current stepmother, Mrs. Gloria Stickles, née Slitz, of Wichita.

The bride-to-be's sister, Marla, will serve as maid of honor, while Duane Tadlock of Milwaukee, Wisconsin, will stand up for the groom as best man.

US Graduates to Wed

Mr. and Mrs. Willis T. Hendershot
request the honour of your presence
at at the marrige of their daughter
Cheryl Margaret
to
Airman Spec. 4
Gary Dennis Stickles, USAF
on Thursday, the second day of August
at four o'clock p.m.
St. Barnabas on the Plaza
701 South McCormick
and afterward at
The Best Rest Motor Lodge
Republican Room
338 Great Plains Boulevard

Reply S.V.P.

Wrong address! We had to call up everyone the night before and never did get ahold of Pam or Uncle Jim!

The Proposal

Gary had just come back from his 6-weeks A.I.C. training in Texas when he came over to my apartment and asked me for a beer and when I opened the refrigerator there was a box sitting on top of the cans. To my surprise there was a diamond ring inside it with a note saying it was for me! It was really beautiful. We planned to go to Butler to celebrate, but Gary's alternator broke so I drove him back to the base barely in time.

Parties and Showers

SILVER PATTERN _Baronial Dubloon_

CRYSTAL PATTERN _Tradewinds of the Rockies_

CHINA PATTERN _Star Wars_

ONE-YEAR UNCONDITIONAL WARRANTY

Your LUNCHEON FORK

from the Baronial Doubloon collection by Aero-Craft is guaranteed

to perform without metallurgical or structural defect for a period of one year or as long as the utensil remains in the possession of the original purchaser, whichever comes first. Due to limitations of the forging process, and the nature of certain ferrous metal compounds, any and all spurs, pits, and minor variations in weight and color are considered usual within the terms of this warranty, and are therefore excluded from it. Use by owner of Baronial Doubloon utensils for purposes other than the consumption of food—e.g. jimmying doors when you're locked out of the house, scraping dried syrup off counter tops, and opening paint cans—shall automatically invalidate this warranty. It is advised that manufacturer's recommendations as to regular washing

To keep her bedroom
lovely,
And her burners
always hot.
I'm having a Budoir
and Butane shower
For Cheryl Hendershot!
July 16, 1979
4 o'clock at
Poly Lynn's.

IT'S A STEEL WOOL
SHOWER FOR
CHERYL
HENDERSHOT

July 22, 1979

Two p.m.

Michele Doyle's
House

R.S.V.P.

Shiny floors,
And cookware too,
Won't you bring
A pad or two.

Everything was so pretty and we even got a regulator from Charlene.

The highlight of Michele's shower she gave for me was the Kitchin Fishin game she thought up. I caught many a lovely gift and then Gary and his friends came by and we really had a party then.

The Wedding Day

10:38 a.m.	A Cup Cake	Bandage	"We've Only Just Begun"	I expected money
GOT UP	AND	SOMETHING NEW"	WEDDING MUSIC	BECAUSE
White Bathrobe	Gary	Still cloudy-97°	Bill Conti	The Government
PUT ON	THOUGHT ABOUT	WEATHER	BY	FROM
The Wigwam	11:45 a.m.	St. Barnabas	Epic/Reprise	they lost my forms
BOUGHT AT	STARTED TO GET READY	DROVE TO	ON	HOWEVER
$13.88	"Mocao" by Mrs. G	Marla	my eye medicine	white
FOR	PERFUME	WITH	COULDN'T FIND	COLOR OF MY DRESS
Low Clouds-85°	Breck (79)	her 76 Blue Cutlass	in my travel bag	The Wigwam
WEATHER	SHAMPOO	IN	IT WAS	BOUGHT AT
50%	Candees heels	Big parking lot	left with landlord	4:12 p.m.
HUMIDITY	PUT ON "SOMETHING BORROWED...	CHURCH HAD	WHICH I	SAID VOWS AT
Gary	Lipstick	A curved roof	my rent was late	A jet flew over
THOUGHT ABOUT	SOMETHING BLUE...	AND	BECAUSE	JUST AS
The Bathroom	Marla's Timex	air conditioning	I left it as security	A F-5, Gary says
WENT TO	SOMETHING OLD...	PLUS	SO	IT WAS
Ate some yogurt		Gary	It wasn't my fault	My dream apt.
THEN I		THOUGHT ABOUT	BUT	THOUGHT ABOUT

St. Barnabas on the Plaza   Rex Baumgartner, Pastor

First Church Lutheran Saints
"The Biggest Little Church in Kansas"

101 S. McCormick (1 blk. N. of V.A. Hospital)

Handwritten notes on card: Alternator $85 rebuilt · Coil $15 · Rocker arms $12 each · Blood test $25 · Me-frost (joint) $7 · Wax (Keira oral) $14.50 · Ring $38 plus loan · Oil @ 4.80/qt · Bratwurst #5?

Mom snapped this picture in the middle of the confusion just as I was trying to get ready. Dad loaned us their window air conditioner unit for the wedding night, but the freon was real low, so he had to work on it right up to the last second, but it still didn't work. Also, my dermatologist stitches got hair spray on them because the bandage was loose, so Marla had to change it while I was trying to do my eyes. I never thought I would make it, but I did!!!

AUGUST 2, 1979

Being in Love means....

...Not getting mad at the other person even if you have to turn on the TV channel with a pair of pliers when the knob is broken because you can't afford to replace it and it's real hot and you don't have any air conditioning.

Cohen's Golden Hanger
Formal Wear for Every Affair

DEPT. 022
CLASS 143
ITEM TUXEDO   SIZE MED
STYLE RIVERBOAT FLORENTINE
RATE $15.99/DAY

The Wedding

"The Shutterbud"

At first Gary thought it was the alternator again, but it was just a belt.

"The Shutterbud"

"With this ring I thee do wed" said the minister as Gary and I were both really nervous.

"The Shutterbud"

Oh, Gary!

"You are now pronounced man and wife."

"The Shutterbud"

Mom, dad, Reverend Baumgartner, Gary's step-mom and Gary's dad posed for a group picture in front of the church just before the ceremony.

The Reception

"The Shutterbud"

The food was out of this world!

Gary gets the traditional first piece.

"The Shutterbud"

And the music was heavenly— with a little help from Reverand Baumgartner!

"The Shutterbud"

We share a dance as man and wife.

Wedding Gifts

GIFT	MADE OR SOLD BY	FROM
"Swiss Miss" Multi-Fork Fondue Set	Yodel-master	Marla Hendershot
Money Order ($15.00)	7/11	Aunt Diane
Mix 'n' Match Fashion Extension Cord Set (Rainbow Pack)	Volt-Age	The Wright's
Cup and Saucer - "Star Wars" - Every-day China	Table-top Chinaware	Claudia Hendershot
"Margarine Blast" Nuclear Pop Corn Furnace	Micro-Beam	The Thatcher's
Baronial Doubloon Luncheon Fork	Aero-Craft	The Crowley's
Souvenir Bean-Bag Dinette Set	Sulfer Spring St. Park	Mom and Dad
Willie Nelson's "Best of..."	Columbia	Michelle Doyle
Grip 'n' Sip "Pride-o-the-pulp" Paper Cup Refills	M'Lady	Poly Lynn Sturgis
2 "Manager's Choice" Rubber-Belted Plainwall Radial Tires	Lifo Inventory-King	Mr. and Mrs. Stickles
"League of Beers" International Lazy Wheel	Not Sure	Duane Tadlock
"Steam-Glide" Ironing B... Cover	Scorch-King	The Brenner's
"Pro-Tune" Timi...	J.C. Whitney	The Squad
2 Rubber ...		
...air ...		
Grip ...		

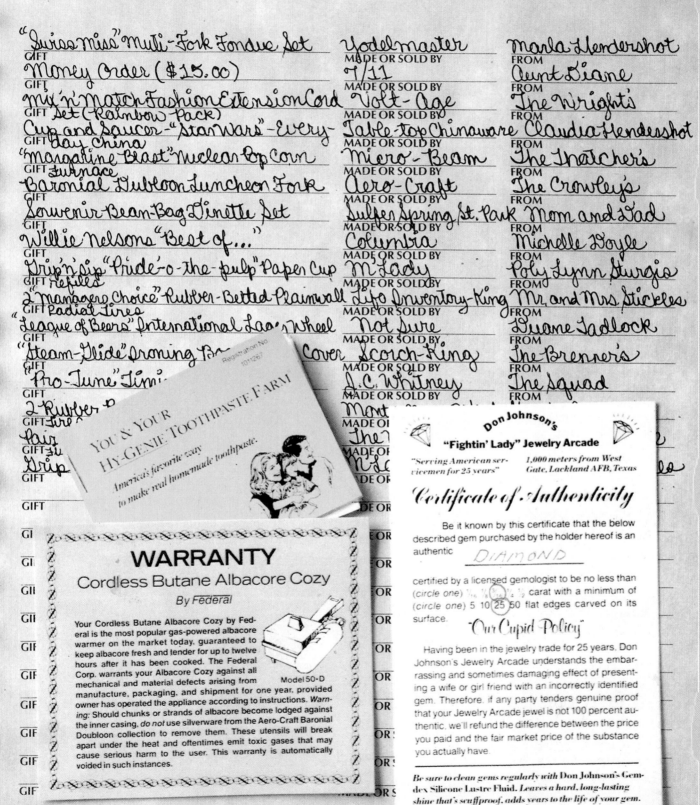

YOU & YOUR HY-GENIE TOOTHPASTE FARM

America's favorite way to make real homemade toothpaste.

WARRANTY

Cordless Butane Albacore Cozy

By *Federal*

Your Cordless Butane Albacore Cozy by Federal is the most popular gas-powered albacore warmer on the market today, guaranteed to keep albacore fresh and tender for up to twelve hours after it has been cooked. The Federal Corp. warrants your Albacore Cozy against all mechanical and material defects arising from manufacture, packaging, and shipment for one year, provided owner has operated the appliance according to instructions. *Warning:* Should chunks or strands of albacore become lodged against the inner casing, *do not* use silverware from the Aero-Craft Baronial Doubloon collection to remove them. These utensils will break apart under the heat and oftentimes emit toxic gases that may cause serious harm to the user. This warranty is automatically voided in such instances.

Model 50-D

Don Johnson's "Fightin' Lady" Jewelry Arcade

"Serving American servicemen for 25 years"   1,000 meters from West Gate, Lackland AFB, Texas

Certificate of Authenticity

Be it known by this certificate that the below described gem purchased by the holder hereof is an authentic   *DIAMOND*

certified by a licensed gemologist to be no less than (circle one) 1/16 1/8 1/4 1/2 carat with a minimum of (circle one) 5 10 25 50 flat edges carved on its surface.

"Our Cupid Policy"

Having been in the jewelry trade for 25 years, Don Johnson's Jewelry Arcade understands the embarrassing and sometimes damaging effect of presenting a wife or girl friend with an incorrectly identified gem. Therefore, if any party tenders genuine proof that your Jewelry Arcade jewel is not 100 percent authentic, we'll refund the difference between the price you paid and the fair market price of the substance you actually have.

Be sure to clean gems regularly with Don Johnson's Gemdex Silicone Lustre Fluid. Leaves a hard, long-lasting shine that's scuffproof, adds years to the life of your gem.

Registration No. 101167

The Honeymoon

This is Lagenheimer's Lodge of Love in the "bewitching Ozarks" where we were supposed to spend our honeymoon except that something happened with the Arabs and the oil again and by the time we got to Arkansaw there wasn't any gas, not _anywhere_. We were lucky, though, I guess because the little town that we ran out in called Russellville was where a Fair was going on with prize hogs (razorbacks they call them) and a little ferris wheel so we had something we could do until we got some gas again.

First Anniversary

We are in Kirikkale, Turkey now because Gary was transferred here, and Gary Michael will be 6 months in two days, however he has a hole in his heart and so we want to take him back to Wichita but the goverment keeps making us fill out new forms, probably because of all the money they had to spend on Gary when he hurt his back. Gary bought some Turkish donuts without holes for our anniversary, then we walked around the neighborhood and planned to visit Sgt. Burke whose also from Kansas and said he had a '73 Dart for sale. Our neighbor came by later and took a picture of us. We never made it to see the Dart.

by Commander Barkfeather

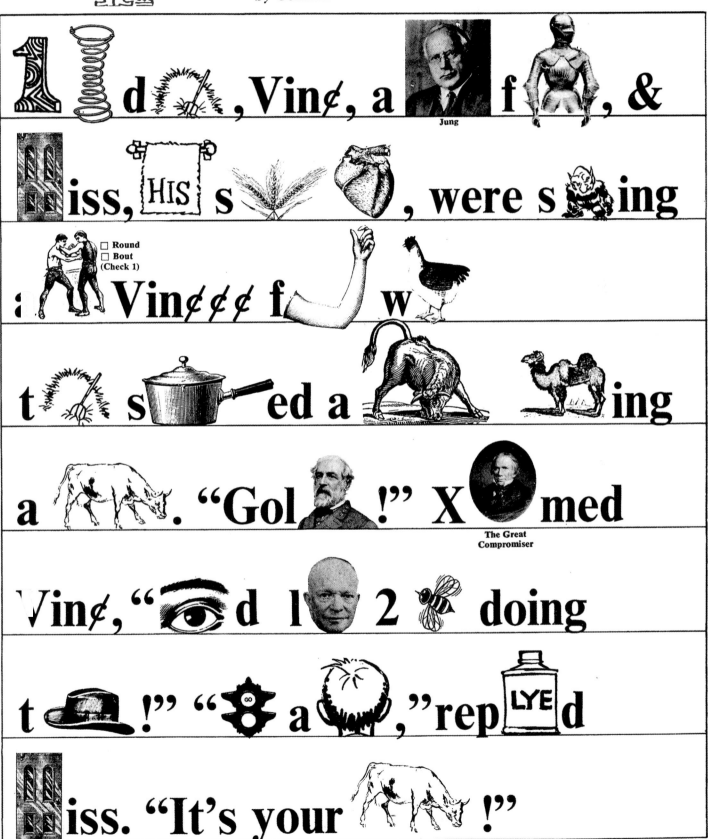

On her wedding 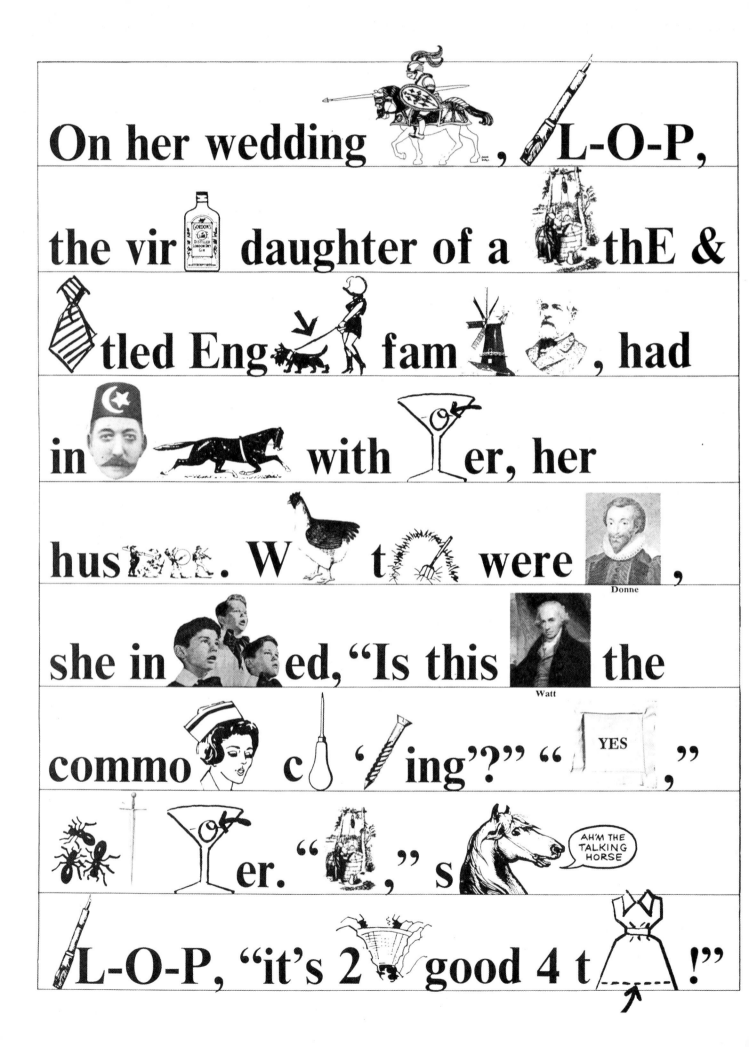, L-O-P,

the vir daughter of a thE &

tled Eng fam , had

in with er, her

hus . W t were ,

she in ed, "Is this the

commo c 'ing'?" " YES ,"

er. " ," s

L-O-P, "it's 2 good 4 t ！"

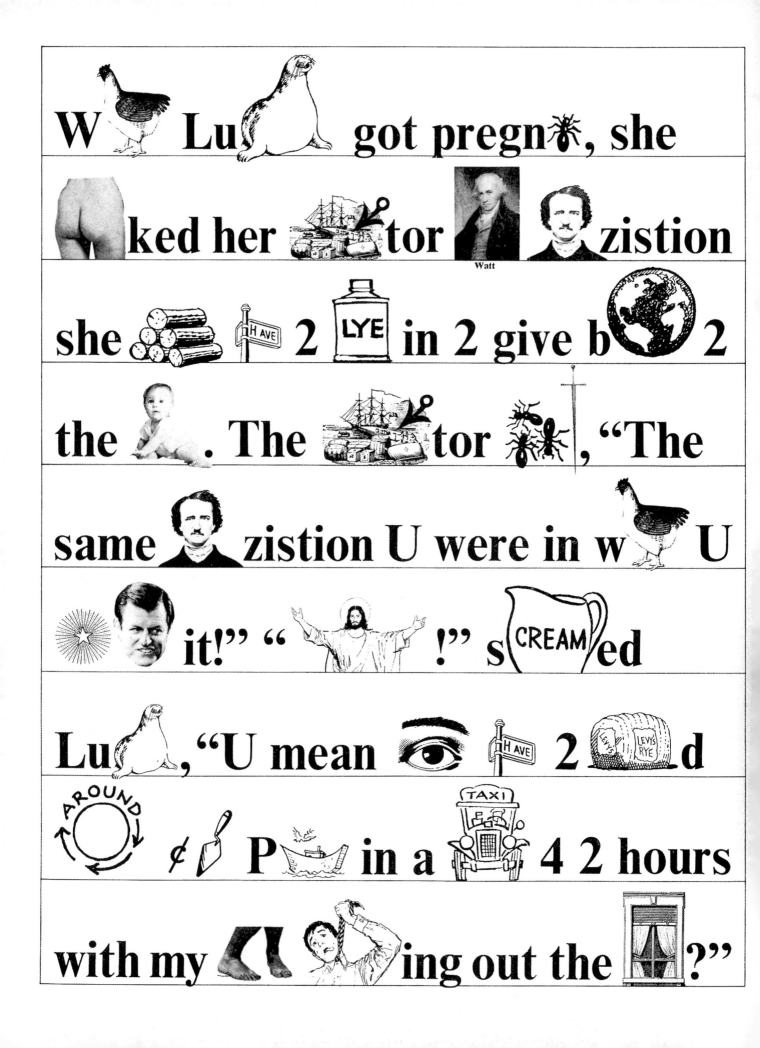

W Lu got pregn, she ked her tor zistion she 2 in 2 give b 2 the . The tor , "The same zistion U were in w U it!" " !" s ed Lu , "U mean 2 d ¢ P in a 4 2 hours with my ing out the ?"

ART OR PORNO?

A Photographer's Guide to Naked Ladies

Every year, thousands of fledgling shutterbugs want to break into the rewarding field of glamour photography. "And why not?" one might naïvely say, ". . . all you need is a camera, film, a room with a lock on it and some gullible broad, right?" *Wrong!* The rewarding field of glamour photography is not as easy as it looks! There is a vast difference between the delicate, evocative nude portraits by Wingate Paine and the grainy, unappetizing pastramis splashed throughout seamy skin mags like *Keyhole Pix* and *He-Man Sewage Monthly*. (continued)

BY GEOFFREY DE MANDEVILLE

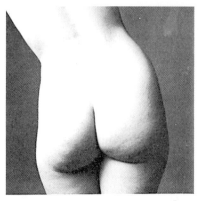

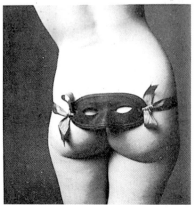

HISTORY

The art of nude photography has come a long way since that historic day in 1826 when Nicépoher Niépce trained his crude camera obscura upon some naked pigeons lolling about the quaint rooftops of Chalon-sur-Saône, France. But it was not until noted fashion photographer Richard Avedon's famous *au naturel* portrait of socialite Christina Paolozzi appeared in the glitzy pages of *Harper's Bazaar* in 1962 that fusty Victorian morality concerning the female form was finally overthrown. Despite the fact that *The N.Y. Social Register* dropped Miss Paolozzi from its listings like a live grenade, photographers everywhere finally declared open season on every undraped classy chassis in the world. Nude studies blossomed in dozens of "respectable" publications, and famous personalities, from Pablo Picasso to Hayley Mills, fought their way in front of every agreeable Nikon zoom.

THE TEN QUESTIONS

But what are the guidelines to follow through this wilderness of freedom curtailed only by certain stick-in-the-mud postal authorities? Well, first of all, every tyro should begin by asking himself these 10 questions:

1. Do I really have an abiding fascination with truly serious compositional studies of the female figure?
2. Am I sure I am not just out to cop a few cheap thrills and fast bucks?
3. Am I aware of the professional respect due female models?
4. Am I aware of the professional respect due female animal models?
5. Will I pay my animal models the same rates as my human models?
6. Do I know what the words *"ars gratia artis"* mean?
7. Do I know what the words, "You're under arrest," mean?
8. Do I keep my lenses clean and my f-stops to myself?
9. Would I let my mother see these photographs?
10. Would I let my mother pose for these photographs?

If you answer "no" to three or more of these questions, you are not qualified to take genuinely artistic photographs. (If you answer "no" to eight or more of these questions, you *are* qualified to make highly profitable *8mm motion pictures*, however, so don't despair.)

MODEL RELEASES

Passed that hurdle, eh? Good. Now you must consider the Model Release. The Model Release, as you may know, is a specially prepared form that gives you signed permission to publish the photographs you have just taken. In most cases, the standard release will put you in good stead, but should your shooting require . . . unusual demands of your model (say, the use of such props as lead-weighted whips, live seals or trapeze equipment), she may become skittish after the shooting and unnecessarily suspicious as to the exact wording of your release. In such rare cases, you should always carry some special forms in Gaelic, Esperanto or very fine print. Also, you would do well to look into the remarkable properties of disappearing ink.

BEAUTY IN MOTION: *Stroboscopic techniques can capture*

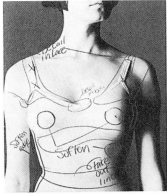

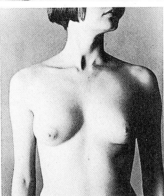

DON'T BE AFRAID TO RETOUCH: *Your model refuses to peel for $1.98 an hour? Just a dab or two of darkroom hi-jinx magically transforms this drab subject into a dramatic (and enjoyable) composition.*

MODELS

The proper choice of model cannot be stressed too much. To get the "right" picture involves a lot of preliminary preparation (or "horsing around," as the pros like to call it).

Make sure, above all, that you have completely informed your model *in detail* of what will be expected of her during the shooting. If she gets cold feet in the middle of an elaborate set shot, you can find yourself stuck with a good deal of half-used film and some very-expensive-to-rent trapeze equipment.

To insure full cooperation of your model, then, it is of the utmost importance that you *establish rapport with her.* This rapport can be established in a number of ways: soft music, chatty, getting-to-know-you small-talk, etc. Photographers of long experience, however, will usually rely on such tried-and-true ice-breakers as sodium pentothal or any number of animal tranquilizers.

and grace of a moving nude, but care must be taken that the model herself doesn't break the mood with any little awkwardnesses.

*Pamper Your Body...
with Flotzo's Bath
Balm*

CROP YOUR PICTURES ARTFULLY: *One of the most common photographic tricks is judicious cropping of excess detail from your composition. Notice how this glossy advertising photo on the left creates an entirely different mood from the original, cluttered composition on the right.*

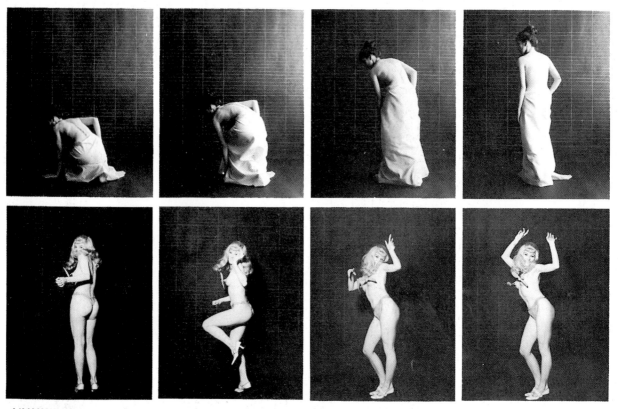

CHOOSE THE RIGHT MODEL: *The old motion-study series by Eadweard Muybridge (above) may have been all right in its time, but the stark, detached model lends a rather cold and sterile look to his pictures. A livelier, more animated subject can transform the same situation into a memorable portrait*

CAMERAS

Well, you've got your model, your Model Release — but aren't you forgetting something important? That's right, the camera! You may have spent hours preparing your setting and days finding just the right model, but what kind of pictures do you hope to take without that most important piece of equipment?

"What kind should I buy?" you may ask. For starters, don't be intimidated by those darkroom know-it-alls who tell you that you *must* have an expensive Hasselblad or Leica to capture your subject. *Not true!* While fancy 35mm units with supersonic shutter speeds and elaborate doodads can often come in handy, there's absolutely nothing wrong with less complicated varieties. Polaroid "Swingers," Kodak kiddee-kameras and various 98-cent Japanese miniatures can all produce prints of excellent clarity, and there are more than a few who staunchly swear by the quality pictures snapped with a homemade unit constructed from old shoe boxes and a salvaged binocular lens. Because of its relative simplicity, beginners are often better off with such units rather than the more complicated ones laden with sophisticated gimcracks like "lens openings" and "shutter speeds," gadgets guaranteed to baffle and confuse the novice.

A FINAL WORD

Lastly, here are a few Dos and Don'ts you would do well to remember as you embark on your first shooting.

DO refer to your subject matter as "art studies" or "figure composition."

DON'T call your finished work "pictures of naked ladies" or "hot stuff."

DO use such terminology as "bounced floods" and "stroboscopic timer."

DON'T use such expressions as "Chilly, isn't it? Heh heh," and "Watch the birdie! Heh heh."

DO discuss the use of framing in the early works of Stieglitz and Callahan.

DON'T discuss the use of hands and gutteral sounds in the early works of Russ Meyers and Guido Pombozzi.

THERE YOU HAVE IT

Well, there you have it! Now you're ready to load up and shoot on your own! It's only a matter of time before you'll hear opportunity knocking at your studio door and those long-awaited words of recognition: "Okay, buddy, *this is the police.*" □

DON'T BE AFRAID TO BE CANDID: *On the left is a rather typical and somewhat boring "set" shot. Pretty, but it lacks a certain something extra. You can get that extra* with the same model *by waiting for that fleeting, unguarded moment when model, situation and mood all seem to click just right.*

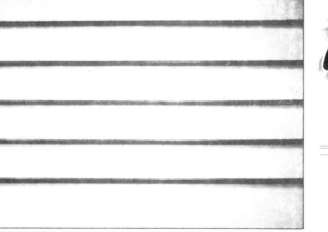

Try a Little Tenderloin

You are meat, I am meat,
We are all Grade A.
Touch me, fill me, grill me, fry me,
Broil me, boil me, shepherd's pie me.
The rest is gravy.

More Meat by Tony Hendra and Ron Barrett

You are mine. . . .
We are together. . . .
I knead you.

You see a rich green meadow,
and you stop the car. You both
remove your clothes and begin
to run. Faster and faster the
breezes swirl between your
legs and lift your hair. Arching
through the air, your speed
accelerates and you find the
strength in this purity to go
even faster and you . . . yes . . .
YOU BEAT YOUR MEAT.

The contemplative afterglow
day when nothing need be said.
Your thoughts are together
and in peace. In silence your
reverie recalls the gristle on
the rind, the pork chips of
Trebbia, the chaos of head-
cheese. These things will we
become till all things are one.
Flanks for the memories

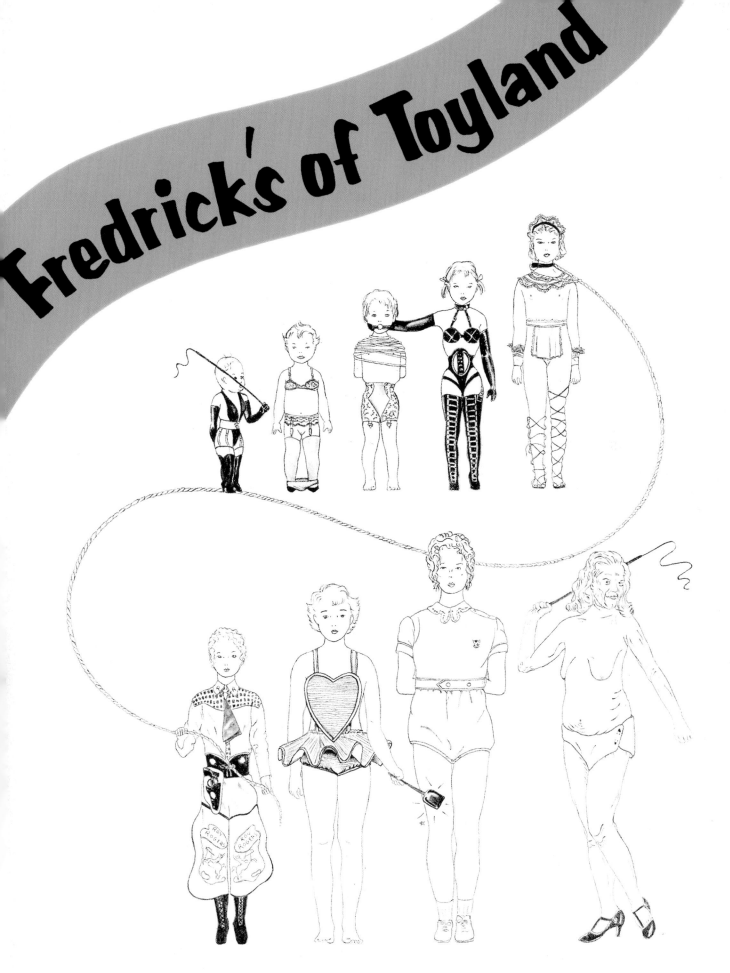

Fredrick's of Toyland

by Michael O'Donoghue and Mary Jenifer Mitchell
illustrated by Neke Carson

A #3-4113 LITTLE RED RIDING CROP

"Why, Grandma, what a big **** you have!" "And getting bigger every second, my dear!" But don't worry, because she'll tame the baddest wolf in these inviting vinyl togs that require no washing. Just wipe clean with a sponge. Five pieces include a sassy halter, crotchless corset, "spanking new" gloves, Betty Bedwetter Boots, and spurs like a kitten. Flail extra. Black or Rust.

$18
Flail $4.50

B #3-4061 LITTLE BO PEEK

Ooooooooo la la! To make frogs out of tadpoles, our designers capture the spirit of Paris, France, in an enticing ensemble that "bares looking into." What moppet wouldn't be utterly molestable in this clingy 100% Orlon acrylic *peignoir*? And when worn over a tiny bra, a tiny garter belt, tiny panties, tiny nylons, and tiny shoes, you have an eye-catching combo that makes short work of childhood's innocence. Available in Aqua, Lilac, Coral, or Hot Pink.

$16

C #3-4377 LITTLE MISS MUFF

Just sit back and enjoy the view when the "apple of your eye" dons this no-holds-barred, all-holes-bared creation from our Toys-'n'-Debasement collection, including a provocative cutaway Flirt Skirt and a daring lace-up Drop Top that unties in a jiffy, all styled from sturdy, machine-washable stretch satin. And Dad, if you wish your son would prefer Fire to Treasure Island, don't pass on this one! In Slinky Black with matching Purple gloves and lining.

$18

D #4-2294 CRIB BAIT

Calling all cradle robbers! When it's just you and your baby, slip some Layette Lingerie on her, and before your eyes she's magically transformed into a goddess full-blown from the brow of Seuss. Classically crafted from luscious lace and Dacron polyester, this comely costume features see-thru bikini Scant Pants and the Pixie Cup Bra, sizes 10 AAAAA to 18 AAAAAAAA. In Red, Orange, Black, or Nude.

$12

E #8-1829 GOODY TWO-BOOTS

With two gleaming thigh-high boots, a sensuous shaped-bodice leather top, and, "lash but not least," a durable plastic miniwhip, this toddler is dressed to beat the band . . . or baby sister . . . or even you. As the old nursery rhyme put it, "One, two, lick my shoe!" (non-toxic, of course). Black only.

$27

F #8-1717 BOTTOMS UP

"Make it brief!" was the byword when we fashioned this open-tip training bra that reveals all her endearing young charms. Then we left our pint-sized pinup "stripped for action" in only 3½-inch heeled pumps with stockings fastened to the skimpiest of elastic bands. The results? A "derrière-to-be-different" minor with morals just begging to be impaired. One size fits all. Assorted colors.

$9.50

G #8-1832 SINDERELLA

Time to change the baby? Begin by rubbering her the right way with a soft and supple zip-backed Rubbertex Romper Top, discretely padded with curvaceous Kodel Fiberfill. Then toss in a hint of midriff, a French maid's apron, sultry net stockings, a pair of black patent-leather shoes with shiny spiked heels and—*voila!*—your baby is changed into an alluring *enfant fatale*. No wonder so many parents are saying as we do: "Children should be obscene and not heard!"

$45

All our garments are certified flame-retardant by the American Council on Child Safety.

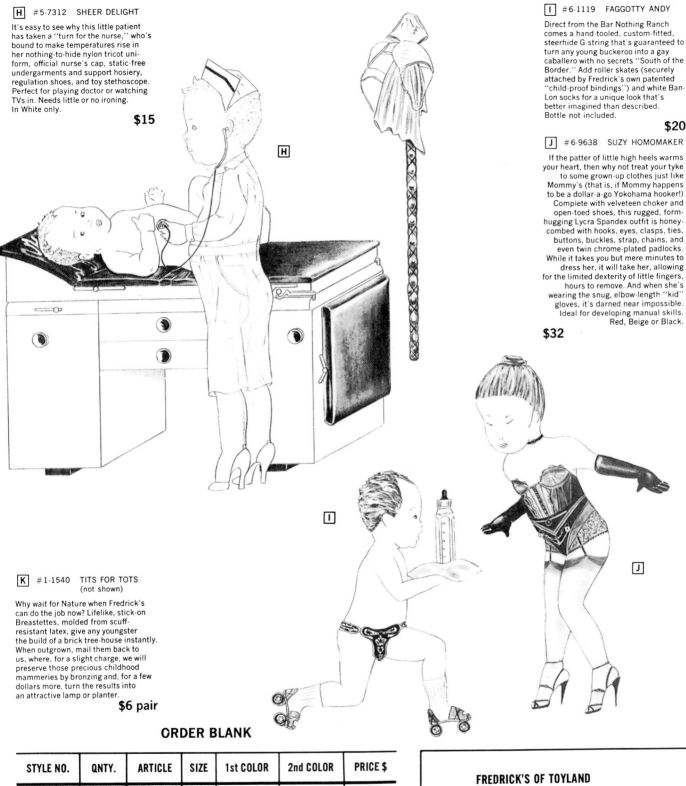

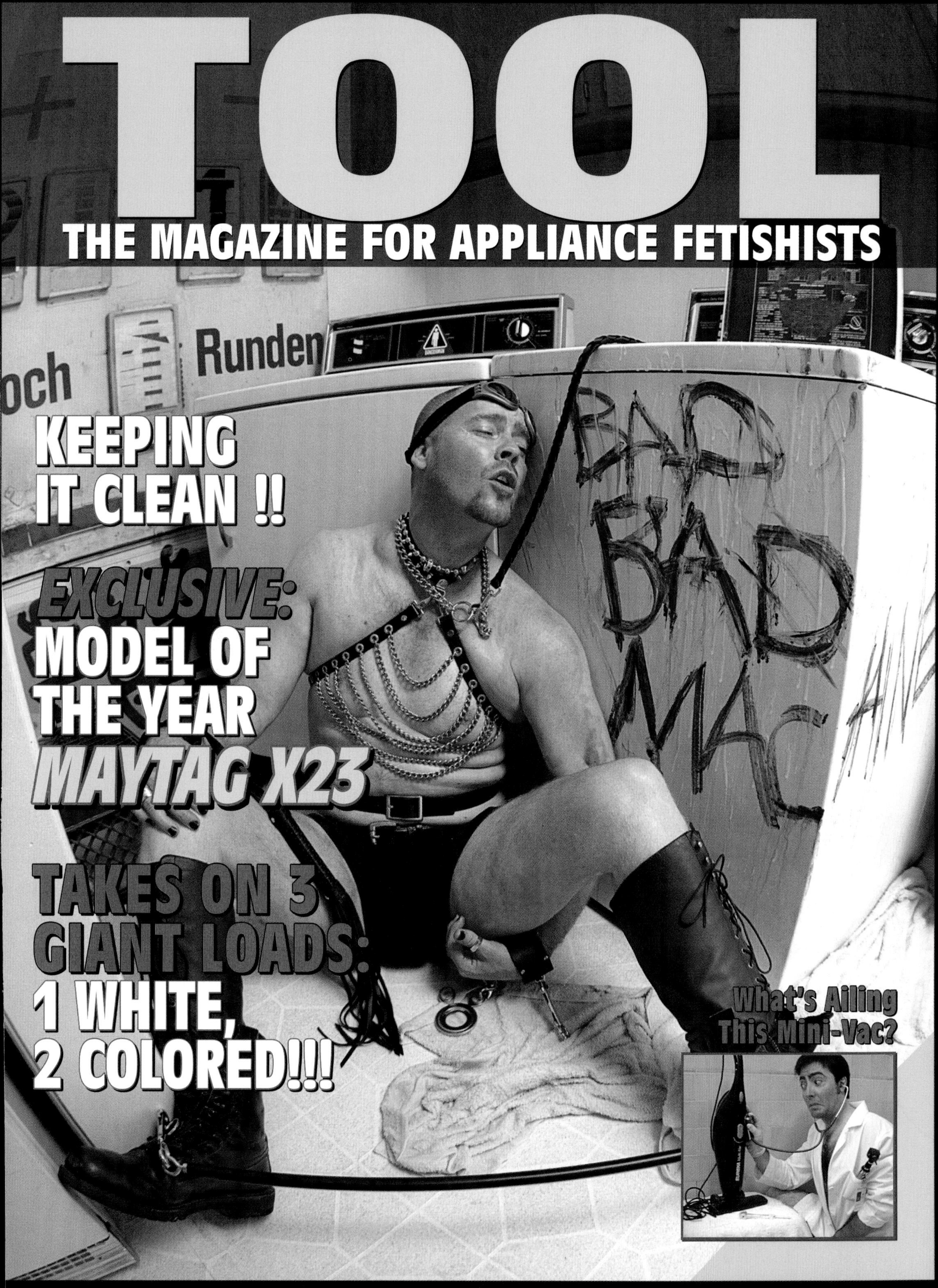

TOOL

THE MAGAZINE FOR APPLIANCE FETISHISTS

KEEPING IT CLEAN !!

EXCLUSIVE:
MODEL OF THE YEAR
MAYTAG X23

**TAKES ON 3 GIANT LOADS:
1 WHITE,
2 COLORED!!!**

What's Ailing This Mini-Vac?

by Steve Brykman

CONTENTS

8 Pictorials
Keeping It Clean—Machines that Suck!
Popular Mechanics—Find out Why They're So Popular!
Extreme Appliances—Food Processors & Exhaust Fans

23 Crafts
Martha Stewart Shows Just How Much You Can Do
with a Pair of Serving Tongs and Some AA Batteries!

42 Science Milestones
George Taylor—inventor of the Steam-Powered Vibrator

55 PlayMachine of the Month
Maytag's X23 Washer—can it possibly get out *these* Stains?

62 Forum
Rube Goldberg Devices—Are They
Really Worth the Trouble?

68 Travel
Coping with International Voltages—
without Losing Your Shorts!

72 Movies
The Camera Loves Meg Ryan—literally!

75 Technology
Q: Can Cell-Phone Abuse Lead to Genital Cancer?
A: Only If You're Doing It Right!

A Brief History of Appliance-Aided Masturbation:
Part XI: the '80s

Encouraged by the emergence of SoftSoap, in 1986, Americans nationwide learned the simple pleasure of a remote showerhead with six-foot hose. By varying the force of pulsation, it was discovered, the ever-increasing intensity of coitus could be approximated.

The introduction of the video cassette recorder (VCR) to the home market was a milestone in American Masturbational Practices as it afforded the user the ability to pause the action or to view the events frame by frame (even in reverse, should such a need arise).

Suddenly, our citizens were empowered. No longer need they sit endlessly in front of the television, waiting for that elusive Prince video or Yoga lesson. Onanism became interactive. And with a single week's investment, one could easily compile a masturbatory mix-tape of favorite hits.

FICTION
Hard Copy

The first time Jim fucked a photocopy machine was back in spring of '89. But perhaps *fucked* is too vulgar a word to adequately capture what transcribed between Jim and the photocopier. Perhaps it was more than just a *fuck*. Indeed, in Jim's mind, the two had had a trusting, mutually respectful relationship. Jim was always loyal to the machine, always attentive to its needs — allowing the copier to power down for an hour each day, as recommended by the quick-reference card. He even brought it flowers once, in a tall glass Bud bottle.

Jim was alone in the Kinko's that warm spring evening. The Sanyo M146 was chugging along tirelessly. Jim, on the other hand, was exhausted. It was three a.m. He leaned against the machine to check how many pages it had left to copy (250) and how many sheets of paper were left in the tray (about 30). His first instinct, of course, was to tear open a new ream and fill the tray.

But Jim's eyes shivered with sleepiness and before he knew it the vibrations of the copier against his crotch had given him an enormous erection. Jim stepped away from the machine. There hadn't been a customer in over four hours. He locked the entrance, dimmed the lights, and turned to Sanyo. The soft glow of the exterior flood lamps through the windows rounded the copier's hard edges and lent a rosy hue to its eggshell exterior. No doubt about it – for a copier, Sanyo was downright sexy. Jim strode past the more squarely masculine Canons and Ricohs, shutting the power down on each machine as he passed.

He caressed Sanyo's ventilation slits, then teasingly, but firmly, tugged on her paper tray. It gave way to his pull. Jim ripped open and fanned a ream of paper, the breeze ruffling his hair. He filled the tray, and solidly, but considerately, pushed the cassette into Sanyo's port.

continued on p. 57

BOOK REVIEW
2004 Gas Turbine Generator Maintenance Mechanic's Manual

If you love gas turbine generators, you'll really love the 2004 Gas Turbine Generator Maintenance Mechanic's Manual! Talk about steamy!!

Despite a slow open (safety & loss prevention, etc.), this book soon gets into the good stuff — gaskets, anchor shackles, and feeler gauge sets! Worth buying for its full-color turbine gallery & fold-out hydraulic wrench torque conversion charts alone! You've never seen wire rope sling ratings like *these*! One-nut studs, anyone?

> "The developer's creamy whiteness contrasts with the heady red of the penetrant, revealing a bounty of hidden crevices."

The Doctor is IN...

Part IV of our *Machines That Suck* Series

Ordinarily, this petite Japanese model loves it wet & dry. But when things go wrong, it's time to call in the doctor.

Are we worried? Not at all. We know she's in good hands. After all, he did graduate Summa Cum Naughty from Hooverd Med School!!

But hold on now...something something smells fishy about this doc. Call it a hunch, but something's telling us Dr. B's bedside manner is anything but professional. We can't put our fingers on what it is, but we suspect he's pushing the ol' Snake Oil!

Now sit back and relax as we get the dirt on Dr. B.!

Eureka Stick-Vac...................$39.95
suggested retail

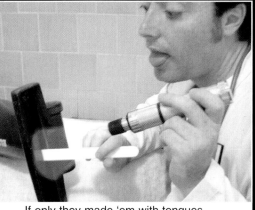
If only they made 'em with tongues

'Let's see how that ol' exhaust hole's doin.'

For once, fillin' the ol' dustbag doesn't mean your wife!

Goes places larger vacs can't reach!

ART INSTITUTE OF MONTECITO'S

SURVEY OF MODERN MASTERS, #12
"Love Is" - The Art of
Kimberly Grove Casali

Often decried as maudlin and kitsch, the art of Kim Casali (nee Grove) is seeing a resurgence among art historians as more and more of her work is brought to light.

Even among her harshest critics, her uniqueness remains unchallenged. "No one who sees a Casali ever confuses it with the work of an artist," stated Robert Hughes in what could almost be construed as a backhanded compliment if it weren't so obviously an insult. "It is blessedly her own."
—Professor's Mason Brown and Joe Oesterle

The Early Years

As a youngster in New Zealand, Kim Casali was driven by an insatiable compulsion to draw the world around her. Though her mature style would not arrive for many years, even in her earliest drawings, we can begin to make out the through-line that would give her entire life's work its unmistakable coherence.

Casali's "Food is..." series delved into the mysteries of physical sustenance, and soon placed her squarely in the top rank of New Zealand's art community. But after her "Lamb is..." series insinuated that beef was slightly tastier than sheep, the Kiwi community quickly cast her out.

food is...

ICE CREAM CONE

HAMBURGER

... *something to eat.*

America!!!

Rejected and humiliated by her homeland, Casali sought out America as a refuge. But while the Land of the Free did provide her with the artistic license she so desperately required, Casali quickly found herself perilously short of funds.

Forced by cruel circumstance into secretarial work, Casali found office life unbearable, escaping the banality of administrative tasks only through the soaring imagination that was her art.

Not unlike Gustave Courbet's "The Stone Breakers," Casali's art embraced a gritty social realism that forced the viewer into a confrontation with the brutal nature of modern employment.

the assistant to the head of human resources is...

... helping Mr. Johnson in his daily tasks.

Despair

Unfortunately, Casali's employer construed her efforts as "communist" and, in a misguided attempt to do his part for the American war effort in Vietnam, abruptly dismissed her. "The dominos stop here!" he raged as he sent her shamefaced out onto the street.

Betrayed and confused, Casali spiraled into the first of the deep depressions that would mar her later years. Her sense of identity fragmented, her art suffered a shocking parallel disintegration of identity. Note how the works from this period evince a change both in subject and predicate, a jarring disconnect that would never again be seen in her pictures.

gigantic robots are...

... sometimes friends, and sometimes enemies of humanity.

Yet, it was here, at this lowest point in her life, struggling somehow to make ends meet, and oddly ambivalent towards gigantic robots, that Casali discovered the key syntactic formula that was to be the backbone of her glory years.

At last, Casali had discovered "Love is..."

...$ 50, kissing is extra.

A New Beginning

And, as if the mere saying of the words had a talismanic effect, within weeks Casali had met the love of her life, Italian immigrant Roberto Casali.

Her new happiness spurred her into the most intense creative period of her life, and by the time they were married, Casali had given the world such enduring monuments as her unforgettable "Cherish" triptych:

...a cherished treasure.

...a treasure to be cherished.

...a cherished treasure to be treasured and cherished.

Golden Handcuffs

The nation soon became enamored of the "Love is..." series and she became syndicated by the *Los Angeles Times*. T-shirts, coffee mugs, and calendars provided a steady stream of income, upon which the Casalis soon came to depend.

Saddled by ever-greater debts, Casali began churning out "Love is..." pictures on an hourly basis just to stay afloat. This huge effort took its psychic toll on Casali, who became increasingly desperate in her search for metaphors, often relying on bizarre combinations of the fantastic and the mundane. In one particularly productive afternoon in April 1973, Casali wrote that "Love is..." over 276 different possibilities, including... "an alligator with wings, but with sharper teeth than a regular alligator would have," "A reclining chair that spins, but not so much that you get dizzy," and "Pretending you're a pirate all day just to stay sane, aaaarrgh!"

...an alligator with wings, but with sharper teeth than a regular alligator would have.

Stagnation

Yet amazingly, despite what she deemed to be a decline in the quality of her insights, her adoring public continued to clamor for Casali cartoons.

Disheartened and disillusioned by the public's over-enthusiastic appraisal of her art, Casali turned to the California hyper-realists in an attempt to recapture the authenticity of experience that had permeated her earliest works.

The *Los Angeles Times*, however, was less forgiving of her forays into Post-Modernism, never running what many consider her finest work, "Love is... big-headed, etc."

...big-headed, prepubescent mongoloids. who may or may not be related, sitting on a big heart, surrounded by many smaller hearts.

Tragedy

In 1976, Casali's devoted husband died of cancer. In her grief, Casali turned to a reputable San Fernando psychoanalyst, Dr. Charlie Tan. Through Dr. Tan's sessions, Casali began a voyage of self-discovery consisting almost entirely of recovered memories brought out while under hypnosis.

These "dream" sessions gave Casali's later work a darkness that proved disturbing to many. Indeed, her popularity slowly declined throughout the '80s and '90s as she explored the deepest reaches of her sexuality.

In 1995, Casali produced her least popular piece, sold to syndication as "Love is... the world's greatest uncle."

... keeping a secret.

Love Is...Forever?

Tragically, Kim Casali died in 1997 at the age of 55. Yet her legacy did not die with her.

Fueled by the same passion as his mother, Stefano Casali has taken up the challenge of "Love is..." and already his work is being compared favorably.

The burden of continuing the work of this century's most prolific and beloved artist obviously weighs heavy on the young man, who attempts to deflect the pressure through humor.

"No one can ever fill my mother's shoes," stated Stefano in a 2001 interview on the Oxygen Network. "Oh, who am I kidding, she was a perfect size 7B."

Nonetheless, the impact of such enormous expectation has already transmogrified itself into a refreshing new vision in Stefano's art, at once both a fitting homage to the past and a bold new step into the future.

We are fortunate, indeed, that the age-old questions about love are constantly being redefined by such a distinguished line.

... mailing it in.

FOTO FUNNIES

Special Danish Section

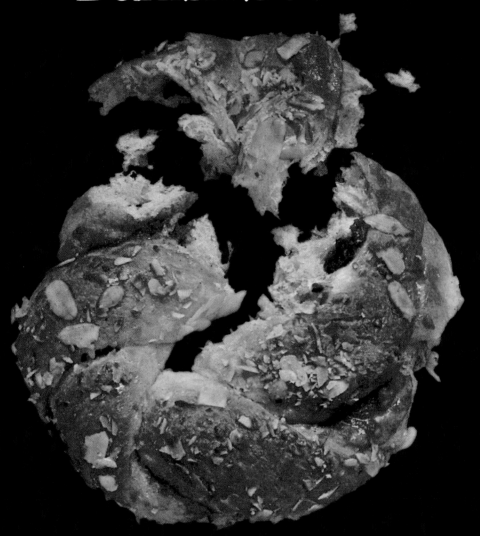

Denmark, the southernmost of the Scandinavian countries, is located in Northwest Europe and is bordered by West Germany, the North Sea, the Skagerrak, the Kattegat, and the Baltic. It is a low-lying land with coastal plains and rolling hills, inhabited by 4,870,000 people, 95 percent of whom are Evangelical Lutherans. The Danish national anthem is "Der er et yndigt land" ("There Is a Lovely Land"). The chief rivers are the Stora, the Skjern A, the Varde A, and the Gudena. Exports in 1968—chiefly machinery, meat and meat products (especially bacon and ham), dairy products and eggs, ships, pharmaceutical products and other chemicals, clothing, and metal furniture—totaled $2.58 billion. Exploited resources include peat, lignite, diatomaceous earth, chalk, marl, kaolin, limestone, granite, flint, and salt.

So much for Denmark.

Kinky Kutouts

Have hours of fun with Bennie, the unisex doll. It can be Barbie, it can be Ken, it can be anything in between. And next Christmas tell your mommy you want a complete set of fetishes and an S & M kit and rubber clothes . . .

Kinky Kutouts

Turn those boring snapshots into scenes
of wanton depravity with these
handy paste-ons.

Make that vacuum cleaner or Water Pik into a weird sexual device.

UNITED STATES POSTAL SERVICE **APPLICATION FOR LISTING PURSUANT TO 39 USC 3010**	*SEE INSTRUCTIONS BEFORE COMPLETION*	**APPLICATION NUMBER** 444927	DATE SIGNED YEAR MO DAY

I hereby state to the U.S. Postal Service that I DO DESIRE to receive sexually oriented advertisements and material through the mail.

NAME

PRINT LAST NAME BELOW   PRINT FIRST NAME BELOW   MI

ADDRESS

PRINT STREET NO. BELOW   PRINT STREET NAME, ROUTE, OR P. O. BOX NO. BELOW   PRINT APT. NO. BELOW

PRINT CITY OR TOWN BELOW   PRINT STATE ABBREVIATION   ZIP CODE

CHILDREN

PRINT LAST NAME BELOW   PRINT FIRST NAME BELOW   MI   YEAR   MO.   DAY

DATE OF BIRTH

Signature _____

A TRUE STORY

MARY

The TWO PATHS

MONA

Hard-Core Geography

Manuel, what have you got if you have a mothball een one hand and a mothball een the other?

Caramba, José! The beegest moth in all of Spain!

INDEX

Abasement 1–98, 100–159
Abatement 99, 160
Aberrations (see Perversions)
Absolution 160
Aisles, laying in the 4, 78, 91
Akimbo, arms 46
  legs 87
  breasts 89
Amanda, achieves apogee with ape 148
  repents 160
Angela, among the aborigines 65
  among the Amazons 124
  among the monks 159
  wins sainthood 160
Apertures 1–159
Arlene, sees skyrockets 136
  sees stars 158
  vomits 160
Backlash injuries, chiropractic attitude toward 68
  orgies as cause of 76, 90, 156
Backwoodsman (see Perversions)
Bagpipes, and Betty 18
  and Florence 18
  and Helen 18
  and Marjorie 18
  use as multiple dildoe 18
Bandwagon, Arnold gets on the 87
  Alice gets on the 87
  Adrian " " " 87
  Andy " " " 88
  Betty " " " 88
  Brenda " " " 89
  Charles " " " 90
  Claire " " " 90
  collapses 90
  splinters removed by surgical team 91

Bella, in the barracks 65
  in the fieldhouse 78
  in the stockyards 89
Bestiality, with cassowary 89
  piranha 118
  porcupine 56
  tarantula 116
Boobs (see Knockers)
Bookmark, Randolph leaves in Bella 78
  Randolph leaves in Ellen 111
  Randolph leaves in Vincent 147
Brenda, and Murray 115
  and Murray and Philip 118
  and Murray and Philip and Sam 123
  and the U.S. Seventh Fleet 136
Chastity (see Lorna Doone)
Counterclockwise (see Orgy)
Diaphragm, effectiveness of 97
  use as trampoline for parakeets 119
Dildoes, aluminum 66
  bulletproof 87
  chrome 20
  diamond-studded 118
  licorice 114
  notched 157
  rustproof 113
  saw-toothed 75
  stainless steel 119
  warp in 88
Dinosaurs, organ size 77
  sexual response to volcanoes of 118
Fetishes:
  Empire State Building 55
  gorgons 63
  hangnails 86, 114

left eyelid 13
marigolds 41
pencil sharpeners 117
rotisseries 12
wisdom teeth 16
Gloria, attends Bryn Mawr 2
  establishes meaningful relationship with Bill, Harry, Mike, Ned, Phil, Tom, and Vincent 3
Going steady, and bestiality 3
  and flagellation 12
  and restraint in disembowelling 14
Joan, and Aaron 14
  and Mack 16
  and Bernard 28
  and St. Bernard 37
Knockers (see Zelda)
Lila, shyness of 1
  reticence of 2
  succumbs 3
  whorishness of 4
Margarine, as lubricative substitute for butter 67
  views of laundries toward stains of 68
Mathilda, and community singing 1
  and necrophilia 8
  and voodoo 92
  and sacraments 160
Oatmeal, restorative value of 114
  disadvantage of lumpiness in 118
Orgy, all odd-numbered pages
Oona, and orality 16
  and Olivia 97
  and onanism 110

Perversion 1–159
Phallus, colossal 3
  elephantine 43
  enormous 5
  monstrous 8, 90, 116, 118, 125
  monumental 11
  stupendous 2, 147
  titanic 14
  towering 90
  unbelievable 40, 87, 91
Redemption 160
Sky-diving, in combination with *soixante-neuf* 3
  as an antidote to impotency 16
  as a diuretic 18
Socially redeeming value (see motto "Mother Knows Best" 160)
Stewart, feelings of rejection 1
  feelings of worthlessness 1
  feelings of despair 1
  first sensual stirrings 2
  first sexual experience 2
  turns egomaniac 3
True love 160
Ukulele, as contraceptive device 112
  as purveyor of erotic music 111
Vera, versatility of 22, 45, 68, 97–99, 112, 148, 157
  vilification of 159
  vindication of 160
Zelda, as a virgin 1
  reaches depths of depravity 2–159
  reforms, finds true love, gets married, has baby, learns meaning of true happiness 160

4

5

Dirty books should have indexes. Write your pornographer.

How to Make
"No Lump" Mashed Potatoes

Combine:
    ½ cup shortening
    4 lbs. instant mashed potatoes
    ¼ lb. saltpeter or potassium nitrate powder
    1 lb. sugar
    2 lbs. baking soda or commercial bleach

Mix thoroughly and heat over medium flame for one
hour. Use additional bleaching agent if yellow color
persists.

Serves twenty-five. Allow six hours before beginning
of dance or other social activity.

No, it doesn't affect your vision, but we know you won't take our word for it, so go
ahead, hold the magazine at arm's length and read the eye chart. Feel better now?
How these old wives' tales persist is anybody's guess.

Kinky Kutouts

Don't take no for an answer.

CERTIFICATE OF STERILITY

This is to certify that Mr. _____
has voluntarily submitted to sterilization procedures
approved by the Department of Health and has been
examined for latent potency within the last six months.

D.O.H. Form 2630
1 May 1970
Not to be used for
purposes of identification.

_____
Certifying Physician

5/27/71
_____
Date of Examination

Calm her fears without resorting to clumsy and uncomfortable preventive apparatus.

WOMEN

Sick of the anonymity and coldness of big-city life? Cut out and paste on office or apartment door.
Remove "WO" portion or not, depending on sex and/or personal preferences.

Down Mammary Lane

or Where You First Saw It

671049

Is this your lucky number? Sniff here and see! Catherine Deneuve sat on this spot on one copy of this month's press run.

Turn page for the most pornographic picture ever printed!

Hey, Manuel, did you hear about the cross-eyed seamstress?

Si, José, she couldn't mend straight!

Hoy, Manuel, do you know the difference between the cha-cha and pea-green paint?

Si, José. Anyone can learn to cha-cha!

The 5:18 to Peyton Place 67

was on his, her tongue pushing deeper, harder, with a desperate longing she had never known.

"Love me," she moaned. "Love me now."

"Now," he repeated, as his trembling hands came slowly up and found her heaving breasts. He fought the buttons of her blouse, then tore them away with a muffled curse. She groaned and pulled him down, their bodies locked together in a rhythmic throbbing ecstasy. As their passion reached its peak, she shuddered, then exploded with the wild and blinding fury of a dying star.

Their passion spent, they fell breathlessly apart and listened as the first light drops of rain splashed softly on the windowpane. Another rainy afternoon in Peyton Place.

Manuel, what ees the difference between an old nun and a señorita taking a bath?

That ees easy, José. One has hope in her soul, and the other has soap in her hole!

Goode Christians Take Heede
Seven Signes of Infestations bye Devilles

1. Glassey and shiftie eyeballes.
2. Unhealthie complexion.
3. Dark ringes beneathe the eyeballes.
4. Listlessnesse and lacke of ambitione.
5. Sallowe and pale countenance.
6. Nervousnesse.
7. A feeble bodie.

Parents Take Note!
The Seven Signs of Self-Abuse

1. Glassy, shifty stare.
2. Bad complexion.
3. Dark rings under the eyes.
4. Lack of "get-up-and-go."
5. Face pale and sallow.
6. Nervousness.
7. General physical weakness.

Police Officers! Look for These
Seven Sure Signs of Drug Use

1. Glassy-eyed expression.
2. Poor complexion.
3. Dark rings under the eyes.
4. Lack of ambition and motivation
5. Pale, drawn features.
6. Nervous, jumpy state.
7. Underdeveloped physique.

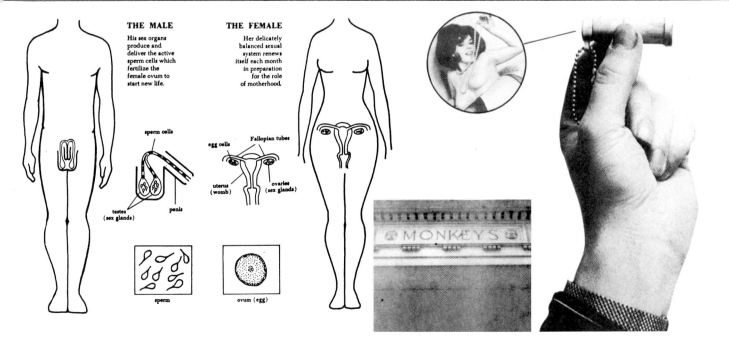

THE MALE
His sex organs produce and deliver the active sperm cells which fertilize the female ovum to start new life.

sperm cells

testes (sex glands)

penis

sperm

THE FEMALE
Her delicately balanced sexual system renews itself each month in preparation for the role of motherhood.

egg cells

Fallopian tubes

uterus (womb)

ovaries (sex glands)

ovum (egg)

MONKEYS

Quite a picture, wasn't it? Well, now, do you remember how annoyed you were the last time you found the pages of a magazine you were trying to read just a little hard to separate? 'Nuff said. A little courtesy goes a long way!

Is there a parent, teacher, brother or sister, draft-board member, drill sergeant, bureaucrat, employer, business rival, or former object of affection whose discomfiture would be a source of satisfaction to you? Obtain his or her telephone number and insert the appropriate ad from the list below in the Personal section of your local smut rag, porn paper, or scuz sheet.

Parents or married couples:

WEIRD STUFF

Adventurous, liberated older couple seeking other couples interested in the unusual. Accent on S & M, animal lore, dessert toppings, nude bumper-pool, etc., but we'll try anything once! Tel:

Sister or single female:

I CAN'T GET ENOUGH!

Doctors at a fancy Swiss clinic say it's something in my glands, but the way I see it, it's something that isn't in my glands! Either way, I'm open to suggestions! An inch of prevention is worth a pound of cure to me! Call me anytime, day or night. Tel:

Brother or single male:

AC-DC

I don't care what it is, as long as it's freaky! I don't care who it is, as long as they're kinky! As far as I'm concerned, if it isn't a morals charge in Tijuana, it isn't worth doing! Give me a try. Tel:

Don't forget what we said about courtesy!

FOUR-LETTER FUN!

1. I've got to go take a ____S__.

2. Of all the girls I know, Sue has the biggest _____T.

3. Do you have Sally's number? I want to ____L__ her tonight.

4. That's the longest ___O_____ I've ever seen!

5. I know a place where you can get a ____O__ job.

6. Jim really eats _____T.

7. What a smelly F_____!

8. Why, Sam, your underwear is covered with _____Z!

9. Stay away from Betty. She's been giving everyone C_____s.

10. I'll say one thing for Sarah: she really knows how to _____K!

ANSWERS
1. TEST
2. FEET
3. CALL
4. ROPE
5. GOOD
6. FAST
7. FISH
8. FUZZ
9. COLD
10. COOK

PROTECT YOUR CHILDREN! KNOW THE CODE!

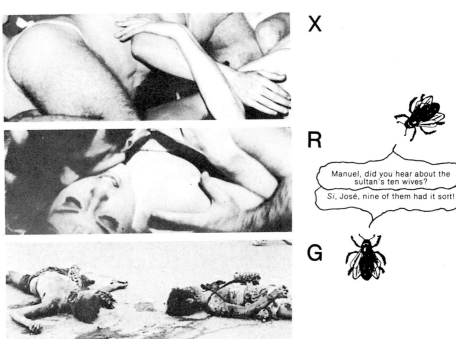

X

R

G

Manuel, did you hear about the sultan's ten wives?

Si, José, nine of them had it soft!

Down Mammary Lane
or Where You First Saw It

If you want to impress her with a war story, don't tell her how you stood off five thousand gooks single-handed, unless, of course, you prefer Meaningful Dialogue on the Immorality of the War to Relating to Her As a Person. Use these handy protest tales!

There we were, completely surrounded by congressmen. I don't know what got into me—I guess it was just plain rage at seeing all my buddies get it—but, whatever it was, I sort of blacked out. The next thing I knew, I was telling this guy from Indiana about the faked medal citations, the black market, the atrocities, the racial incidents—everything. Yeah, sure, I got a bad-conduct discharge, but there were a lot of brave guys out there that deserved it more.

We'd been taking it pretty bad, and along about nightfall me and Kowalski and Greenberg and Billy Joe were at the bottom of a shell hole, just sort of keeping out of the way of things, when the lieutenant comes over and says, "Henderson, I want you to take three men, sneak up the hill, and blow that machine-gun nest. The whole operation depends on it." I don't know who got him first. I think it was Kowalski.

As soon as I got over to Vietnam, I had this medical exam, and the doc said, "It's right on the borderline, soldier," and I said, "Listen, Doc, this means a lot to me. The gooks killed a lot of my friends. All I want is a chance. Can't you just this once kind of forget the book?" Then I slipped him fifty bucks, and I spent the rest of the war in a cushy desk job in Saigon.

Look, I know you've heard this story a million times, but, honest, I never left Fort Dix. I spent the whole two years sitting on my ass in New Jersey, counting canteen covers, twelve thousand miles from My Lai and all that stuff. The closest I got to Vietnam was once I went to Philadelphia and took in The Green Berets.

Are you an effective obscene caller? Test yourself with this scorecard. If you average less than 7, you better get "busy," less than 4, "hang it up!"

First Reaction	Points
Click.	0
Who is this?	1
We already have a subscription to that magazine.	1
Bill gave at the office.	1
You want Al's Body Shop. We always get their calls. It's 3380.	2
Is this one of Sally's friends?	2
If I was your mother, I'd wash out your mouth with soap!	2
If I was your mother, I'd wash out your mouth with Drano!	3
Jeez, do you eat with that mouth?	3
You think you're funny, but you're not. You're sick!	4
I hope you know the Telephone Company has special dogs that can smell out people like you.	4
What are Fallopian tubes?	5
I'd hang up, but I want to give the Telephone Company time to trace you with their satellites.	5
Where have you got that mouthpiece, anyway? I can't understand a word you say.	6
I've heard some disgusting, left-wing, perverted things in my time, but that takes the cake!	6
Mister, they should lock you up and throw away the key!	7
I just threw up all over my shoes! You ruined my shoes!	7
You know what I think! I think people like you should be hung over slow fires on wire hangers and beaten with basting spoons and have jam rubbed in your hair!	8
Hey, Marian! Has Richard Speck broken out of jail?	8
Maybe you think the police won't get you, but God will! He's got millions of tiny little microphones all over the place!	9
I'm warning you, I'm taking down everything you say!	9
Listen, can you hold on a minute while I get a cigarette?	10

lANA does it.

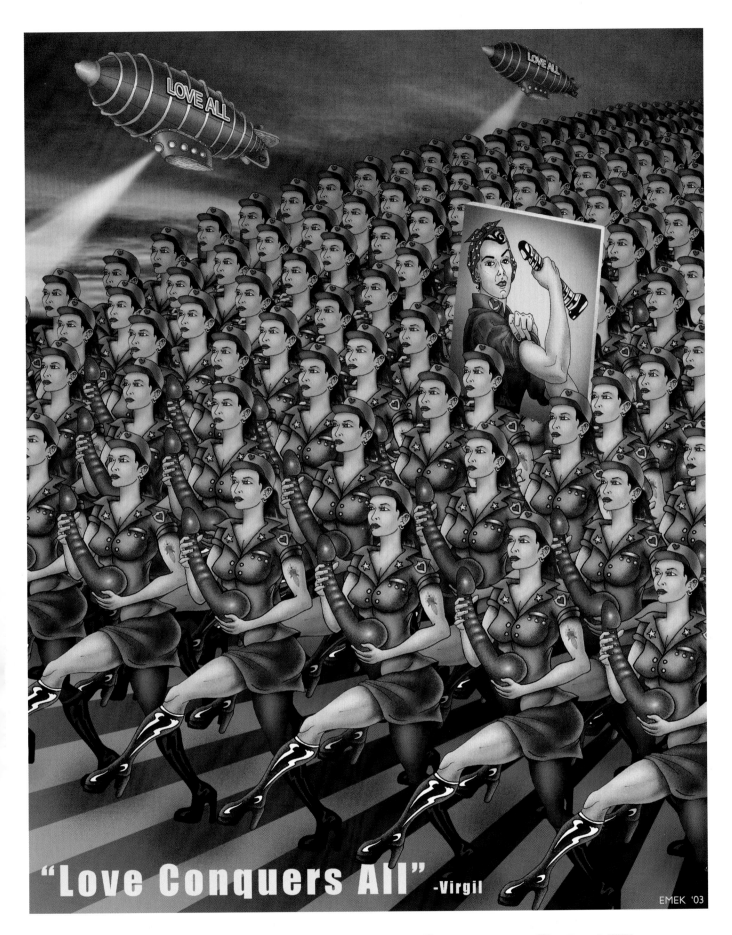

"Love Conquers All" -Virgil

EMEK '03

LITERATURE OF LOVE

I, a Splurch

By Dr. Sexx

There once was a birdie
Named Seymour the Splurch,
Who was born and brought up
On a small wooden perch.

Now the Splurch was a good bird,
He worked hard at school,
And studied, especially,
The Splurch golden rule,
Which told all young Splurches
To learn and to grow,
To wonder and question,
And hunger to know,
To trust other Splurches,
(Even those over thirty),
But to never, Godammit,
Do anything DIRTY!

Now the Splurch always minded,
He did just what they said.
When he flew over nudists,
He'd turn up his head.

He never took birdseed
From drooling old strangers,
Or got into cars
With their unexplained dangers.

Seymour, in short,
Was as good as they came,
A credit, they said,
To the grand old Splurch name.

But one day
While digging for Greebles to seize,
Seymour sensed a strange quiver
Just north of his knees.

So Seymour looked down
At this strange complication,
And found that he'd sprouted
A new decoration.

Where before his young drumsticks
Shook hands with his rump,
He found he'd produced
An elongated lump.

And to go with his growth
He found himself feeling
Several strange new emotions
Which set his mind reeling.

So he packed up his birdseed
(He'd just bought a new shipment),
And went searching for someone
To explain his equipment.

He tried his librarian,
Morris the Glapper,
Who slipped him a book
In a brown paper wrapper.

He flipped through the index,
Found the chapters he needed,
But the relevant pages
Had all been deleted.

He next tried his neighbors,
Two flying pink Frumers,
Whose cohabitation
Had caused many rumors.

They listened politely,
Then shot a quick glance
At the source of his troubles.
(Seymour wished he'd worn pants.)

"Here let us show you!"
They both giggled at last,
But their whips, boots and chains
Told him, "Beat it, and fast!"

He next sought advice
From the fluff-tailed Gazorning,
Who gave him a wallop
And added a warning,
"If you touch what you've got there,
Or give it a tweak,
You'll go blind in the eyes,
And grow warts on your beak!"

This made the Splurch nervous.
His eyesight was ace,
But the urges and surges
Were picking up pace.

He thought of his grandpa,
An aged Splurch wreck,
Who in fact *had* gone blind
And grown warts on his neck.

"But what is it good for?"
Thought Seymour still doubting
The point or the use of
The thing he was sprouting.

But an urgent new yearning
Had flickered and grown.
His claws started sweating;
He let out a moan.

"What I need's a girl,
One's good as another!"
But the only Splurch girlie
He knew was his mother.

Seymour's sex education
I'm afraid had been slight,
And he didn't know doodling
Your mommy's not right.

He'd never been taught
About unnatural sex,
And dozed off
When his teacher read *Oedipus Rex*.

So Seymour took off
In a state of great haste,
For the throbs in his wishbone
Left no time to waste.

But alas for the Splurch,
Fickle Fate held a catch.
When he knocked at mom's door,
His *dad* opened the latch.

"Stand back!" hollered Seymour,
"I've got to see mum!"
And he lunged for the bedroom,
Still not sure why he'd come.

His father, however,
Was not so confused.
He glanced at his son,
Saw he'd no time to lose.
Then a flapping of wings
And a screeching ensued,
Which I'd like to describe,
But it might seem too crude.

At any rate,
Later that evening at nine,
Seymour's two parents
Both sat down to dine.

The dinner was perfect.
The wine was superb.
But the hit of the feast
Was a tender roast bird
With two wings and two drumsticks,
And—excuse the digression,
But Seymour's old dad
Had to carve with discretion.
For although most roast birdies
Are eaten completely,
A small part of this one
Was severed quite neatly.

So, kids, if you liked
This short yarn I've been spinning,
If it set you to twitching
And started you grinning,
Don't miss my next book,
Which tells of the Gringus,
A small furry rodent
Who learns cunnilingus. □

—JOHN WEIDMAN

MY PARENTS MET IN A
CHAT ROOM

by Pete Cummin

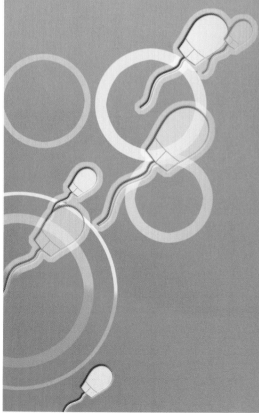

Every Valentine's Day, I am reminded of the greatest love story of all: that of my parents, who met back in 1999, on the verge of a new millennium that threatened to destroy any and all computerized civilizations. It was called Y2K and it had everyone—Americans, Europeans, Asians—preparing for certain apocalypse. As world leaders agonized, private citizens took to building underground bunkers and stockpiling weapons. Overnight, supermarkets were virtually wiped out of supplies, ATMs drained of cash and normally rational people reduced to buying kerosene and drinking water. It was against this backdrop that my mother, a sophomore at Smith College in Amherst, Massachusetts, and my father, a 38-year-old African-American trucker from Cleveland, met and, despite all odds, fell in love, using of all things, a computer.

Years later when I would ask my mother what had made her log onto America Online that December afternoon and enter a chat room with the mysterious call letters of BM4WF; she would simply smile and say, "Fate." But fate can only explain how two people find each other, it does not account for the passion that leads them, after only 20 minutes of typing, to "do phone."

Perhaps my mother, a delicate woman with a penchant for plaid skirts and flowery prose, specifically sought out a protector to help her survive in the post-computer world she was sure to face. She was a woman of strong Victorian influence, which certainly would have been compounded by the fact that she had just completed a Comparative Literature exam pitting the Brontë sisters against each other in a determination of that era's more influential voice of romance. Add to that a young woman's preoccupation with love, the romantic setting of first snow in the Berkshires, and it is not surprising that she rushed back to her dorm room immediately following the exam, turned on her Dell 586 with dial-up modem and began entertaining suitors.

My father, on the other hand, was passing through the Berkshires on his way to Boston with a shipment of

canned corn. With the snow building up, he was forced to pull over on the Massachusetts Turnpike until the morning plows could clear better passage. Y2K and its impending apocalypse meant only one thing to my father: life without consequences. And to a black trucker from Cleveland that in itself meant only one thing: married white women. But alas the room BM4MWF was full, forcing him to enter the room where my mother was. The rest, as my mother would say, is "fate."

But rather than read my woefully inadequate description of their first meeting, I have included a copy of the actual printout from their chat. As I read through it, I am always taken aback by my father's straightforward determination (Oh, how he must have known even then) and my mother's eloquence. While her words may seem old-fashioned to us now, I marvel at the traditions of a generation past—a generation where people still emailed and instant-messaged each other despite a climate of complete uncertainty.

So without further ado: It is 4:00p.m. on a snowy December. A lone knight appears in my mother's chat room. His name is as confident as it is mysterious. Yet he does not introduce himself. He does not even type a word. He merely says…

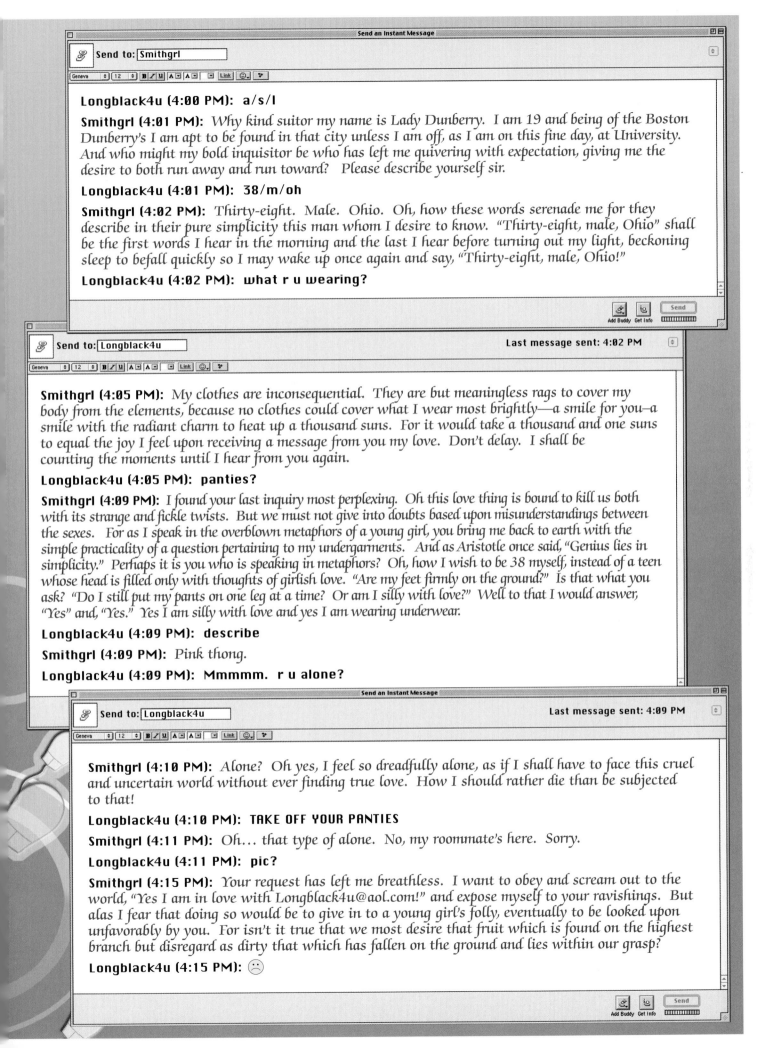

Send an Instant Message

Send to: Smithgrl

Longblack4u (4:00 PM): a/s/l

Smithgrl (4:01 PM): Why kind suitor my name is Lady Dunberry. I am 19 and being of the Boston Dunberry's I am apt to be found in that city unless I am off, as I am on this fine day, at University. And who might my bold inquisitor be who has left me quivering with expectation, giving me the desire to both run away and run toward? Please describe yourself sir.

Longblack4u (4:01 PM): 38/m/oh

Smithgrl (4:02 PM): Thirty-eight. Male. Ohio. Oh, how these words serenade me for they describe in their pure simplicity this man whom I desire to know. "Thirty-eight, male, Ohio" shall be the first words I hear in the morning and the last I hear before turning out my light, beckoning sleep to befall quickly so I may wake up once again and say, "Thirty-eight, male, Ohio!"

Longblack4u (4:02 PM): what r u wearing?

Add Buddy Get Info Send

Send to: Longblack4u   Last message sent: 4:02 PM

Smithgrl (4:05 PM): My clothes are inconsequential. They are but meaningless rags to cover my body from the elements, because no clothes could cover what I wear most brightly—a smile for you—a smile with the radiant charm to heat up a thousand suns. For it would take a thousand and one suns to equal the joy I feel upon receiving a message from you my love. Don't delay. I shall be counting the moments until I hear from you again.

Longblack4u (4:05 PM): panties?

Smithgrl (4:09 PM): I found your last inquiry most perplexing. Oh this love thing is bound to kill us both with its strange and fickle twists. But we must not give into doubts based upon misunderstandings between the sexes. For as I speak in the overblown metaphors of a young girl, you bring me back to earth with the simple practicality of a question pertaining to my undergarments. And as Aristotle once said, "Genius lies in simplicity." Perhaps it is you who is speaking in metaphors? Oh, how I wish to be 38 myself, instead of a teen whose head is filled only with thoughts of girlish love. "Are my feet firmly on the ground?" Is that what you ask? "Do I still put my pants on one leg at a time? Or am I silly with love?" Well to that I would answer, "Yes" and, "Yes." Yes I am silly with love and yes I am wearing underwear.

Longblack4u (4:09 PM): describe

Smithgrl (4:09 PM): Pink thong.

Longblack4u (4:09 PM): Mmmmm. r u alone?

Send an Instant Message

Send to: Longblack4u   Last message sent: 4:09 PM

Smithgrl (4:10 PM): Alone? Oh yes, I feel so dreadfully alone, as if I shall have to face this cruel and uncertain world without ever finding true love. How I should rather die than be subjected to that!

Longblack4u (4:10 PM): TAKE OFF YOUR PANTIES

Smithgrl (4:11 PM): Oh… that type of alone. No, my roommate's here. Sorry.

Longblack4u (4:11 PM): pic?

Smithgrl (4:15 PM): Your request has left me breathless. I want to obey and scream out to the world, "Yes I am in love with Longblack4u@aol.com!" and expose myself to your ravishings. But alas I fear that doing so would be to give in to a young girl's folly, eventually to be looked upon unfavorably by you. For isn't it true that we most desire that fruit which is found on the highest branch but disregard as dirty that which has fallen on the ground and lies within our grasp?

Longblack4u (4:15 PM): ☹

Add Buddy Get Info Send

Send to: Smithgrl

Geneva | 12 | **B** *I* U A A A | Link | ☺ | ✦

Smithgrl (4:15 PM): *Don't be angry my love. For what is captured by the camera's eye is only that light which reflects off the outer surface of my being. What truly belongs to you—my heart, mind and soul—can never be caught on any film. And besides… my scanner's broken. And I don't have a digital camera.*

Longblack4u (4:16 PM): k, describe yourself.

Smithgrl (4:22 PM): *Sick with love is how I would describe myself. But I fear that my suitor wants a physical description. And to that I would reply that my skin is porcelain but it blushes rose upon reading your messages. My hair is auburn and my eyes chestnut. I am nearly 10 hands high, 14 stone and good stock for being both a wife and a mother.*

Longblack4u (4:22 PM): What size are your tits?

Smithgrl (4:22 PM): *36C*

Longblack4u (4:22 PM): phone?

Smithgrl (4:24 PM): *How dare you sir ask a lady such a question!!!! It is both impudent and rude, especially of such a woman as whom you know so little and who herself knows nothing of you save your age, sex and location.*

Longblack4u (4:24 PM): 10" uncut, thick

Smithgrl (4:24 PM): *OMG!*

Longblack4u (4:25 PM): 756-555-7864 - ask for Leo - but give me three minutes to log off.

Add Buddy   Get Info   Send

He had a name! Leo Longblack4u! Perhaps he was from the Philadelphia Longblack4u's, having moved to Cleveland during the stock market crash of 1987? Or maybe he was related to Sir Longfellow of the Dutch explorers by the same name. Oh it didn't matter whether he was the richest software baron or the poorest farmer. She was in love! And as my mother waited for what must have seemed like an eternity—180 seconds can tick by mercilessly slow for a young woman in the throes of infatuation—she wrote with her lavender pen over and over, "Mrs. Leo Longblack4u, Mrs. Leo Longblack4u…" until she got her signature just how she wanted it forever and ever.

Finally, at two minutes and 48 seconds, my mother dialed Mr. Leo Longblack4u, figuring that the mere act of dialing must take at least a dozen seconds. As they spoke, his deep chocolaty voice confirmed what her heart already knew—she must meet this Leo Longblack4u, and she must meet him in a populated, well-lit place. So later that afternoon, wearing a baby T-shirt, short skirt and no undergarments, my mother walked into the Amherst Starbucks and met the man who would become my father. After nearly two lattes and some meaningful conversation about "limits," both knew that a love such as theirs could wait no longer. Out in the parking lot, away from the prying eyes of customers, Leo Longblack4u helped my mother into the cab of his 18-wheeler. And it was there that they consecrated their love for each other… three times.

Sadly, after that night, my mother was never to see Leo Longblack4u again. She had heard stories that all the Longblack4u's as well as the Hungblack10's and the Masterdaddy's had been taken away by Y2K, somehow swallowed whole by their computers before the Great Relief of January 1, 2000. And while I often ask my mother whether it is better to have been loved roughly one night in the cab of a big rig than never to have been loved at all, she just smiles. For standing before her is the ultimate reminder of what she had that night— kinky, unprotected sex with a total stranger—or what on the eve of the millennium stood for TRUE LOVE.

And I, Cynthia Starbucks Longblack4u, am proof of this.

Strange Sex We Have Known

by William S. Burroughs
and
Terry Southern

Southern

My first encounter with "Dr. Benway" (whom I was later to know as the master scribe and film buff extraordinaire, William S. Burroughs) was on the sleepy sands of St. Tropez in the south of France in the summer of '47. I had been suffering from—or rather, *complaining of*—a certain lesion, a rather persistent lesion, on the hinder fleshy part of my left calf, just below the knee. It wasn't *painful*, but it *was* irritating in a *psychological way*, and I was keen to deal and have done with it. An acquaintance of mine, Allen Ginsberg—who later achieved international poetic renown (*Howl, Kaddish*, etc.)—was staying at the same hotel, and when I showed him the lesion, he said: "Doc Benway will put that to rights in double quick order!" (little did I realize at this point in time that it was simply another joke at my expense by the mischievous Al Ginsberg) and he set up a meet at Benway's beach house.

Dr. Benway was (and *is* to this very day) a most remarkable personage.

"Your lesion," he observed in his dry and singular tone, "has the mark of *genitalia*," and he poised a finger near it, just so, not quite touching. I glanced down and noted, with some surprise, that it did indeed resemble a tiny vage, with its puckered pouting lips, half-parted and moistly glistening—but I was reluctant to admit as much to the formidable Benway. "You must be mad," I exclaimed instead with a show of indignation, and instinctively drew back; but the fantastic Benway continued as though not having heard: "Naturally it would follow that the treatment of choice would be to . . . *fuck it away*." And before I could protest, he raised a finger of caution: "*But* an extremely *small sexual member* would be required—perhaps that of a *gerbil*—and by damnable good fortune, hee-hee, I happen to have just such a specimen here in this very lab. . . ." He gestured towards a shoddy complex of small cages nearby, and continued: "You entertain no superstitious qualms, I take it, towards *bestiality*?"

I informed this "Doctor Benway" in no uncertain terms that I did indeed entertain such qualms, and would *not* consider being "fucked in the lesion" by a gerbil, *nor* any other member of his devilish menagerie! I had failed, however, to reckon on the man's powers of persuasion, which border on the veritably hypnotic.

"Similar case a few years back," he went on, unperturbed, "man-of-the-cloth developed stigmata in both hands and both feet, each of the blessed wounds being in the shape of a female cunt, not unlike your own, only larger—so that when the populace filed by in holy reverence to view the miraculous visitation, they found his worship—his coarse mandrill-root pulsating in gross distention—going at it into both hand-wounds like a maddened warthog. They could not restrain him—he finally broke his own back trying to fuck the lesion in his left metatarsus. . . ."

I must admit to being somewhat taken aback by the sheer grossness of this account, but it did put me in mind, a few years later, of a story so bandied about that I dare say it carries no "kiss-and-tell" onus at this late point in time—namely, that curious tale of how LBJ was "caught in the act" (if one may coin) on the Kennedy death-plane from Dallas, trying to force his rude animal-member into the mortal wound of the young President. I recounted the bizarre incident to Benway, but it was apparently old hat to him.

"Hee-hee," he chuckled, nodding sagely, though more through *politesse* if my guess is any good, than through your true humorous enjoyment, "yes, a classic case of . . . *neck-ro-philia*, was it not?"

I'm not too keen on *puns* myself, but I let it pass; after all, a man of Benway's stature (Ginsberg had shown me a lot of weird microfilmed diplomas, citations, credentials, depositions, endorsements, etc.) was not to be challenged unduly.

"Very well, Benway," I said, "if that is your view—"

"It is not only my *view*," he quipped in his inimitable fashion (cross between Ben Jonson and W. C. Fields), "it is also my gol-dang *pur-view*! Hee-hee-hee. . . ."

Needless to say, Benway's "treatment of choice" proved to be less than useless—and, in fact, I very nearly succumbed to a damnable case of the pesky "gerbil-clap."

I was intrigued, however, by the emphasis he placed on what was later to become his infamous "view-syndrome," and when I pointed this out he was good enough to address himself to that very issue.

Burroughs

Yes, the cinematic image is apt, and may be extended. Ungrammatically speaking, what is sexy to humans is a film usually laid down in early childhood on a receptive screen. In my not inconsiderable experience as a physician, I have indeed encountered some strange films. Here is a mild example I cite simply to illustrate the concept of sex as film. This highly placed British civil servant pays boys to don uniforms which he provides and treat him like a boy in a reform school. They are given a precise script with certain words like: "You little bastard." And he reads back his own script: "Yes, sir," assenting with civil leer as he casts himself as a Borstal Boy instead of an old school tie. He is tied to that little piece of film. It is the only way he can achieve sexual satisfaction. He may be bored with it and disgusted with it. He may even laugh at it. But not while it is going on. There seems to be a basic incompatibility between sex and laughter. Sex must be *serious*. Who can laugh during an orgasm? I recall the bizarre case of a boy named Ali I encountered in a remote corner of southern Morocco who could accomplish this seemingly impossible feat. He disappeared before I learned his secret. He is tied to a fear film that is the sexualization of fear, a phenomenon that dates back to our caveman days. It is dangerous to be caught with one's pants down by a saber-toothed tiger, a Texas Ranger, or a house dick. However, if the intruder is on your payroll and acting in your film play, then fear can be converted into the desired end product.

I know of one case of a man whose name I cannot mention because of my deep reverence for his exalted office who can only achieve orgasm by dressing himself as an atom bomb. He is then detonated by a whore disguised as Marilyn Monroe and goes off watching Hiroshima films. Another case of a billionaire . . . (once again my medical ethics prevent me from giving his name) who recreates the 1929 crash, watches his stocks fall off the board, then screams out: *"I am ruined! I am penniless!"* and jumps out a prop Wall Street window all of six feet down into a swimming pool full of gold dollars and achieves orgasm on contact. Many other cases of this nature are in my files: a famous actress who reenacts her greatest role and defecates on stage; a similar case involving an Admiral who defecates on deck and wipes his ass with Old Glory while a chorus of hired tars scream imprecations; a white-supremacist politician who turns into a nigger on TV and drops dead while the White Goddess of the evening says coldly: "Take him outside because he stinks. Take him to the nigger morgue."

The thoughtful reader will detect a common denominator. All of these VIPs achieve orgasm by a *simulated situation* in which the thing they fear most occurs, like the famous author who types out an atrociously written page and screams out: *"My talent is gone!"* and comes all over the critics.

Cases of animal identification are frequent: subjects who dress themselves as horses, pigs, mandrills, leopards, bears. It would seem that renunciation of the human form is in this case the exciting element dating to a time when some nanny called them a filthy beast, or when the patient reflected that perhaps saber-toothed tigers have more fun than people.

I am happy to say that the whole matter of human sexuality has been placed in a new and more hopeful light by recent discoveries in the area of electrical brain stimulation. Once the sex centers in the brain are stimulated by implanted electrodes, everything in sight is sexy, even a psychiatrist. In fact, one subject was able to achieve full satisfaction by looking at an old boot. So we can perhaps change the film and lead our patient back to normality? Enter the psychiatrist with a naked Bunny girl. But the man said flatly, "The boot is cheaper."

And who can say he is wrong? Electrical brain stimulation demonstrates that sex *is* arbitrary and if you can't be normal, why not be arbitrary, especially if it saves you money? With electrodes installed in the brain of every citizen, full sexual satisfaction will be achieved by all and we will enter a Utopia of electronic bliss endangered only by mechanical failures, a very real danger indeed as anyone knows who has waited weeks and even months for electrical repairs, even though he had been guaranteed twenty-four-hour service on his appliance. The answer, of course, is private enterprise and competition. I would like to sound a word of warning, however—and I am sure T. Southern will join me in this—of the *very real dangers inherent in nationalized sex-service.* □

True Facts

ST. LOUIS—A man who allegedly knocked down girls and women, took off their shoes and sucked their toes, was charged yesterday with sexual abuse.

In a recent attack, police said, a 13-year-old girl was knocked down by Edgar Jones, 28, who took off her shoe and sucked her toes. He didn't otherwise harm her before fleeing.

New York Daily News

PETERBOROUGH, Ont. (CP)—A man reeking of excrement was arrested after a woman complained someone leered at her through the toilet seat of a conservation area outhouse.

Const. Bob La Freniere, of the Ontario provincial police, said Wednesday a man apparently crawled inside the holding tank of an outhouse at the Warsaw Caves conservation area to satisfy a bizarre fetish.

"When this woman concluded her private business, she noticed [Darren Laitte, 26, of Richmond Hill] staring up at her from the holding tank.

Brantford Ontario Expositor

NEWCASTLE, ENG.—After a five-day trial, a jury found animal rights campaigner Alan Cooper not guilty of outraging public decency in connection with charges that he masturbated a male blue nose dolphin in full view of a group of boaters.

The prosecutor had produced two witnesses from the boating group who said they had watched Cooper, 39, masturbate the male dolphin for "several minutes."

But Newcastle Crown Court Judge John Johnson pointed out discrepancies in the accounts given by the two witnesses. The judge also cited expert testimony by Dr. Horace Dobbs, a dolphin specialist whom Cooper had consulted about the mammal's behavior and who testified during the trial.

Dobbs testified that he had told Cooper to relax and enjoy the encounter, which Dobbs said sometimes included the dolphin using its penis.

"It is extending the 'finger of friendship' and should not be rejected," Dobbs told the court he had advised Cooper.

Pittsburgh's Out

WARSAW—A philandering Pole was rudely surprised when he took advantage of his wife's absence to visit a brothel in Germany.

The errant husband set off in search of some extramarital activity believing his wife had gone to stay with friends in Germany where she had been offered a lucrative seasonal job. The sexual services he was offered were being provided by his wife.

UPI Staff

Parents
of the Girls
of the
Eastwest
Conference

pictorial essay

By MICHAEL REISS

*if there's anyone who doesn't love
these girls in the same way we do,
it's apparent it's a parent*

LOU AND ANNE DIMEO; Darien, Connecticut

ANNE: "Let's face it; we weren't too happy to see our daughter Virginia turning up in *Nympho* and *Slut* and the *Crabs Gazette* every month; but we understood. She wanted to become a movie actress, and that was the only exposure she could get. But it finally did pay off. She got $1,200 to star in *A Taste of Ginger*. Of course, it's not a classic movie, or even a very, very good one, but it is a start. And while it still has a lot of that nude stuff—what movie doesn't these days?—it does give our Virginia a few minutes to show off her acting ability. Now, I know we're prejudiced, but we really thought she gave a magnificent performance. And since she's the only girl in the movie, she really does stand out from the pack. So now we're sure it's just a matter of time before they offer her a big Hollywood contract. We've waited about six months already, so it should be any day now."

STU GROTH; Tempe, Arizona

STU: "I mean, heck, there's really nothing to be ashamed about, is there? So it's my daughter, so she's naked—what's the big deal? The human body is a very beautiful thing, and if it's handled right, it can be—well—very beautiful. It's art, kind of like those Greek statues; *they're* all bare, but no one says, 'Put some clothes on them, they're so dirty.' Well, it's the same thing with my daughter. Anyway, her photo is really pretty subtle; you can't see just everything. You know, there's still a little bit left to the imagination. After all, this wasn't in some cheap scum porno magazine. It was in *Vulva*. They're pretty respectable. And it's not like this is how my daughter plans to make her living forever; she's just going to do it for a few years, so she can earn enough to go to college and med school. Then she can become a doctor, to keep people healthy and heal the sick. Which, if you ask me, makes the whole thing pretty much all right, all right?"

JACK AND MARY McGILPIN;
Lancaster, Pennsylvania

JACK: "Boy, they grow up fast, don't they? One minute they're just babies in diapers; the next minute, there they are, posing for *Bonér Monthly*. The kids leave home and all you've got left is a bunch of old snapshots. So we spend our time looking at pictures of our Susan, watching her turn from a tiny girl into a big, beautiful woman. Of course, it's tough to pick favorites, but I guess we like her centerfold the best. It's a lot bigger than the others, and it certainly is more professional than anything I could snap with my Instamatic. And it is just about all we've seen of Sue in the past few years, so we're just glad that she's looking so healthy and so pretty and that she's becoming such a big celebrity. No, sir, we couldn't be prouder of our little girl. No we couldn't. No, sir."

FRANK AND EDNA JOYELL; San Diego, California

FRANK: "Ever since she was a little girl, all our little Kathy wanted was to be a model. So we scrimped and saved to have her teeth straightened and her hair styled professionally, and to buy her all the most beautiful clothes. And we hoped and we prayed that someday Kathy would get her big break in modeling. Well, last month our prayers were answered: the people at *Wet Pussy* magazine published this full-page photo of our daughter.

"Of course, there's more to her than this. She's got a beautiful smile, and her mother's nose, and big blue eyes just like her old dad. But I think this shot shows enough. It says here's a beautiful girl, slim, who's very clean and very much at ease in front of a camera. And I think any high-class fashion photographer reading *Wet Pussy* will see the picture and realize that our Kathy has just what it takes. After all, even Brooke Shields and Margaux Hemingway started out this way, didn't they?" □

Father Aikens' Day Planner

by Mason Brown

Father Aiken's
First Holy
Catholic Day Planner

Baltimore, Md. MMII

Day 1

Dear Diary: Ordination Day at last! The Monsignor has given us all diary/dayplanners to keep a log of our good deeds. I can't wait to fill you up!

Seminary was a wonderful experience, but after 6 years I'm burning up to do God's Work. When the Bishop laid his hands on me, I confess to feeling shivers all through my body. I can't believe some people have never felt the presence of God, and yet, for all my life, I have been blessed by the ability to feel His grace surge through me many times.

I'm going to miss the Seminary, it's scheduled life, the firm discipline and regimentation. I'll never forget my classmates. We're going to be spread throughout the globe, and yet... I'll always feel like a part of me goes with each and every one of them. So young, so vital, so full of the Holy Spirit. Is there anything we can't do? Right now, we have the faith to move mountains!

....I've packed everything up now, Diary. And once you go into the bag and I zipper you in, then it's off to Boston and my new life helping runaway teens. I'm so excited I can barely sleep.

...Sorry to take you out again. It's 4 am, and what a blackness fills my soul. After I finished packing, I joined a prayer circle with Father O'Malley, Father Doogan and myself. It was the last time we were going to be together, so it felt right that we should all pray to thank God for bringing us together, and for him to give us Guidance... Fine, so far.... But I still couldn't sleep afterwards. So just to help myself get some rest, when I got back to my room, I engaged in Onanism. Just to help me finally sleep.

What was I thinking??? My first night as a priest, and already I've defiled myself. It's ridiculous.... How weak the flesh is.... Perhaps this is a lesson sent from above. I'm filled with shame... Such shame. Now, I'll never sleep! Must pray for forgiveness. Find a way to soothe my troubled soul.

Day 2

Three times in a night!!! I can't bear to look at my fellow passengers on the bus to Boston. They look at me in my collar, and I can see them thinking that I am a Priest, a holy man, a man of God, perfect....What a fraud I am.... The parallels to Peter and the crowing Cock are almost unbearable. I suppose, Peter went on to great things. I must take heart. At least I am well rested.

...Such joy in my heart upon arrival. The Monsignor greeted me warmly, and showed me to my quarters... They are spartan, but they are better than that of the young runaways lodged only 1 floor beneath me. Those spunky castaways greeted my arrival with suspicion. I surmised that the priest that I was replacing was not well-loved by his wards, for what reason I cannot guess. Nonetheless, there was something about their dirty boyish faces that filled me with delight. Such youth. Such hope. Such promise! I just wanted to bathe each and every one of them, clean them up and fill them with God's promise of enduring love.

Day 3

Do I really have to abuse myself in order to fall asleep? My track record as a priest is 2 for 2 nights. Must break this before it becomes ridiculous. Fortunately, I can always remind myself that as sins go, it's not the worst. Still, I'm not looking forward to Sunday.

On the bright side, I have begun my ministry. I feel like I'm a natural!!!

I mix freely among these "lost boys," reaching out to them on the street, getting them food, shelter... They are so hurt, so broken.... With God's help, I can nurse them back to health. I want to hold each and every one of them. Cuddle them.... Let them know how much God loves them.

Day 5

I feel I may be thinking too much about the boys. Must try to take my mind off of the pressures of adjusting to a new place. At last a chance to resume my hobby of ships in bottles. I have purchased a fine one in Cambridge. A Yankee Clipper. Sleek and fast.

Day 8

Already my first confession, and despite the sanctity of the sacrament, I can tell that the Monsignor is displeased with me. Doesn't he understand that what's said in the confessional, stays in the confessional? Perhaps I have to tone down my fresh-from-seminary idealism, but I mean Puh-lease.... that's basic stuff! Besides 50 Hail Marys is an awful lot for masturbating every night before bed. I know I should stop, but it does help me sleep...

I only gave young Bobby Lofton 5 Hail Marys, and he had masturbated in front of a man for heroin money. Why would I get 50? I wasn't being too lenient, I don't think. I mean, Bobby's just in a hard place, that's all. I can't imagine what a scene that was. How do you even ask a young kid like Bobby to pleasure himself? Who has that kind of guts? I pray for that man. If only he could harness that daring bravado for some good purpose instead of his sickness.

Day 12

I've taken to instructing the boys in all elements of sport. Seeing their lithe, sinewy bodies leap and turn is a testament to the presence of God. Glorious nature herself provides evidence of revelation!

Alas, the bad habits of the street have rubbed off on some of these young foals. They hesitate to bathe afterwards, as if ashamed of their nakedness in front of their peers.

Rather than stand silent, a guilty accomplice to their poor hygiene, I appoint myself shower monitor, and make sure that each of them returns to the sleeping quarters bathed and refreshed.

Day 14

Monsignor gives me another 50! I understand that I must break my cycle of sin before bed, but he must understand that it's hard. My body is begging me to unwind. Nonetheless, this week I shall not, SHALL NOT masturbate. I reaffirm my vow of chastity. I am pure and good.

Day 15

Starting now. No masturbating.

Day 16

Stupid, stupid, weak, weak flesh....

Day 17

Hosanna! Made it all day without despoiling myself!

Day 18

Great blackness! I am undone! Little Bobby Lofton seems intent on tormenting me. How long can one boy shower? His "playful" splashing is anything but innocent. The vision of his smooth buttocks haunts my dreams. I cannot sleep. 3 times in quick succession

already, and still I am awake. What fresh devilry is this?

Day 19

I immersed myself in model-making all day. I had already made good progress, but today's labor was outstanding. The ship appears ready to sail!

Day 20

A new beginning! Baseball Season at last!

We have a strong team. Carl Kocher, Tommy Henman, Tyrone Williams. A veritable murderers row (alas, perhaps literally in Tyrone's case). Bobby Lofton objects when I place him in right field—far, far away from me. How his voice infuriates me! I shall maintain my decency though. In right field he shall stay.

The rest of the kids are really responding to my enthusiasm. I hope they feel how much I love them. I've taken to swatting each one of them on the buttocks as they enter the showers, just like real big-leaguers. We all have a big laugh over that.

...What a dream! Bobby begs for sodomy of the most unspeakable kind, and I find myself unable to resist his command. Just as my manhood is about to be desecrated by the supple mouth of deceit, I awake in horror, only to find myself awash in a pool of my own foulness!

Day 21

In the confessional, Monsignor presses me for more details of my weakness. He lets nothing go, asking for graphic details of anything that might have spurred me on to break my chastity.

I have decided that Monsignor's interest in my sexual phantasms seems unhealthy. I fear that he might have a prurient desire to listen to my mind's night wanderings. I omit my Onanism from my confession to him. He has the gall to ask me if I am leaving anything out.

Day 28

The Monsignor still presses me at confession. He is unwilling to believe my assertion that I have been pure. The fact that I am lying is irrelevant! How

can he imply that I am! The outrage!

I tell him that I have been too busy with sport to have carnal thoughts. Yet, Monsignor wonders aloud whether I am spending too much time with the boys! Would he have me go back to my long bouts of sin at night? Does he wish to destroy me?

Day 30

Bobby Lofton, Bobby Lofton, Bobby Lofton! I find myself correcting him at every turn. Now there's a boy in need of mentoring. The other boys taunt him, calling him "Bobby Softon," and he immediately resorts to fighting. I have benched him. He shall sit beside me during the games. I shall teach him to respect the game and himself. He shall be my private pupil.

Day 34

Another horrible dream! Young Lofton sails the ship into regions where it should not go. Shall everything I hold pure be corrupted?

Day 35

Invited Bobby to my quarters. I thought I could talk to him in a place of such holiness, but his attention wandered throughout the whole of my instructions. Finally, when I touched him, I received his undivided thoughts. I had to touch him. He had to listen. It is for his own good. I just must not... Not next time. The damage is slight to him, and the wisdom gained immeasurable. Still, I should not have. Definitely not. I must make it up to him.

Day 41

Bobby loved the baseball glove I gave him. I told him that I would show him how to oil it properly, then tie it, and place it under a pillow to sleep on. He seemed excited by the prospect.

Day 42

My love for the boy outstrips my reason once again! Ah, Linseed, you dangerous unguent, you betray me at last.

Day 43

Bobby asks me for a baseball and I am powerless to resist his request.

Day 44

The boy has an insatiable appetite!

Voracious sexually, he is driven also by greed! He wants me to get him another present. As if I were exchanging gifts for loving. Like some kind of John, with a boy hooker! Does he understand nothing of the purity of my feelings for him? To be sure, the flesh sullies the clear water of the spirit, but how deep runs the current? How powerful the stream? My love is so close to pure. Surely, he must realize the difference!

Day 50

Will Bobby even look at me? I fear his heart is hardened!

Day 51

Can he not feel the depth of my love for him? For it is love, and a good thing that I feel. So powerful my love, it must be good. It must be.

Day 52

What have I done? I forced young Lofton to his knees. To his knees! It was wrong. If only I could undo the dread act... but why did he spurn me? How could I have done otherwise? I prayed for hours for guidance, but it seems as if the whole heavens have fallen silent. Even my beloved boys seem to avoid me now. I could have sworn that I heard Tyrone hiss "queer" behind my back, as if I were gay. I am so alone!

Day 53

The little urchin wants money! I shall teach him a lesson indeed.

...My palm hurts, so I can only imagine the pain of Lofton's backside. Still, I will not be found guilty of sparing the rod. I shall not allow him to be as a painted Jezebel. He is my love, my life. He is my Son and I the Father.

Day 60

Treachery! Bobby Judas has told the Monsignor everything! The bishop comes tomorrow.

Why did I trust a wretched boy such as him to hold precious the confidence of my love?

Day 61

The Bishop seems a kind and understanding man. I am to leave Boston immediately. I swear a solemn oath to be ever watchful of my desires, and how they appear to others.

Before I go, I have one thing left to do with a certain snitch.

Day 62

Squeals from the squealer linger with me still. Why didn't I let him go earlier? There was time. Then again, why didn't Bobby Lofton let me go? He should have known the power he possessed over me. That I wanted to help him, and he twisted my desire. He twisted it, that monstrous little creature! He has ruined me, and I am lost.

Day 62

I am reassigned to Cleveland. At last, a fresh start.

Day 65

New Brunswick here I come. Best not to speak of Cleveland. Never again!

Day 67

The Cardinal himself has intervened this time! I find myself in Cerritos. He has absolved me, and I am clean at last. The clouds are lifting and the sun breaks clear. God indeed looks after his own, and never a Psalm was written that did Him justice!

Southern California is a far finer place than the Northeast. It is not just the weather that is less oppressive. It seems I have a clean slate. The new Monsignor appears to have no idea of my recent difficulties. Nor shall he ever, as I, too, have learned lessons from New Brunswick. I shall not make such a mistake again.

Day 68

I have computer access here! Wonderful thing, the computer. So much power to help. So many things to see!

And, thanks to Yahoo, I have ordered plans for a model of the warship *Bonhomme Richard* to occupy my time. With skill, it shall fit into a large-mouth 5-gallon jug. My hands shall not be idle. Get behind me, Satan!

Day 69

I have received the most disturbing e-mails, without requesting them!!! Suffice it to say, I almost expect to see pictures of Bobby Lofton when I click on the "hyper-links." But even he might shy away from such depravities as I have seen!

Day 80

I spend almost all my time online now. I am engaged in "chat" with a troubled youth from Texas. Alas, he is so far away.... I feel the need to lay my hands on him.... to heal. To heal!!! No more than that, I say, I swear! To Heal!

Day 89

Praise be to God! "Trevor1988" has agreed to come to Cerritos! I have sent him my picture and a bus ticket. Happy shall be that meeting indeed.

Day 92

Treachery once more! The FBI seized me in the Greyhound station.

Fortunately, the Church has paid for my bail. But I fear, Diary, that you must go to a hidden place, and there remain until the ill-winds pass. With God's help, I shall overcome my sickness. I shall write to you once more in happier times.

Thank the Lord at least my ship building kit has arrived in the mail. I will throw myself into this project.

Day 150

Ahhh, Diary. So much to tell you.... The plea bargain. The transfer to Senegal, never to return. The darkness of the boys here. The chocolate of their skin. It's true what they say about the sons of Ham.... Delightfully true!

I have a native boy, 'Ngala, as a manservant now... 'Ngala - how like my angel that sounds to my ears. 'Ngala, I shall instruct in the ways of fealty, of true devotion. He is more beautiful than any Bobby Lofton....

Day 159

At last, the *Bonhomme Richard* is ready for her maiden voyage!

Day 160

'Ngala has been taken to the hospital. The doctors say that there's a 90% chance he shall regain continence. Lucky lad. I can't help but feel partly responsible. Oh I rue the day that I took up ship-in-bottles! Ah, how I miss my Bobby Lofton... My Bobby.

ED. NOTE: Here the diary ends. Father Aikens' naked body was found hanging in a closet with the diary in front of him opened to this page.

How to write dirty

by Justice Thurgood Marshall

Thurgood Marshall, the first black appointed to the U.S. Supreme Court, tells you how to write dirty.

One of the most time-consuming tasks a Supreme Court justice performs is reading through mounds of pornographic material, to determine if it is protected by the First Amendment right to freedom of speech. The Court has ruled that such material is protected only if it possesses "redeeming social value."

What is "redeeming social value"? To me, it is something that puts "lead" in your "pencil." Pops a "bone of contention" in your "legal briefs." In other words, something that makes your pecker stand up and say the Pledge of Allegiance.

Of course, it takes some hot and steamy writing to get a rise out of a few of those old droopy drawers on the Supreme Court. But don't despair; just follow my simple Marshall Plan for How to Write Dirty. Soon, you'll be able to crank out pornography that a judge will want to review in his chambers time and again. That judge is me.

Keep the reader in mind

How would you like to read a book entitled *A Man Called Homo* or *My Girl Friend Flicka?* Well, I've read them, and they're terrible. Seems too many pornographers these days write stories that appeal only to homos, horses, or other degenerates. They have forgotten that the typical reader of dirty books is a normal, heterosexual, black, elderly Supreme Court justice.

To write dirty well, pick topics your audience will be interested in, like fellatio, blow jobs, and white women. Especially white women. They're my favorite. Oh, yeah.

Write what you know

A man once wrote a book entitled *I Was a Hooker on the Moon.* It did not have the ring of authenticity, and sold few copies. "You should write about what you know," I advised this aspiring author, who just happened to be Justice Felix Frankfurter. His next book, *Suck My Wiener,* was on Thurgood Marshall's Best-seller List for a full five months.

So write about subjects you are familiar with. If you are a mailman, write sexy stories about delivering the mail. If you are a homo, write stories about what your straight friends do. If you are a white woman, write to me. Here is my address: Thurgood Marshall, Supreme Court Building, Washington, D.C.

To illustrate the principle of writing what you know, I have composed the following example. It is based on a true incident— only the names have been changed slightly:

Handsome Thurgood X. was sitting in his chambers one day, reading *A Man Called Homo.* Suddenly, he was interrupted by Sandra Day O., a distinguished white woman. "You certainly look foxy in your big, black robes," Sandra purred. "I've got something even bigger and blacker underneath," replied Thurgood.

Thurgood had always had a way with women—you could say he was a sort of Afro-disiac. Soon the two were lying on the bench, Thurgood preparing to enter Sandra's private chambers. "Here *come* da judge," he shouted, as his groin gavel banged away. Finally, they finished, furiously collapsing in the sweat of their ecstasy. "That was sure good, Thurgood," Sandra cooed.

"Oh, yeah," he replied.

Don't be afraid to exaggerate

In my 200 years on the bench, I have handed down judgments so brilliant that the Statue of Justice once came to life, ran off her pedestal, and gave me a big wet kiss on the lips.

Of course, most of this story is not true, but is actually a subtle use of the principle of exaggeration. Clever exaggeration can prove quite useful in pornographic stories, as well. It can turn a dull novel like *Moby-Dick* into the porn classic *Moby Huge Dick.* Observe how exaggerating the truth makes the following story a million times more interesting: Thurgood was sitting in the New York State Bar and Grill, finishing his twentieth bottle of champagne. He had just returned from Washington, flushed with his victory in the

Marshal Thurgood Marshall declares Marshall law on those sidewindin' polecats who write boring pornography.

After scrutinizing a copy of Playboy *during a desegregation trial, Justice Marshall proudly declares: "I call this magazine Exhibit A—for 'Arousing.'"*

case *Brown* v. *Ten Boards of Education.* Suddenly, a beautiful woman, with bosoms the size of watermelons, walked into the bar.

"Don't be impartial, Mr. Marshall," she implored. "Take me, take me now." In half a second, they were both naked. "I had no idea they'd painted the Empire State Building black," she gasped. "That's not the Empire State Building," Thurgood replied, "that's my fifty-two inches of manhood." With one motion, Thurgood thrust his entire Shaft into her awaiting body. Three hundred orgasms later, they finished.

"That was great," she purred. "Just wait'll I send my ninety-three teenage sisters to see you." All in all, it was a typical day.

Edit yourself

There's an old joke that runs something like this: "A sexually inexperienced couple are on their honeymoon. Not sure what to do, the husband asks his wife for advice. 'Stick it in,' she commands. 'Now pull it out. Stick it in. Pull it out.'" I forget the punch line to this anecdote, but it hardly matters—we've already heard the good part.

Similarly, careful editing can improve your writing. Who wants to read a boring law book when the Cliffs Notes will do just as well? In the following example, a fine pornographic story is made even better by carefully editing out the less essential passages:

Handsome Thurgood ~~X. was sitting in his chambers one day, reading *A Man Called Homo*. Suddenly, he was interrupted by~~

Sandra ~~Day O., a distinguished~~ white woman. ~~"You certainly look~~ foxy ~~in your big, black robes,"~~ ~~Sandra purred. "I've got something~~ ~~even~~ bigger and blacker ~~underneath," replied~~ Thurgood.

Thurgood ~~had always~~ ~~had a way with women—~~ ~~you could say he was a~~ ~~sort of~~ Afro-disiac…

Humor your audience

One day, I mistakenly broke into Lyndon Johnson's bedroom while Lady Bird was preparing to give him a blow job. To mask my embarrassment, I made a couple of ribald jests. First I turned to Lady Bird and quipped, "I guess you put the BJ in LBJ." Then I pointed to the president's groin, and added, "Boy, you sure got a big Johnson, Lyndon." LBJ was so amused by these remarks, and so eager to get me out of the room, that he appointed me to the Supreme Court.

Just as a few great jokes helped my judicial career, so can they help you with your dirty-writing career. Check out this example:

The justices and I were sitting in closed session, deliberating. Suddenly, who should walk in but

Justice Byron White's wife, Lucy. "You sure make me juicy, Ms. Lucy," I quipped. "I love Lucy, " I added, elbowing Byron in the ribs.

I was on a roll now, so I turned to Justice Harry Blackmun and hollered, "I'm the real hairy black man around these parts." This prompted Chief Justice Burger to call for order. In response, I whipped open my robe (I had nothing on underneath) and said, "Hey, Chief Justice Cheeseburger, did you order this big black whopper?"

All the justices excused themselves and returned to their chambers, unable to match my brilliant repartee. I was alone in

Swearing an oath on his personal "Bible for Swingers," Thurgood Marshall testifies that he is a porn-again Christian.

the room, except for Lucy, whose arm I had a firm grip on. "Baby, you sure got big torts," I joked, "and there ain't nothing I like better than White's woman." Then I screwed her eighty-seven times.

The defense rests

Well, I hope you liked my helpful tips on how to write dirty. So, if you follow my rules, the next time you pop up in court on an obscenity charge, maybe something on me will pop up too. Oh, yeah.

Thurgood Marshall

Obligatory Sex Scenes

Three famous men, authors all of recent important novels (Spiro Agnew William F. Buckley, and John Lindsay) have lately and often appeared upon prestigious talk shows to plug their respective books. Each member of this august trio has unblushingly observed that, yes, his tome does contain the "obligatory sex scene."

Clearly, these writers, all men of the world, have seen fit to trim the sails of their creative integrity to the prevailing winds of marketing considerations, motivated not by greed but rather by the desire for their significant and redemptive fictions to reach a wider audience than your ponderous and semiliterate political potboiler usually does.

Lest any of our readers, ever eager for sensual sensation, dash out and buy the Buckley book — thereby subsidizing further the man's unnatural tastes and politics — we excerpt and reprint here the entire of his "obligatory sex scene":

"Oh, yes," she expostulated. "Oh Supreme Being, oh my Supreme Being, yes!"

Always keen to follow the example of our elders and betters, we have taken it upon ourselves to write the "obligatory sex scenes" which, if included in the pages of well-intentioned but, alas, for the most part ignored classics of literature, will return these works to the popularity they deserve.

THE REPUBLIC
by PLATO

"I do not understand how that can be so," replied Thrasymachus.

"Perhaps we should take an example," said Socrates, "to see if what I maintain is true in common nature."

"Very well."

"We have said that Love cannot be purely physical, and therefore mortal, for it is eternal and cannot die. Look at those birds over there. Their parents are doubtless dead, and yet they themselves, the embodiment of their parents' love, live on, and fly beautifully against the sunset, do they not?"

"They do, I agree," answered Thrasymachus.

"Just so. Then we must also agree that Love itself is Eternal, Beautiful, and True, must we not?"

"We must," agreed the chastened boy.

"Fine," continued Socrates, gathering his robes up before him. "Now bend over, and I'll drive you home."

The House at Pooh Corner
by A.A. MILNE

Kanga?" said Pooh, in his I'm-Rather-Shy sort of voice.

"What is it, Pooh, dear?"

"Well, Kanga, Owl said that he . . . that is, someone said that you and Owl . . . I mean, Kanga, would it be alright if I put my Tiddleypom in your verywarmplace?" Pooh said this last part very fast, because he was Excited.

"I think that would be Very Nice, Pooh," said Kanga. "I was hoping you'd ask. In fact, I put rather a lot of Honey in there this morning, Just-in-Case." This Unexpected News made Pooh a Very Happy Bear indeed, and so he hummed a little Hum of Lust.

Oh in I hum
And out I hum
And up and down I'm humming
Titty bum titty bum
Titty bum bum bum bum
Sweet Christopher Robin! I'm coming!

WALDEN
by Henry David Thoreau

There are those who ask me about modern "fancy fucking," an illusion as great as "modern improvements," such as the magnetic telegraph from Maine to Texas. I would rather fuck a squirrel on a bed of thorns than lie on a mass of velvet cushions being serviced by a painted octoroon from New Orleans.

Man in the primitive ages fucked simply, with a free circulation. When the desire seized him he found an orifice and put his tool into it until he was satisfied. He did not engage in so-called fashionable positions, as useless as the gewgaws on the mantlepieces of Boston's mansions. He thrust his member in and out in a straightforward, honest manner with no ornamentation but his own body.

When I am asked whether I can live by fucking squirrels, I am accustomed to answer such, that I can live by fucking anything, a mole, a ferret, a hole in a maple tree. The human race is capable of finding strange bedfellows. But I went into the woods because I wished to masturbate. I wanted to commune with my own cock. Instead of fucking one hundred squirrels, stroke your own shmekel! Simplicity! Back and forth, up and down. Squeeze it, stroke it, make it harder than a ha'penny nail. Who needs to spend a king's ransom on female flesh when you can use your imagination and your sturdy two hands? And so I jerked off as frequently as the church bells rang in Concord, and I was not worse off for it. And I did not go blind, as my friend Emerson warned. My eyes have never been better.

Sherlock Holmes

by Sir Arthur Conan Doyle

*"The Adventure of the
Extreme Unpleasantness"*

It was a cold and foggy day in September of '98 when I next had occasion to call upon my remarkable friend Sherlock Holmes. I was greeted as usual at the entrance to my former, and his present, lodgings on Baker Street by the worthy Mrs. Hudson. "Do come in, Doctor," she said. "Mr. Holmes has been expecting you." So saying, the good housekeeper led me up the well-worn and familiar steps to the door of 221-B.

Holmes answered my discreet knock with a peremptory, "Ah, Watson. Do come in," his extraordinary powers of observation having doubtless informed him of his

visitor's identity sight unseen. I entered, and beheld a singular tableau.

Holmes was engaged in an uncommonly spirited bout of sexual intercourse with a woman whom I immediately recognized as "*the* woman," the magnificent and enchanting creature whose acquaintance my friend had made during the adventure I have described in my journals as "A Scandal in Bohemia." Her dress and coiffure in disarray, Miss Irene Adler—for it was indeed she—thrashed and writhed upon the divan beneath Holmes's persistent thrusting.

"Sherlock, oh Sherlock!" she cried in the extremity of her passion, addressing my friend with a familiarity I found both unusual and impudent. "I am spending, I am spending! Ah! I am spent!"

"Holmes!" I sputtered. "What the devil—"

"Orgasm, Watson, and a clitoral one, I believe," Holmes remarked.

"Yes, but...now see here, Holmes, this is the very limit. How can you—"

Without missing a stroke, and continuing despite his paramour's obvious state of exhaustion and satiation, my friend directed his steely gaze toward me and explained, "My dear fellow, the physical symptoms could not be more obvious. The intense flush in the cheeks. The labored breathing. The spasmodic quivering in the loins. After observing these plainly apparent symptoms, and taking into consideration the woman's sudden and rather passionate expostulations which you yourself have just heard, one would have to be a perfect fool not to conclude that Miss Adler has just experienced a delirious and ecstatic explosion of pleasure like a thousand pounds of nitroglycerine detonating in her love chamber."

"But it's so absurdly simple!" I cried in admiration. The endurance of my friend would have astonished a layman, but I, as a medical man, mentally ascribed it to the effects of tincture of cocaine injected just prior to the carnal engagement. Whether this accounted for the great detective's near-superhuman capabilities or no, Holmes would not divulge. Without ceasing his rhythmic penetrations, he reached into the pocket of the old smoking jacket he had evidently dropped to the carpet during the

erotic revelries, removed a piece of foolscap redolent of cheap French perfume, and extended it to me.

"But come, Watson," he said, the excitement of what surely was a new case beginning to color his cheeks. "Have one of Mrs. Hudson's excellent buttered scones. Then direct your attention to this—a most intriguing missive, I think. I'll be done here in a moment, and then to work. The game's afoot!"

Shortly thereafter we were seated...

Contact Bridge

BY CHARLES GOREN

South opens.
Seeing her vulnerable, North immediately raises.
South passes.
North finesses.

South sees that her partner is now fully raised and ready for action in her suit. She knows that if he completes play while she is still weak, he will dummy and her hand will have to be strong enough for both of them. She has opened and it is up to him now. She passes.

North responds by leading with all he's got.
His club is stronger than she had dared hope.
He trumps her solidly once and then again.
North doubles and redoubles.

South is sure he is out of tricks.
He makes the grand slam, amazing her.
South responds by spreading her remaining cards, flushing royally.

Pride and Prejudice

by JANE AUSTEN
CHAPTER XLIII

The winding path that they had been following had grown narrower, and was overhung with branches that tore at Elizabeth's gown; soon it was but three feet at its widest part, when she espied, in the distance, an old summer house, dilapidated and overgrown with weeds and mosses, of a lonely and slightly forbidding aspect. As the first drops of rain began to fall, Mr. Darcy turned his steps towards the building, quitting the path and taking a shorter way through the tall grasses;—Elizabeth had little choice but to follow. He murmured something about the weather as they reached their destination; the door yielded easily to his touch, and they reached their haven just as the rain began in earnest.

The interior was empty of any furnishing, save for a small settee, towards which Darcy let Elizabeth;—and when *she* had seated herself, much to her amazement, he flung himself to his knees before her, and, in a change of mood that seemed as abrupt as the change of weather, began ardently to express his admiration for and devotion to her person. Elizabeth hardly knew how to respond!—was this the cold, arrogant Mr. Darcy, who had expressed such scorn for her on previous occasions? She was attempting to reply when an even more strange event took place;—to her great consternation, he lifted up her skirts, and disappeared beneath them!—in breathless accents did she beg him to desist; in ardent though muffled tone did he make negative reply, as he attempted, with no little difficulty, to undo her drawers; when he had succeeded in the latter, he stopped attempting the former; and Elizabeth was filled with the most delightful and confused sensations; she allowed to herself that they were certainly pleasurable, but at the same time wondered with rising alarm if she had, by her momentary weakness, allowed too much familiarity in their previous intercourse.

But her pleasure mounted to such an extent that she soon lost her fears in that direction. "Oh! Oh!" she cried, when she could contain herself no longer—"I am all in a flutter!—Mr. Darcy, your unexpected cordiality has left me quite speechless;—my previous coldness was unpardonable;—oh, my dear, *dear* Mr. Darcy;—how can you ever forgive me?—oh, oh, *oh!*"—and Mr. Darcy, whose head now emerged from beneath Elizabeth's petticoats, although *another portion* of his anatomy remained hidden from view, joined his voice to hers in an outpouring of sentiment to which no one, knowing his proud, aloof manner, might have responded without a great deal of amazement.

Amendment I

Congress shall make no law respecting an establishment of religion, or prohibiting the free exercise thereof; or abridging the freedom of speech, or of the press; or the right of the people peaceably to assemble, congregate, and come together in such form and manner, comprehending but not limited to fornication, copulation, coition, venery, adultery, incest, bestiality, concubinage, cunnilingus, fellatio, and such concomitant acts of sexual congress as buggering, humping, sucking, thrusting, squeezing, biting, sweating, swearing, and screaming, as the people in their sole discretion shall deem appropriate.

ABRAHAM LINCOLN: THE PRAIRIE YEARS

by Carl Sandburg

It was early in the spring of 1819. Young Abe had barely turned thirteen, but he already had a piece of manly equipment that had earned him the nickname *the Railsplitter*. Strong as Indiana maple it was, and straight and true as half a cord of good Michigan pinewood. Young Abe loved to read books, never mind if he understood them, and young Widow Harless would pay him for chores around her place with the loan of one of her French books, filled with pictures that set the young boy to dreaming. It was one day while Abe was walking on the ceiling that something happened to the boy that he would remember as a man. "Would you like to take a bath, Abe?" asked the widow. In those days country people would bathe together because water was scarce, and Abe was not abashed at the widow's request. "I cannot tell a lie," said Abe, who wanted a cleaning, because he was dirty. "But there is hardly room for you, me, and this sturdy Aspen between my legs in that small tub."

"Never you mind," said the widow, offering to suck the sap from out of that tree until it lay down as innocent as a limp radish when the wind rises out of the west and the scent of Jesus is in the cloud drift. So they bathed together, and another thing or two did they, and that was the first time that Abe understood the word Union. On the way home, he scratched a poem on the back of an owl, using some chewed sassafras leaves for ink;

Abraham Lincoln visited the widder.
Split her rails and then her beaver.
He would write more as the years went by.

"THE SONG OF HIAWATHA"
by Henry Wadsworth Longfellow

HIAWATHA'S HONEYMOON
Verse DCCLXXXVIII

By the shore of Gitche Gumee,
By the shining Big-Sea-Water,
At the doorway of his wig-wam,
Hiawatha stood and waited,
With his loin-cloth at his ankles,
And his manhood rigid standing,
Ready for the promised blow-job,
From his new bride, Minnehaha.
Minnehaha ho-ho hee-hee,
Laughing spread-out wide her
     cunt flaps,
Fingered hard her fur-fringed fun
     knob,
Took his wang within her
     mouth-hole,
Humming on his come-flushed
     coupstick,
Slip slop slurp slurp suck suck
     gobble.
With a rhythm repetitious,
Slipped her lips along his tent-
     pole,
Forth and backward like the
     metre
Of the third-rate verse we're
     reading.
But forgotten were the plodding,
Boring, hackneyed lines of poesy,
As his load shot out her nostrils,
And she flopped back on the mud
     floor.

MOBY DICK
by HERMAN MELVILLE
CHAPTER 101
The Pequod Meets the Delilah

"Ship ahoy! Hast seen the White Whale?"

So did Ahab cry his peremptory greeting to the snug three-master that bobbed in lanquid placidity abaft our port beam. She sported British colors, and appeared to be a ship unlike the whaling variety as constructed by either English shipbuilders or those of America, but rather seemed laden with a tamer cargo, be it textile or jute or breadfruit. Likely she was accustomed to milder climes and glassier waters, such as those we now mutually sailed. But the *Delilah*'s—for that was her name—pleasure was proving Ahab's curse.

"Ahoy, ship!" cried the *Pequod*'s commander. "Hast seen Moby Dick? Or do ye not know of the beast?"

"Aye, sir!" called the *Delilah*'s captain, a red-faced, swart man clad in rough bluecloth and jovial in expression. "Lower me, lads, and I'll pay this *Pequod* a visit." To Ahab he called in conspiratorial tone, "I've a yarn to spin for ye, sir. So make ready yer welcome. Will ye have me aboard?"

"I will," replied Ahab, his leathery hands working a belaying pin as a constable manipulates his billystick. "Lower, then, and be welcome."

The captain and mate of the *Delilah* were presently lifted aboard and met on the main deck by Ahab, accompanied by the mate Starbuck and the jocular Stubb. During this the crews of the two ships would peer across the narrow gulf that stretched between the vessels and exchange intelligence, as is a seaman's wont. "Halloo, there! *Delilah*! Where are ye bound, and with what cargo?"

"Ahoy, *Pequod*! To San Salvador, with caskets of rosewater, and talc! And what of yourself?"

"Outward bound, and in search of the white whale! No less!"

"What! Are ye daft, then, my laddies?"

"Avast! Avast, and shove it!"

Meanwhile Captain Bammer, for so was the *Delilah*'s commander called, complimented Ahab on his vessel, and the two men exchanged discussion of climatic conditions and the mood and manner of the adjacent seas. But Ahab was greatly impatient for word of his quarry, and soon could restrain himself no longer. "Come, sir, what word have ye of the White Whale? You've a yarn to spin, ye tell me. Spin it, I say, for I am sore eager to lower for the beast and have at it."

"Mayhap you've already met the monster a time previous, hey, Captain?" Bammer asked, his eye studying Ahab's leg of white bone. "We of Britain are as familiar as any Yankee with the proclivity of this leviathan to gnaw the limb of whoever happens—"

"Proclivity be damned, sir!" spat Ahab. "Have ye a tale to tell, or no?"

"My apologies, sir." And here Bammer did smile, but whether to placate the temperamental Ahab, or at some private recollection, no man could say. "For a tale I do have to tell, sir, and by your leave will now reveal it.

"It was nigh onto a year ago that I was homeward sailing from a ten-month mission in search of the spermaceti, and a blessed voyage it had been, gentlemen: for we were loaded to the mizzen with good sperm. We had a clean wind, a happy crew, and the promise of prosperity awaited us in Portsmouth, come landfall. All omens declared the success of the venture—"

"Avast!" Ahab cried. "And 'twas then you spied the beast, is it!? Aha, yes! I know him—and in the prettiest of weather, does he arrive to torment and—"

"Bless me, sir, no!" Bammer laughed. "Never saw the creature. For we reached our port with three days to spare, without mishap. No, sir, neither shark nor storm, nor any whale, white or red or green, did disturb our progress. My point is this, then: two days we were docked in Portsmouth harbor. The lads were nearly all in town, visiting wives or sweethearts or making merry over meat and ale . . . and my mate, Mr. Sprocket—pardon, Sprocket, Captain Ahab, Captain, Sprocket—Mr. Sprocket here suggests that I hie myself ashore and celebrate with my own wife.

" 'Well, Sprocket,' says I, 'I'd take yer advice, saving for the fact that the wife is dead and buried for three years. And a pretty lass she was in her time, by God.'

" 'Well then, sir,' he says, bold as brass, 'every seaman knows what dalliances can be had in Portsmouth by a healthy sailor with a bit of silver in his pocket . . .' and he winks at me, Sprocket you rascal! Ah, Sprocket, you are a rogue."

"Hist, man!" Ahab interrupted impetuously. "What of the whale! What of Moby Dick?"

"In time, in time. So. It strikes me that this first mate's suggestion is as tantalizing as it is impudent, and with Sprocket minding the ship I betakes myself for a constitutional along one of several byways through the city that boasts various . . . establishments, if you comprehend me, gents."

"Aye, and too plainly, sir. For there's no good in such dalliances," Starbuck opined.

"But more, sir," Stubb urged. "And pray be specific."

Again Bammer laughed, apparently oblivious to Ahab's silent fury and frustration. "You've an ear for detail, is it? Very well, then. I betook me to an establishment called The Cask o' Sperm,

and can ye not tell by the place's very name how welcome a whaling man is made to feel therein? And after certain . . . *arrangements* . . . I found myself in a nicely appointed room, all frills and lace and satin divans, don't ye know, and a comely lass barely eighteen summers old ready to do my bidding. A gay young thing she was, too, and sporting—"

"The teats!" Stubb cried, unmindful of the man's rank. "Tell of the teats!"

"Ay, lad! Teats there were, and a full complement of them, two in all. Hefty as casabas from the Carribbee they were, full round and—"

"Damn your eyes!" Ahab bellowed. "Did ye or did ye not see the White Whale?"

"Have patience, Captain, for I tell of the beast in but a moment. So, gents: here was I, ten months from the sight of woman, and now before me kneeled this angel of mercy. 'Shall I disrobe, my dear,' say I. 'If you please, your honor,' she replies. And does so as well."

"The flukes!" Stubb panted, meaning by this the legs. "What of her flukes?!"

"Twin monuments to alabaster purity, my lads. And at the sight of one another did we commence into heavily respiring, and each ardent caress I gave her she returned—aye, and with more fervor than you'd expect from one so professionally engaged!"

"What of Moby Dick?" wailed Ahab, near apoplexy.

"And then we were on her couch," Bammer continued, not heeding the Captain. "And as I made to ram home the harpoon, she balked and said, 'A moment please, your honor,' and in a trice the damsel had taken me into her mouth!"

"Huzzah! Huzzah!" cheered Stubb, and slapped the dubious Starbuck on the back. "And then you lowered away, my hearty! You lowered away!"

"What of the whale, damn ye!"

"Nay, but hold, lads. I was preparing to lower away, but my pike was still gripped by the girl's jaws, when all on a sudden I clap eyes on her marvelous rump. And idly—idly, I say, to *myself* it was—I murmur, 'Ah, my dear, but ye are as white as the White Whale himself, as white as Moby Dick, who every sensible seaman does fear.' And suddenly she starts! And gags! And gurgles! And in a jiff had bitten clean clear through my pin and clove it in twain!"

"No!" gasped Stubb, and nearly swooned, holding onto stolid Starbuck's arm for support.

"Aye, lad. And when the shouting and bleeding and the apologies were subsided, did she explain to me that her own uncle was an American whaling captain who some time previous had lost a limb to the maw of the leviathan, and any mention of the whale disturbed her to the point of spasms and fever. Her uncle! Are ye this same man, sir?" This last he addressed to our captain, who merely stared at the man with a blank gaze and nodded slowly.

"Then behold this bony substitute for as stout an organ as ever traveled a deck," Bammer said, and produced from his trousers an ivory appendage fashioned of whalebone similar to Ahab's leg. "For no longer can I sail for whale oil and the sperm, gents. My vital powers are sapped, and I now deliver cargoes of scented water, and talc, and the like. I am not ashamed of my fate, mind you. But to whosoever does finally kill this white monster, let him know I join in his pursuit. More than one captain has he done injury to, this Moby Dick!"

And with that Bammer hoisted himself down into his boat, and made his way back to the *Delilah*. Ahab, his monomania again kindled and stoked, scowled, and disappeared below decks.

———————————————

CONSUMER REPORTS

We tested five cameras in this range. A target area was chosen and lighting conditions were standardized to give the best possible view of the interior we had selected.

The *Kodak Trimline* is a popular model at around $30.00, and has a three setting zone focus system. On the first setting two people were visible as vague

shapes within the picture frame, while on the second setting a surprising improvement in resolution was achieved. All testers were high in their praise for the third and highest setting, features of the room and characteristics of the two females being observed.

The *Rollei 400* was judged difficult to adjust (see chart next page), but demonstrated its superior design. On all settings, we could observe such refinements as the patterned fabric of the thin silk dress one of the subjects was peeling from her supple form, impressive for a zone focus mechanism.

The Minolta Standard fared poorly. Even with the superb 500-X tripod (C.R. May '74), the best it could do was a somewhat fuzzy image of two pale bodies entwined in languorous embrace.

The *Fujica* we tested was another story, the improved image quality well worth the extra 2.6 lbs. in weight. Though difficult to use with eyeglasses, the patented viewfinder showed a generous and clear spectacle of Sapphic love. Indeed, the scene seemed a lot nearer than the figure shown on the useful built-in distance indicator (also standard on *Fujica* models). Even with a poor lens fine points were visible; wisps of blonde hair cascading over creamy thighs, nails digging into flesh, details so vivid that one had the feeling of being in the target room.

The *Minox 280* boasts a variable range finder that enables rapid focusing. This makes position changes possible, and we found it a pleasure to be able to change from firm breast to quivering buttock without losing time in resetting. With this addition we could visually explore the environment so freely we felt we could almost hear the pleasure cries of the two women, almost taste the ripe love juices that now flowed freely in the heat of the mounting passion.

As we began shooting in earnest we found the thumb-slide film advance a nuisance, requiring a complex series of actions to cock the camera after every shot. Both the *Kodak* and the *Minox* had viewfinders which tended to fog at the worst times. As events surged to a fiery climax, all shooting ceased as we busied ourselves wiping and recocking.

By the time we refocused, we found ourselves disappointingly gazing at two supine forms lying in quiet repose, skin flush and sensual smiles ironically clear images of opportunities missed.

The Pickwick Papers

by CHARLES DICKENS
CHAPTER 28

A good-humored Christmas chapter, containing an account of a wedding, and some other sports beside, which, although in their way even as good customs as marriage itself, are not quite so "rigidly kept up" in these censorious times.

...if anything could have added to the interest of this agreeable scene, it would have been the remarkable fact of Mr. Pickwick's appearing without his gaiters, or anything else in the habilimental way, for the first time in the memory of his oldest friends.

"Do you mean to frolic?" said Wardle.

"Of course I do," replied Mr. Pickwick. "Don't you see I am ready for the purpose?" Mr. Pickwick called attention to his manly part, which was indeed at the ready, and while not of the largest construction, had a healthy glow about it which showed it to be still a formidable engine of merriment.

The family was by this time assembled, according to an annual custom on Christmas Eve, observed by old Wardle's forefathers from time immemorial. From the center of the ceiling, old Wardle had just suspended with his own hands a huge branch of mistletoe, and this same branch of mistletoe instantaneously gave rise to a scene of general and most delightful struggling and confusion; in the midst of which, Mr. Pickwick, with a gallantry that would have done honor to the oldest of noble European families, took the elderly Lady Tollimglower by the hand, led her beneath the mystic branch, gently spread her nether lips and, liberally embellishing this venerable aperture with fresh butter from the dairy, mounted her in all courtesy and decorum. The old lady submitted to this politeness with the dignity which befitted so important and serious a solemnity, but the younger ladies, not being so thoroughly imbued with a superstitious respect for the custom—or imagining that the value of a pleasant tumble is very much enhanced if it cost a little trouble to obtain it—screamed and struggled, and ran into corners, and threatened and remonstrated, and did everything but leave the room until some of the less adventurous gentlemen were on the

point of desisting, when they all at once found it useless to resist any longer and submitted to be mounted with a good grace. Mr. Winkle mounted the young lady with the black eyes, and Mr. Snodgrass mounted Emily, and Mr. Weller, not being particular about the form of being under the mistletoe, mounted Emma and the other female servants just as he caught them. As to the poor relations, they were mounted by everybody. And the plainer portions of the young lady visitors, in their excessive confusion, ran right under the mistletoe, as soon as it was hung up, without even knowing it!

Now, the screaming had subsided, and faces were in a glow, and bodies in a tangle, and Mr. Pickwick, after mounting the old lady, as before mentioned, was standing under the mistletoe, looking with a very pleased countenance on all that was passing around him, when before he distinctly knew what the matter was, he was surrounded by the whole body and squeezed, pinched, fondled, sucked upon, or penetrated by every one of them.

It was a pleasant thing to see Mr. Pickwick in the center of the group, now pulled this way, and then that, first taking one person's part within his mouth, then another's in his hand, and then someone else's up the backside, and to hear the peals of laughter which were raised on every side.

"This," said Mr. Pickwick, looking around him, "this is, indeed, sport!"

"Vell!" said Sam Weller, "there'll be a deal o' hole-fillin' yet afore this here passes, as the Verger says to the Sexton at the first outbreak o' plague."

OUR TOWN

by Thornton Wilder

STAGE MANAGER: "Mr. Webb is publisher and editor of the Grover's Corners Sentinel. That's our local paper, y'know."

MR. WEBB enters from his house, pulling on his coat.
STAGE MANAGER: "Have you any comments, Mr. Webb?"

MR. WEBB: "Very ordinary town, if you ask me. But our young people seem to like it well enough. Ninety percent of 'em graduating from high school settle down right here to live—

even when they've been away to college."

STAGE MANAGER: "Now, is there anyone in the audience who would like to ask Editor Webb anything about the town?"

MAN AT THE BACK OF AUDITORIUM: "Whaddaya do for a piece of ass in Grover's Corners?"

MR. WEBB: "Well...there's Mrs. Gawalski, she runs a house over in Polack town. 'Course, that'll cost you two dollars. Then there's Abe Bingham down at the stable—he'll suck your pecker. Abe's not quite right in the head, though. To tell the truth, I guess most folks just hump the old lady or yank on it."

Being and Time

by MARTIN HEIDEGGER
V. Being-in as Such

26. Throbbing-Memberhood and Its Potentiality-for-Exploding-in-White-Hot-Orgasmicity

At first glance the Being-in (*In-sein*) of Throbbing-member appears to us as a latency. Throbbing-member stands before us as a phenomenon of Itness, i.e., Throbbing-memberhood-in-its-Selfhood-as-merely-ontic Being. The Being-in of Throbbing-member attains facticity as an ontological verity when, with eager hands and low urgent moans, she guides Throbbing-member into her hot, pulsing womanhoodness. Then, too, does Throbbing-member discover the Being-present-at-hand-along-with (*Mitvorhandensein*) of breasts, mouth, clitoris, etc.

Thus, Throbbing-member enters "into" the spatio-temporal nexus of her love-drenched pussyhood and is present (*zugegen*) to its potentiality-for-attaining-orgasmhood. This is what I call Throbbing-member's *Being-toward-orgasmicity*. Her verbal characterization, "Oh my God, you're in me!" has ontological content only insofar as by "in" we understand "the entity inside" (*Das inwendig Seiende*) in its ontological selfhood as Throbbing-member, exclusive of the theirness of other "throbbing-members" merely ready-to-hand, i.e., mere equipment.

"Oh God, I can't stand it, I'm coming, I'm coming, I'm coming..." is, therefore, not only a phenomenological statement, but has existential-ontological meaning as well. □

FOTO FUNNIES

LOOK, SUPPOSE YOU HAD NEVER EATEN A STEAK BEFORE, BUT YOU HAD HEARD IT WAS REALLY GOOD...

EONETTE

...WHAT YOU'RE DOING IS SAYING THAT YOU'RE GOING TO STARVE YOURSELF AND NOT EAT ANYTHING SO THAT WHEN YOU EAT THAT STEAK, IT'S REALLY GOING TO BE DELICIOUS...

...THE TROUBLE IS--AND HERE'S THE PITFALL A LOT OF YOU GIRLS FALL INTO-- THAT WHEN YOU FINALLY SIT DOWN TO EAT THAT STEAK...

...AFTER STARVING YOURSELF FOR SO LONG, YOU'VE BUILT THAT STEAK UP IN YOUR MIND SO MUCH...

...THAT NO MATTER HOW GOOD IT TASTES, IT'S NEVER GOING TO MEET UP WITH YOUR EXPECTATIONS. SEE?

NOT TILL I'M MARRIED.